THE POLITICS OF THE PANTRY

The Politics of the Pantry

Stories, Food, and Social Change

MICHAEL MIKULAK

McGill-Queen's University Press

Montreal and Kingston • London • Ithaca

ISBN 978-0-7735-4276-1 (cloth)
ISBN 978-0-7735-9017-5 (ePDF)
ISBN 978-0-7735-9018-2 (ePUB)

Legal deposit fourth quarter 2013
Bibliothèque nationale du Québec

Printed in Canada on acid-free paper that is 100% ancient forest free
(100% post-consumer recycled), processed chlorine free

Financial support has been received from Wilfrid Laurier University's Contract
Academic Staff Research Fund.

McGill-Queen's University Press acknowledges the support of the Canada
Council for the Arts for our publishing program. We also acknowledge
the financial support of the Government of Canada through the Canada
Book Fund for our publishing activities.

Library and Archives Canada Cataloguing in Publication

Mikulak, Michael, 1980–, author
    The politics of the pantry: stories, food, and social change / Michael Mikulak.

Includes bibliographical references and index.
Issued in print and electronic formats.
ISBN 978-0-7735-4276-1 (bound). – ISBN 978-0-7735-9017-5 (ePDF). –
ISBN 978-0-7735-9018-2 (ePUB)

1. Food – Social aspects. 2. Food – Political aspects. 3. Food writing. I. Title.

GT2850.M54 2013   394.1'2   C2013-903223-1
                                                              C2013-903224-X

This book was typeset by Interscript in 10.5/14 Sabon.

Contents

Acknowledgments

Writing a book is not something that happens in isolation. I would like to express my deepest gratitude to the many people who contributed their time, support, and encouragement throughout this process. It has been a long time coming, and there are perhaps too many people to thank, for the deepest influences are often the most indirect.

First, I would like to thank Dr Susie O'Brien. I cannot even begin to express my gratitude for your patience, incredible dedication, and the care you put into my work. You provided the anchor I needed and prevented this book from reaching beyond its scope, even while encouraging me to weave together an improbable set of problems and approaches. I am so grateful for your influence, and will carry the lessons you taught me throughout my future work. I would also like to thank Dr Imre Szeman and Dr Petra Rethmann for the crucial dialogues you provided through this process. Thank you for your enthusiasm and support, and for encouraging me to pursue every wild tangent. A big thank you to Dr Timothy W. Luke for your advice and support during my post-doctoral work.

I would also like to thank my wonderful wife and daughters. You have been my foundation, and in times when I thought I would never finish, you reminded me that there is so much more to life, and this is what kept me writing. When it seemed like everything was over the horizon, you were my reminder that everything I need is right here. I would also like to thank my parents, sister, and family in Winnipeg for your words of encouragement and for always believing I would succeed. It has taken many years, but I always knew your support was unconditional.

Too many friends and colleagues have been instrumental in writing this book for me to mention them all. I would like to thank my colleagues and friends Christina, Lauren, Dilia, Daniel, Jeff, Jamie, Evan, and the many others for your counsel, sympathy, and friendship. When I write about the shared table and conviviality, it is your company that I think of. Many ideas within this book emerged from our many dinners together. A special thanks to Kyle for your keen eye in the final stages and for helping me get over some of those editorial bumps that, at the time, seemed like mountains.

Finally, I would like to thank SSHRC and Wilfrid Laurier University for their financial support. SSHRC generously funded the postdoctoral work from which this book has emerged, and Laurier has helped offset its publication. I also want to thank Jeffrey Brison and Jonathan Crago for helping me hone the text with your keen editorial senses and for guiding a new author through the maze that is the publishing world. All the staff at McGill-Queen's were always helpful, patient, and a pleasure to work with. Jane McWhinney, your editing work was especially sharp and insightful.

And to those whom I do not mention, but who spent hours listening to my meandering ideas, know that you are appreciated and that your influence marks these pages in many ways.

THE POLITICS OF THE PANTRY

INTRODUCTION

Telling Stories with Food

What do you hunger for? What's eating you? What's for dinner? Decisions about eating have always been complex, but today they seem to be even more complicated. What for most of human history has been a relatively transparent affair has become as convoluted as any other aspect of the global economy. Books celebrating local food, examining the root causes of obesity, and speculating about how we will feed ourselves in the future are sprouting like proverbial weeds from popular and academic presses. Cookbooks, gardening gurus, and lifestyle television shows extolling the value of eating and living slowly all have something to say about what, where, how, and with whom we should eat.

There seems to be an insatiable hunger for what I call *storied food*, a genre of literature, film, and new media that attempts to reveal the "truth" behind the veil of incomprehensible ingredient lists, transnational foodways, and genetically modified organisms, in order to trace the hidden worlds of agriculture. What for most of human history was quite evident is now often as inscrutable as the workings of the electronic device in your pocket: who can fathom the mystery of the immortal Twinkie, let alone the near absurdity of bumper stickers that remind us that "Farmers Feed Cities" or Michael Pollan's invocation to "Eat food"? Even the need for a so-called real-food movement speaks to the state of our industrial food system, and the cultural disconnect that is fuelling this rise in popular food literature. Celebrity chefs such as Jamie Oliver, Mark Bittman, and Alice Waters offer compelling narratives that invoke

authenticity, family values, frugality, community, and the benevo-
lent citizen-consumer who supposedly changes the world every day
by voting with his or her dollar. Eating has never been so politically
charged, emotionally vested, or misunderstood.

Unlike many things we consume, food is unique in its irreducible
materiality: without it, we die! Although many in the world know
hunger and are deeply affected by issues of food security, most of
us holding this book experience anxiety about food in a different
way. I personally have never known deep hunger, and yet, I worry
about the future of food. My hunger extends into imagining the
future of a crowded, hot, and changing planet: how will we feed a
growing population? Should I eat meat? Where should I source my
food? Which is better, local or ogranic? Can individual and planetary health ever be reconciled? What are my obligations to future
and current eaters? Carlo Petrini, founder of the Slow Food movement, argues that we are all bound by the "gastronomic axis," the
web of life that connects all things in a conjugation of the verb to
eat.[1] As a metaphor, the gastronomic axis suggests the centrality of
food and also its violence. To eat is to simultaneously consume and
produce, to destroy and enliven. Eating connects us to plants
and animals, landscapes, histories, gendered politics, memories,
pleasure, and pain.

Humans currently use half of the world's fresh water, have transformed one-third to one-half of the planet, and use two-fifths of the
planet's primary productivity.[2] The question of what to eat has res-
onances far beyond the seeming triviality of that everyday task,
since agriculture is among the largest contributors to a typical individual's or nation's eco-footprint.[3] Industrial agriculture has transformed what was once a solar economy into one saturated in oil, to
the point where, on average, ten calories of fossil fuel are consumed
for every one calorie of food energy produced, without considering
transportation or the fuel used to cook the food once it gets to the
household.[4] It would seem that the gastronomic axis also binds us
to another irreducible materiality – the limits of a finite, overflowing and overworked planet.

From the standpoint of equity, the world's richest consumers use
"four to eight times the cropland required by the poorest of the

world's poor."[5] The capital-intensive, unseasonal, global food system championed by the West simply cannot feed the world at the level Westerners are used to. The typically meat-heavy, processed, and calorie-intensive diet of a North American eater requires too many resources to be adopted globally, and externalizes too many environmental costs in the form of soil degradation, habitat loss, and carbon intensity. The UN Food and Agriculture Organization warns that 2013 may see a food crisis as severe as the riots in 2008, as droughts in the United States, Ukraine, and other countries have reduced global grain reserves to historic lows.[6] Environmentalist Lester Brown warns that climate change will lead to even thinner margins as extreme weather leads to a new and prominent geopolitics of food scarcity.[7] We are poised at a crossroads when it comes to food and, as many commentators have pointed out, business as usual is simply not an option if we want to avoid widespread riots, environmental degradation, and even social collapse. So where do we go from here?

One of the most dynamic environmental movements to emerge in the last decade has been the sustainable, local, or alternative food movement. With its focus on connecting people, developing communities, spurring economic growth, and helping address a mounting environmental crisis, it offers a solution to many of the problems encapsulated above. The works of Michael Pollan, Gary Paul Nabhan, Barbara Kingsolver, and Alison Smith and James MacKinnon have catapulted food to the centre of the sustainability debate and articulate a compelling case for a "politics of the pantry." For many in the movement, food needs to become the central node for creating a green economy capable of addressing issues of employment, economic development, and environmental sustainability. Bill McKibben's book *Deep Economy* prioritizes the development of a local, sustainable agriculture in a new economic model based on zero growth and an acknowledgment of the implications of peak oil and the mounting environmental crisis. The Oxford Dictionary word of the year for 2007 was "locavore," a word designating a person or a practice that captures people's desire to know where their food comes from and take control of a system that many feel has become too complicated and industrialized. The last decade has seen the emergence of a unique social and literary movement dedicated to telling the stories of our food. With less than 2 percent of the population living on farms in North America, it is easy to understand why so many have become interested in those accounts. We hunger for more than just what goes into our stomachs; we want to know its history. Whether it comes to us in the form of advertisements, sensuous experience, organic labelling, farmers' markets, or lifestyle television, we yearn to understand our food as a narrative experience.

Because food exists on the boundaries between different realms of our lives, it touches on numerous tensions and anxieties. Food represents the most basic transformation of nature to culture, and culture to nature; defines and shapes social and gender relations; reveals global and local inequities; organizes entire sectors of the economy; gives focus to anxieties about family and community life; organizes and mobilizes cultural identity; and embodies the tension between public and private subjectivity within the global everyday. It is more than just a byway through which we can understand issues of social justice, environmental degradation, culture, identity, and economics; it is the very substance of life. Food is not only good to eat, it is good to think with. We eat with our mouths, minds, hearts, and stomachs. Perceived connections and disconnections, absences, presences, stories, and shared meals reveal crucial dimensions of what it will take to adapt to climate change. Questions about who gets a seat at the table, what will be served, and who will serve it are all entangled with a much broader question: how will we survive? How will we adapt to the growing and apocalyptic implications of climate change, financial instability, increasing inequality, and the large-scale degradation of entire ecosystems and the planet? The politics of the pantry offers a way of understanding how we can transform capitalism so that it does not consume the planet. It also gives us crucial insights into the problem of developing a green consensus in a world where affluent countries must contract their consumption while allowing poorer countries to grow. The gastronomic axis runs through our stomachs and minds, through our wallets, and into our very ability to (re)imagine what a sustainable and just agriculture and economy would look like.

Despite the recent surge of attention in various media, the basics of food production and preparation are absent from most lives. Few people have the skills it takes to farm, cook from scratch, or preserve their food, and even fewer have the time, resources, or freedom to make food central in their lives. I grew up in a Ukrainian household that emigrated to Canada in the early 1980s after my father dodged the Soviet draft for the Afghanistan war, a conflict he was sure would end in his untimely death. As a Ukrainian living in an occupied country, my father has always harboured a fierce nationalism. After fleeing across the Berlin Wall toward safety in West Germany, we were sponsored by a Ukrainian cultural organization in Winnipeg and my family was given accommodation in exchange for custodial duties. When we arrived in Canada, my father's nationalism manifested in an intense desire to become Canadian, as he worried about the prospect of being deported and sent to a Soviet gulag. As immigrants to this new safe-haven, we were pulled toward a new identity, while still firmly rooted in our heritage and culture. Although my earliest memories are mostly within Canada, my ties to my culture, past and present have frequently been rooted in food.

For my mother, food was always a source of profound pleasure and anxiety. Even though my parents both worked long hours, alternating evening and day shifts so that one of them could stay home with us, we always ate food that was prepared from scratch. I have vivid memories of my mother coming home from work, tired after a long shift at the perogy factory. The perogy is a typical peasant food; made with little more than flour, water, potatoes, onions and some cheese, it embodies a time when women stayed in the kitchen and could labour all day to transform basic ingredients into something magical. Perogies take a lot of skill and time to perfect: the centre must be dry enough to not affect the dough, and wet enough to cohere into a ball. The dough has to be silky smooth and glutinous, so that it can be rolled out to a perfect thinness – just thick enough to hold up to boiling and frying, but thin enough to melt in your mouth. Making perogies is one of those day-long affairs involving generations of women who convene in a kitchen and make hundreds to be frozen for later use. Learning to make them involves a deep form of sensual knowledge – a constant search for a particular texture, the right ingredients, a specific feel to the dough. It is artisanal in the full sense of the word and no recipe can tell you how to make a perfect perogy.

Occasionally, my mother would bring home some of the factory-made perogies. This was perhaps my first experience with industrial food for, like many immigrants, my mother was anxious to feed our bodies and minds with tastes of home, and conscious of the expense of convenience food or eating out. To her horror, and perhaps later to her pleasure, her two young children rejected those manufactured perogies, having been tuned to a wholly different sensual experience. I have never developed a taste for industrial perogies – what should involve a seamless transition from dough to potato and melt in your mouth is frustratingly dense and chewy. My mother tells us we would spit them out and beg her to make the handmade version. And she would. On her days off, I remember her taking the time not only to make our favourite food, but to teach us about the process and encourage us to get our hands into the dough so we too could understand the tactile experience as an extension of our taste buds – to understand that taste doesn't just happen on the tongue.

In his excellent book *Embodied Food Politics*, Michael Carolan argues that food preferences are produced, that our bodies are "tuned" to industrial flavours and textures, and that we learn to recognize those flavours and textures as good and pleasurable. The corollary is that we need to be re-tuned "toward alternative foods and food systems if we want those alternatives to be sustained over the long run."[8] Pleasure is not just a bourgeois affectation to which we turn to after the hard political battles are won. It arises at the nexus of the personal and the global, where advertising, family, habit, and preference intersect. Pleasure can in turn provide friction against the global food system, a way of instantiating habits, tastes, and desires for something else. For that to occur, alternative food must involve a re-education of the palate, what Petrini calls taste education. While political-economic analyses of food related to class, privilege, and cultural capital are vital, Carolan reminds us that "social change also requires bodies that think social change ought to occur."[9] Knowledge alone will not suffice when it comes to changing the food system or addressing the environmental crisis more broadly.

Most of us have seen commodity biographies such as Robert Kenner's *Food Inc.*, filled with tragic tales of the "true costs" of cheap food in the form of obesity, environmental degradation, the death of the family farm, and the torture and confinement of animals. These cautionary tales suggest that we can attain salvation through enlightened shopping, and that decisions to buy local, sustainably produced food can literally change the world by turning us into co-producers. While economic arguments based on hidden costs are necessary, they often fail to incite more than a momentary pang of guilt. Like the over-used images of starving African children in advertisements imploring us to sacrifice less than the price of a cup of coffee a day, the guilt they arouse lingers for only a few days, perhaps a month if we are particularly sensitive. But we soon find ourselves back in old habits, craving chicken McNuggets even after seeing the pink slime YouTube video, or being enchanted by Jamie Oliver's fierce desire for a food revolution and his generous glugs of the finest extra-virgin olive oil.

Guilt can never be enough. People have to want to eat better; they have to crave change and feel the need viscerally. As Elspeth Probyn says, "the question of how to live today can be best seen at a 'gut' level."[10] Eating ethically will always involve both a push and a pull, acknowledging the multifaceted and often contradictory layers of history, meaning, and taste that tune our bodies toward certain kinds of foods. For me, the industrial perogy simply did not resonate with my experiences; I have an almost involuntary response, a gag reflex: my body refuses to acknowledge that this thing is actually food. And yet, at the same time that I was begging for Mom's homemade perogies, I also became obsessed with McDonald's. As a recent immigrant, McDonald's was something I had never experienced. Nothing of the sort existed in Soviet Ukraine in the 1980s, and what was more, my mother had an almost irrational fear of fast food, so the golden arches had a special attraction for my five-year-old mind. In addition to objecting to the cost, which was too much for a family of four that had come to the country with only five dollars to their name, she seemed to believe that I would be corrupted by the food – literally poisoned. I remember spending my first allowance on a set of McDonald's *Fraggle Rock* toys that a friend of mine had collected from his much more gastronomically lenient mother. I didn't even know what *Fraggle Rock* was, or anything about the power of cross-marketing, but the toys were a talisman from the golden kingdom. My mother was, to say the least, not pleased by my purchase for, while the food had not passed my lips, I had been sullied by the empire. Some time later, I came ever so close to tasting the forbidden fries when my school bus driver, in a fit of generosity, offered to treat the few kids on his route. I was overcome by a giddiness that was swiftly crushed when one of the kids on the bus said he didn't want to stop, and we glided past that beacon of capitalist food nirvana, the smell of grease leaving a faint taste of salt on my lips and teasing me as I was once again denied entrance.

I tell this story to make a point about food and the accumulated layers of meaning that flavour our experience of eating. I suppose my mother was successful in tuning my body, for to this day, I too have a strong aversion to fast food. But the meaning of McDonald's in that context, the power it had over my imagination, suggests something about the nature of food and the stories we tell about it, about what that knowledge feels and tastes like. Like the onion, food has layers of meaning that not only provide insight into how individuals relate to wholes, but also suggest something about how desire, pleasure, taste, and politics become entangled in everyday life. I did eventually get a chance to fulfill my dream of the golden arches, and in a rite of passage typical of many Canadians and Americans, I went to a birthday party, complete with the Ronald McDonald army, Happy Meals, and brightly coloured toys. I honestly don't remember the food so much as the experience, and my mother continued her campaign against fast food for my entire childhood. Coca-Cola, strangely, was permitted, but only as a solidification of our heritage, when the children were allowed to quench their thirst at the soda fountain after Ukrainian dance classes. For a few minutes, the rules were suspended and I was given access to an almost unlimited flow of pop. For the longest time, that sweet nectar kept me performing my nationality like a dutiful little addict secretly awaiting his next hit of sugary bliss.

What strikes me now about my early experience with fast food is the polysemous nature of eating. It was never solely about the food, but rather about what it represented to my young mind. Even at that age, food was already good to think with. McDonald's was exotic and forbidden: an idea as rooted in the toys as in the meal. The story of food is perhaps as important as its physical substance, and the newfound current interest in that narrative is revealing some fascinating possibilities – and perils – for imagining and putting into practice alternative and sustainable economic relations based on conviviality, mutual aid, and the shared table. My mother's rationale was always negative: fast food was bad for us, expensive, and simply should not be eaten. But in the end, it was pleasure that won me over to her side. It wasn't fear of McDonald's, for I think this actually made the food more appealing – it was the pleasures of her cooking and the pride she took in her skills. And once my initial fantasy had been fulfilled, I realized something: McDonald's didn't taste good.

This tension between pleasure and anxiety is at the heart of the sustainable food movement, and represents a key impasse for environmentalism in general. The environmental crisis forces everyone to consider a very basic question: how shall I live? How shall *we* live together? The contrasting concepts of utopia and apocalypse are the polar forces that structure most environmental critiques. Whether in the discussions of "The End of Food," the spectre of Malthusian hunger, or conversely, in the possibility of a green-energy future powered by the sun, or the joys of gardening, we seem to be stuck between the promise of a better future and the reality of a capitalist system incapable of curbing its lust for perpetual growth. On the one hand, there is a deep anxiety that we are on the precipice, that the blandishments and opulence of global food are a mirage – a temporary technological transmutation of oil into loaves. On the other hand, there is the pleasure of ripe seasonal fruit, the vibrant flavours of home preserves, or the commensality of a bustling farmer's market that pulls people toward local food.

When I began research for this book, I realized that, in addition to reading the literature, it was crucial that I become as deeply entangled in my own foodshed as possible, and thus I decided to commit to a locavore *annus mirabilis*, a year of eating only foods grown within a hundred miles of my home in Hamilton, Ontario. It would be a way of getting to know the limitations and possibilities of eating as a form of knowledge and connecting the literary and the material world. One of the most immediate effects of placing a geographical constraint on my diet was that it transformed the grocery store from a place of abundance into a relative wasteland. All of a sudden my choices were reduced from some forty thousand items to maybe a hundred, and the conveniences of packaged food, bread, and canned goods disappeared overnight as I was forced to cook from scratch and find alternative ways of provisioning my dinner. Initially, this was very difficult, but as I became more adept and my knowledge grew, what began as an artificial dystopia of industrial abundance just out of my reach, soon became a lively and delicious world of local food, heirloom vegetables, riotous summer gardens, and gleaming mason jars lining my basement shelves. This tension between abundance and limitation, utopia and apocalypse – between pleasure and knowledge, and the local and global – will be a central dialectic organizing the subsequent chapters. I encourage the reader to put aside any inclination to read these poles as mutually exclusive, and instead to focus on points of convergence where theory and practice can add up to something more. I think it is in this excess, in what can be neither contained nor counted, that the politics of the pantry can find its true voice.

My mother came from a family that suffered great casualties in the *holodomor*, the human-made famine imposed by the Russians before and around the Second World War that claimed the lives of millions of Ukrainians. My grandmother was one of two survivors of eight children because she was "lucky" enough to have been taken by an Austrian to work as a maid in an upper-class home during the war. The legacy of hunger had a profound effect on my mother, although she experienced it in a different way. She recalls from her childhood that my grandmother would be tremendously anxious if she didn't have 10 kg each of flour and sugar in her pantry. For my mother, in her adopted country, this anxiety took on a different manifestation. She would return from the grocery store with a manic glee, stuffing sale items into an ever-growing pantry and freezer, hoarding in a way that, to an outsider, looked as if we were preparing for the apocalypse. We always had sacks of potatoes in the garage, canned food in the basement, home-made pickles and sauerkraut, and multiple freezers' worth of food. For me, the ghost of famine has manifested in an abiding interest in food scholarship and cooking. Although not quite as extremely filled, my pantry also tends to be well stocked, and during my locavore year, I began to feel the same dialectic tension between apocalypse and utopia that runs through so much writing about food.

For those of us writing, reading, and eating from privileged positions, it can be difficult to reconcile the luxury consumption of artisanal, organic products with a politics of equal distribution and climate change. And yet, this is precisely what we must do, for the gastronomic axis also binds us to a shared future. When I started the 100-mile diet I planned to record everything. I wanted to write down where I got every piece of food and keep an account book so as to make comparisons between costs, convenience, location, and so forth. Very quickly, however, I realized the absurdity of the premise and stopped my notations. I had been trying to reduce the experience to numbers, hoping to convince people that eating locally wasn't more expensive, or that it really didn't take more time. I figured that, as I was writing a book about the green economy, global warming, and food, these were the statistics that would convince people that any inconvenience or cost was worth it. Without realizing it, I had participated in a habit of mind that reduces the world to quantities and numbers, and tries to bridge the gap between economics and ecology by appealing to objective metrics.

The dismal science had infected my mind with hope that the numbers could speak for themselves, that supported with the right figures, the truth would be impossible to ignore. Like Paul Hawken, Anthony Van Jones, Nicholas Stern, and many others, I participated in what I call the *economic turn*, which refers to an increasing, and often necessary reliance on the language of GDP, natural capitalism, and green growth to frame the environmental crisis.

While, generally speaking, the environmentalism of the 1960s and 1970s focused on rejecting consumer society as a model of agency and economic activity, twenty-first-century environmentalism is more geared toward finding ways to make consumption sustainable.[11] Whether in the growth of organic food, ecotourism, fair trade certification, eco-labels, or the popularity of Slow Food, we are seeing a shift from efforts to regulate industry and other sites of production, to a recognition of the power of ethical and green consumption.

Local food, whether seen as what Barbara Kingsolver calls "edible patriotism," or in the form of local economic development, agrotourism, or farmers' markets, is popular precisely because it works so well within the logic of capitalism. Farmers' markets providing small-scale, community-based alternatives to alienated forms of capitalism have become exemplary models of the future green economy. In locavore literature, the farmers' market is interpreted as a utopian space of possibility, representing a more authentic and human economy in which producers interact directly with consumers, and responsibility takes on a decidedly local flavour. Whereas globalization implies an alienation from the here and now, local food brings politics, consumerism, and ethics into a fraught, but potent combination of the "citizen-consumer hybrid."[12] Farmers' markets become spaces where we can atone for our carbon sins, voting with our dollar for a better world and building community at the same time. For McKibben, they are a hub of community activity: "a simple change in economic life – where you shop – produces an enormous change in your social life."[13] But with the language of markets and choice comes a deep cost. As I trace in chapter 1, the attempt to account for nature in economic terms leads down many different roads and, as shown by the development of organic food from counter-culture cuisine to large-scale industrial products available at Walmart, something is lost in the process.

So how should we value food? What stories are the most effective in achieving change? Why is the sustainable food movement catching on and how can we promote it without losing something in the process? While I am sympathetic to critics such as Chad Lavin, who states that the politics of local food "reflects more than anything else a deep suspicion of conventional politics and the wholesale colonization of the political imaginary by the logic of the market,"[14] I am unwilling to throw the proverbial baby out with the bathwater. No matter how privileged, contradictory, or classist consumer-based environmentalism may be, the surge of interest in storied food suggests that there is something powerful about the ability of these narratives to capture the collective imagination. The values that impel people to eat better, to shop at farmers' markets, to buy organic, and to drive hybrids are not inherently about consumption or status display; nor can they be dismissed solely as artifacts of an impoverished political imaginary. They are for the most part based on care: for the earth, one's family, and the community. And yet, these values are being sold back to us in the form of artisanal products, "authentic" experiences, and greenwashed commodities. Slow and local food are currently available only to those with the income and time necessary to express these values through consumer means. Where I disagree with Lavin is that I strongly believe that this limitation does not reveal a deficiency of the movement, but rather, its next phase.

I teach a class called "Consumerism and Identities," whose goal is to introduce students to an array of theoretical approaches that will help them appreciate the role consumerism plays in the economy, the environmental crisis, and identity formation. We speak a lot about the local food movement and green consumerism. At a certain point, I invite the class to create a journal entry in which they calculate their ecological footprint and consider their own impact on the world. The ecological footprint is a measure developed by William Rees that helps to spatialize the environmental impact of an individual by providing a land-equivalent for individual consumption. Most of the students found that universalizing and sustaining their lifestyles would require between three and five planets of resources. The range of response is telling: some react with horror, others with indignation, but all are stuck in a similar way. The indignant seem to take the measure of their footprint as a personal affront – the environmental equivalent of George W. Bush's infamous claim that terrorists simply hate the American way of life. These students see no alternative, and immediately begin to justify their lifestyle: "I'm a student who must commute from my parents' house out of town"; "I eat out a lot or on campus because I don't know how to cook, or don't have the space"; "it's inconvenient to take public transportation." The excuses are no different: "it's too hard to change and I'm not even sure it would do anything." Many suggest that the "system" needs to change before individuals can, and to a certain extent they are right – or at least, they capture one of the central problematics of contemporary environmental critique: how do we start? How do we get from here to there? What tools are required to break free from the tyranny of the present, from the sense of dread that so many share in their inability to even imagine an alternative to capitalism.

Fredric Jameson has famously written: "it is easier to imagine the end of the world than the end of capitalism."[15] I think this is precisely the impasse that my students face; they have no idea where to start. They have all grown up during the neoliberal era for which, among claims of the end of history and a triumphant dismantling of the welfare state, the future is simply a mirror of the present. History hasn't ended, our future has! In a very real sense, the future no longer exists, either as an imaginary construct pulling us toward a shared goal or – increasingly – literally. With James Hanson declaring that mining the Tar Sands will mean game-over for the climate, and study after study showing that climate change predictions have been much too conservative, we are approaching an indistinct yet terrifying tipping point that could mean the end of planet Goldilocks.[16] With overwhelming numbers of humans living in cities, disconnected from the tactile realities of food production and other natural cycles, we forget how precarious civilization truly is, and that a mere 10,000 years have passed since the agricultural revolution changed the face of the planet. Even less time has passed since the industrial revolution initiated a series of events that have led Paul Crutzen to dub this era the anthropocene, a new "human-dominated, geological epoch supplementing the Holocene – the warm period of the past 10–12 millennia."[17]

Civilization as we know it developed during the Holocene. Agriculture relies on a very precise temperature gradient: too cold and crops fail, too warm and they whither. The drought of 2012 in the United States and around the world is a window into the future: a glimpse of McKibben's *Eaarth*, a new world we have created by ushering in the anthropocene and finally killing off Nature. But the endpoint I most fear is echoed in the response of horror that some of my students have to their own footprint. When they see the number, they simply cannot believe the impact they have, and immediately ask what they can do. Often, however, they reach the same impasse: how do we start? They simply do not see how one person, or even one group, could derail the juggernaut of capitalism. Even if they agree that we need a better, more sustainable, more just system, they cannot see how achieving it would be possible. And this is perhaps the most tragic outcome, as this sense of impotence will prevent them from seeing what can be done and stop them from using one of the most vital and necessary faculties they have at their disposal for solving the problems they face: their imagination.

Hopelessness only arises by being manufactured: it needs to be produced, advertised to the population, and sustained. The last thirty years have seen the development of a vast machine of hopelessness centred around the basic idea that no other future is possible. The response of the global elite to the economic crisis has revealed the terrifying momentum of a capitalist system declared "too big to fail," and in need of only minor tweaks and regulations but no systemic changes. In *The Uprising*, Franco Berardi argues that the future is no longer a promise but a threat. The neoliberal revolution has transformed relations between bodies into relations of competitiveness and ushered in a crisis of the imagination. What remains is an "image of modernity as disenchanted … as a place of dearth and alienation."[18] One reason I use the ecological footprint in my class is that it allows me to visualize two things. First, it helps students realize the extreme waste that goes into even a modest student lifestyle. This is the part that usually leads to despair. But it can be turned around rather easily with a simple point: if one person can have such an impact in ruining the planet, then surely they can have an equally positive one if they simply try. The anthropocene did not occur intentionally; nor was it guided by a collective will or desire. It was largely the accidental byproduct of trillions of small decisions made by billions of small people, and it has now acquired a momentum that has become attached to certain class positions, institutions, and systems of production. Global warming thus causes an apocalyptic rupture of the imagination – an impasse that is as fundamentally psychic as it is physical.

After the ecological footprint calculation, my class begins to discuss the sustainable food movement, and this is the point when a slow, but persistent hope begins to creep into their expressions. There is something about the politics of the pantry that feeds their hunger – it satisfies them on the level of the gut. I draw heavily on my experiences during my locavore year, and it isn't economics that brings hope. I may have begun the 100-mile diet thinking about quantities and economic arguments, but that soon began to fade away. It was perhaps a mistake to have begun in the middle of winter, with no provisions to speak of, and only enthusiasm and root vegetables to satisfy my hunger. But when the spring came, I began to work at a local CSA (community-supported agriculture) farm that agreed to allow a work-share arrangement whereby I came in once a week and worked on the farm in exchange for my food. I was able – literally – to feed off the fruits and vegetables of my labour, and proceeded to carve out a utopian space of possibility where money did not mediate my relationship with food. My first year of the locavore *annus mirabilis* was intentionally strict. I cut out everything not produced within my arbitrary limit (except chocolate, for in its absence life is indeed not good!) as a way of getting deeply involved in my local foodshed, of bringing food back home. I biked to the farm, thirty kilometres each way, sustained by a kind of masochistic spirit of possibility.

Although I have been an environmentalist for a long time, there was something pure and enchanting about this year that still sustains me. I spent afternoons rambling through the woods learning to identify plants and forage. I would work all day under the sun and then bike home with panniers loaded with fresh vegetables and eggs. I lovingly tended exotic-sounding heirloom tomatoes, with lineages longer than my own, into Jurassic-sized plants that gained me considerable respect from a group of Italian seniors who lived up the street from my apartment. I started a sourdough culture and diligently baked loaf after loaf until I finally had something that could be called bread. I still have that culture eight years later, and now my daughter helps me make her favourite sourdough waffles every Sunday morning. I learned to pickle everything, to make jam with fresh fruit, and to prepare for the winter in the summer. My life became realigned with the seasons in a way it never had been, and I felt a sense of empowerment and possibility in the impossible simplicity of making sauerkraut with a group of friends.

Unlike so many aspects of my life, these experiences were unalienated. I saw them through from seed to plant, from dough to bread, from start to finish. For that year, I became the embodiment of the politics of the pantry. But the time it took to sustain this rhythm, the purity of the utopian enclave, could not be sustained. I was privileged as an academic funded generously by the government, had access to a car when I needed to get larger loads of vegetables for preservation, did not have kids, marshalled the social and cultural capital of a PhD student, and did not have to do it every day. Unlike migrant agricultural workers who do much the same, but for sixty to eighty hours a week, and do not have the ability to stop or change the pace, I was undertaking an experiment. I was not stuck in the local by force of economic circumstance, but by choice. I was a tourist.

Fredric Jameson identifies two political functions of utopia. First, they create an enclave, an imagined space, from which the "root of all evil" can be banished.[19] In this form, the utopia functions as a diagnostic tool, identifying what the author believes to be the efficient cause of the problems society is facing. In order to do this, the utopia, from the Greek meaning "no place," must be isolated on an island or another planet, or in a different time. Utopias also function as collective wish-fulfillment fantasies that draw us toward a better future by maintaining a radical alterity. It is in this form of collective dreaming that utopias can invigorate a politics of the pantry and break from the deadening prospect of history ending upon the pyre of neoliberalism. However, because they exist on these islands, because they are dreams and not a reality, utopias are trapped in the space of the utopian leap, "the gap between our empirical present and the utopian arrangements of this imaginary future."[20] I want to return to my students for a moment. Immediately after completing the ecological footprint exercise and watching documentaries about the environmental crisis, they often sink into a pit of apocalyptic despair, imagining a future of resource hoarding, competition, or some combination of the zombie apocalypse and *Children of Men*, where the best-case scenario involves an authoritarian regime that stops us from destroying the planet by stripping us of many of the rights and pleasures we currently enjoy.

I think part of the power of the politics of the pantry lies in its emphasis on pleasure, conviviality, and the central metaphor of the shared table. So, the tension between apocalypse and utopia brings up the question: how can contemporary environmentalism stir people into action? How can it find a means of disenchanting the public with the narrative of modernity, progress, and capitalism as the end of history, while offering a vision of an enchanted world worthy of saving? As Jane Bennett asks in regard to disenchanting narratives, of which an imagined apocalypse is perhaps the purest form: "what's to love about an alienated existence on a dead planet?"[21] People must want change. They must hunger for it! Within neoliberalism, the future is increasingly imagined as foreclosed, as a world where austerity and limits dominate, and expectations must be curbed in order to get the economy growing again. Environmentalism is empty without a compelling narrative that reconciles limits with generosity and a sense of the possible. This is precisely what my year of local eating did for me. What began with scarcity and anxiety was in the end much more about pleasure and generosity.

For example, when I got my first half pig from the farm, one of the skills I was forced to learn was how to use the nasty bits. Most of our meat comes highly processed. It has been plucked, shucked, gutted, and cleaned. But when you order directly from a farmer, you have the option of getting everything. My first order included a large part of the pig's jowl, and as I looked at my meat face to face, I wondered what on earth I would do with this disgusting, slightly hairy, misshapen reminder of my dinner's animality. This was no disembodied package of boneless, skinless pink flesh of the kind you get at your grocery store. I had been a vegetarian for over a decade, so dealing with this was not an easy task; slightly repulsed, I had to figure out what to do with the parts I frankly would rather not have considered. Once I got over the shock, I started to explore, and the face has now became one of my favourite parts of the pig. The cheeks are utterly sublime, and the jowl gives you an opportunity to practise the nearly lost art of making guanciale, or what I like to call face bacon. Guanciale is a cured but not smoked form of bacon that is very hard to find, but extremely tasty. Curing it is one of the simplest tasks for an amateur – it requires only salt, sugar, some herbs, and about a month of hanging time. Guanciale contains less fat and more collagen than traditional bacon made from the belly, making it ideal for thickening sauces. It makes the most ethereally smooth carbonara, and teaches you how to find pleasure in limits by making use of every portion of the animal – by transforming the nasty bits into delicacies that connect you with the most basic aspect of food: the translation of nature into culture.

From the perspective of global ecological politics, we are poised at a similar moment. We have the ability to turn things around now, to change because we want to, because we believe that a better world awaits us. We can choose to redefine economics within the limitations of the planet by harnessing the utopian impulse within the politics of the pantry; otherwise, the choice will eventually be made for us, and under conditions that will no doubt involve a scramble for resources, hoarding, and famine. To recall the example of my grandmother and mother: the desire to learn food-production skills stems from dialectically opposed impulses. One is conservative and apocalyptic: I acknowledge that the future of food looks dire, and that climate change will fundamentally begin to unravel our ability to feed everyone on the planet. This response tends toward a rugged individualism and the kind of apocalyptic hoarding made popular by shows like *Preppers* and *Living for the Apocalypse*. However, the other impulse derives from the pleasure of food and the belief that the enchantment and the conviviality of the shared table form an important counterpoint to the disenchantment narrative of modernity. The true power of the politics of the pantry lies in this dual movement:

utopia as a diagnostic tool, and the power of enchantment to pull people toward a change they desire.

The space of the utopian leap is like the crack in the pavement that quickly becomes colonized by weeds. It starts off small, barely noticeable. Soon, soft plants, probing roots, and verdant green begin to break apart the hard concrete. The world is inverted. What is hard becomes soft! We need more grand utopian visions; but we also need to nurture the practices and values, the *micro-utopian embodiments of alternative values* that have the ability to break through the concrete materiality of the present. That feeling of heaviness, oppression, and totality that comes with the conviction that capitalism is too big to fail can be broken down little by little. It is perhaps best to think like a weed, to exist on the fringes and find every opportunity to invade those spaces that capitalism abandons in its restless drive toward dematerialization. On these edges, in the wasted spaces of creative destruction, in our devalued urban cores and post-industrial suburban wastelands, and in the wasted lives of redundant workers, the politics of the pantry can thrive by offering physical and spiritual sustenance. As a locus for rebuilding community, schemes such as urban farming and co-ops, CSAs, and small-plot intensive (SPIN) agriculture have the potential to provide employment and purpose for millions of disenfranchised people feeling the sword of austerity dangling above them. Greece is currently seeing a farming renaissance as ex-bankers, financial workers, and others facing economic redundancy return to rural areas to make and grow things with their hands. Like the victory gardens of the past, growing food on the margins can help buffer one against the cruel indifference of capitalism and mobilize a shared vision of what is possible.

Chapter 1 will take the reader through a history of environmentalism over the last four decades. I discuss the economic turn by examining the tension between economic and non-economic representations of nature, and investigate how the capacity to be (ac)counted and valued aligns along the poles of nature and capitalism. The tension between value systems is a crucial site of struggle for the coming decades as humanity attempts to restructure the world along less socially and ecologically destructive modes of production. Looking at such examples as industrial organic agriculture, vertical farming, and ecological economics, I consider different stories about how we got here and where we are going. I am especially interested in the wide range of responses to the environmental crisis that they animate, especially in the relationship between capitalism, growth, and economic arguments in general.

The second chapter enquires into the stories we tell about food by treating the recent proliferation of texts that try to "lift the veil" on our industrial food system as a genre. Following a format similar to that of the preceding chapter, I consider each sub-genre – the commodity biography, nostalgic pastoralism, utopian pastoralism, and the foodshed memoir – for what it brings to an understanding of production and consumption, knowledge, and agency in relation to capitalism. In addition to providing a map of the genre, I consider the role of food experiments and life writing, and the autobiographical nature of many of these texts as an attempt to traverse the space of the utopian leap.

In the final chapter, I work through my own embodied attempts to become a locavore in order to consider how food can become both a subject and an object of knowledge. By recounting my experiences and trying to look squarely at some of the contradictions of scale and scope, class, gender, and access, I argue that one of the most important aspects of enchantment and embodiment is the way in which it opens up time and space for alternative value practices and utopian thinking to germinate. Without hope for a better world, without the small moments of micro-utopian practice that build upon the pleasures of everyday life, the soil will not be ready for future harvest.

There is a truism in organic farming: feed the soil and not the plants – for a good harvest, a foundation needs to be prepared. Industrial agriculture does the opposite: it uses fertilizers to feed the plants instead of enriching the soil and as a result, has been degrading the soil at alarming rates around the world. The current bounty is an illusion sustained largely by oil. This is perhaps one of the most unacknowledged and potentially catastrophic consequences of mono-cropping – it treats the soil as a medium of growth and not as a condition of possibility. As a result, industrial agriculture is mining the very basis upon which civilization is possible. By focusing on that soil – on the conditions of possibility – this book takes up the issue of narrative in relation to some key trajectories and ideas relating to food, global warming, and the future of the economy. It is an attempt to understand how we got here, where we are going, and how we can get somewhere else.

I

The Nature of Capitalism:
How Green Can We Grow?

What does it mean to live sustainably? Like nature and culture, the concept of sustainability is immensely complex, and has come to signify a host of social, ecological, economic, political, ontological, and epistemological attitudes and practices that are shaping the emerging ecopolitics of the twenty-first century. The expression begs many questions: What is being sustained? Who is sustaining it? To what end? What obligations and rights are subsumed by the term? And how can humans claim to speak for a nature they are presumably sustaining or destroying?

The concept of living sustainably has simultaneously become charged with meaning and moral content, and almost completely emptied of it. Deployed as a rhetorical device along the entire range of the political spectrum, it is simultaneously used to appeal to a transcendental nature capable of providing a moral compass beyond the human[1] and to justify xenophobia and economic protectionism in various incarnations of both localism and nationalism.[2] The Brundtland Report, "Our Common Future" (1987), twinned "sustainable" with the equally elusive term, "development." Unlike the 1972 Club of Rome, which postulated "Limits to Growth," Brundtland "claimed that economic growth and environmental sustainability could be combined."[3] Sustainable development has now become the hegemonic configuration of green capitalism, a rhetorical means of uniting altruism and profit, and ethics and the market.

We can further see this shift by comparing two images: "Earthrise," the 1968 photo taken from Apollo 8, and the August 2007 cover of *Popular Science*. The Apollo 8 photo, which shows the earth coming up over the horizon of the moon, has been called the most influential environmental photograph ever taken.[4] As the first image of the planet from deep space, it is credited with crystallizing the burgeoning environmental movement by visually demonstrating that we live on a *finite* planet. Although a product of one of the most sophisticated technological efforts ever undertaken by humanity, the image is striking for its simplicity and beauty – the earth hangs over the horizon of the moon, emerging from the black depths of space in a shock of blue and white that seems almost tender and timid. A whole generation perceived it as indicating that "we are in it together," floating through the void on a tiny and insignificant "spaceship earth" that houses all the life that we know.[5] The image inverts the familiar view of the moon from earth, so as to suggest the precarious balance of life, contrasting a desolate moon on the horizon, with a verdant, yet finite and precarious earth piercing the darkness. The photograph has encouraged frameworks of stewardship and care based on the idea of a singular but finite world. The image seems to speak directly to the environmental crisis as a global event in which the line between life and death is as faint and thin as the pale glow of the atmosphere.

The August 2007 *Popular Science* cover shows a contrasting logic at work. Highlighting technological innovation, geo-engineering, market-based solutions, and the overcoming of limits, this picture portrays the earth by means of a composite of satellite and computer generated images. Unlike the indistinct and half-shrouded planet of the earthrise, this one has precise contours, with North and South America and Europe visible in topographic detail. The headline reads "Engineering a Better Earth," and the planet is shown perched precariously on three talon-like robotic calipers, as if ready for surgery or on display in a museum. Another robotic arm, reminiscent of something from an automotive assembly line, holds Europe above the surface of the planet and reveals the mantle below. The arm reads "planetary rescue" and looks weathered, as if it has been working tirelessly to save the earth. While Europe is a lush green, the rest of the planet is arid and desolate.

Although obviously fictional, the pictorial elements – the size of the calipers holding the earth in place, the wounded continent being removed (or replaced?), the absence of any signs of climate or clouds, and the slogans – all represent a shift in focus from the natural to the technological, from reverence to domination, from acceptance to disregard of limits. The geo-engineering focus of the issue showcases various techniques through which science proposes to engineer a better world and save nature. Unlike the "man-made super-trees" that can theoretically absorb more carbon than a real tree, nature is seen to lack the ability to solve the crisis, suggesting that the survival of the planet is contingent upon better engineering and technology. The opening article, "A Realist's Guide to Climate Change," is a catalogue of apocalyptic consequences of global warming which can nonetheless be solved by science and a judicious and rational approach.

These photographs illustrate the profound shift in the way the environmental crisis has been represented over the forty years between them. The first presents a vision of a fragile planet, the object of awe, threatened by growth and limited by its finite nature. The second suggests a new frontier for unlimited growth, a path for reconciling capitalism with nature through technology, markets, and innovation. In 2006 the British government commissioned Lord Nicholas Stern, the former chief economist of the World Bank, to examine the economic impacts of climate change. In his influential report, Stern argues that "climate change presents a unique challenge for economics: it is the greatest and widest-ranging market failure ever seen."[6] The report uses the apocalyptic implications of climate change to argue for quick and decisive action in the name of continued economic growth. "The evidence shows that ignoring climate change will eventually damage economic growth. Our actions over the coming few decades could create risks of major disruption to economic and social activity, later in this century and in the next, on a scale similar to those associated with the great wars and the economic depression of the first half of the 20th century. And it will be difficult or impossible to reverse these changes. The earlier effective action is taken, the less costly it will be."[7] Interestingly, Stern has since stated that he "got it wrong" and had been much too optimistic about the future; what may have been solved by the market valuing climate change, is perhaps too little too late.[8]

Nonetheless, the Stern Report treats climate change and its relationship to capitalism primarily as a question of rectifying market mechanisms that have been skewed by incomplete data. By incorporating the true cost of environmental degradation, especially the effects of carbon, the report suggests, markets could respond effectively and still grow. By invoking the GDP and growth figures, Stern tries to downplay the popular right-wing argument that climate change is simply too expensive to tackle, and that without growth the economic system will collapse.[9] He argues that it would cost the world only 1 percent of GDP annually to stabilize emissions at 500–550 ppm of CO_2 by 2050, whereas waiting will cost much more.[10] Ulrich Beck commends Stern, stating that the report's economic approach "robs the opponents of the political counter-argument as well as the counter-argument of costs. Now there are no excuses left!"[11] By focusing on creating "discourse coalitions"[12] between business, government, and NGOs, the report is important for its effect on the climate of fear surrounding global warming, especially in the business community – and in this sense it is simultaneously beneficial and harmful. What we see here is a domestication of climate change that places it within an economic grammar. In order to make climate change more palatable to the business community, and as a way of reframing what has in the past largely been a moral and scientific argument, Stern appeals to the rhetoric of dynamism, market mechanisms, and cycles of innovation.

Reaction to his report has been divided, with some celebrating it as "realistic," "reasonable," and "a vital step forward in securing an effective global policy on climate change,"[13] and others criticizing it for its economic methodology,[14] its failure to bring in an analysis of power, politics, or the "tense nature of international relations,"[15] or for its economic reductionism and naturalization of growth and cost-benefit analysis.[16] What I would like to focus on is the shift toward evaluating nature through economic means, and the implications of this shift in terms of what Michel Foucault calls an "imperative discourse," which guides and shapes all other discourses in a field of forces.[17] Stern is part of the economic turn in environmentalism in which the grammar of markets, growth, GDP, and cost-benefit analysis dominates the discussion of how best to account for nature. Discourses are more than just words; they imply a set of political and economic relations, and naturalize forms of power and knowledge.[18]

So what does the economic turn imply? How can one actually evaluate nature in economic terms? What is the worth of a butterfly or a coral reef? How can we calculate the ecological services rendered by the respiration of plants? The tempting answer to these questions is to give them a dollar term, often calculated at $36 trillion annually. This number, cited by popular commentators and theorists such as David Suzuki, Herman Daly, and Paul Hawken, was first published in 1998 in the journal *Nature*. That estimate, although rife with methodological problems and likely impossible to verify, is meant to represent what it would theoretically cost us to replace all of nature's services with human labour and technology. It is more important, however, for showing us that the human economy cannot hope to "outproduce" nature's economy and that the two are irrevocably intertwined. The last decade has seen a flurry of economic metaphors emerge and frame the environmental crisis in very specific constellations of power/knowledge that utilize the language of externalities and ecological debt, cost-benefit analysis, ecological services, natural capitalism, and environmental economics to align economics and ecology. The World Wildlife Federation, for example, has been referring to the environmental crisis as the "ecological credit crunch,"[19] suggesting that ecology must trump economy, but that fundamentally the two are inseparable.

This cross-pollination of metaphors does specific work in situating priorities, but it also imports a host of assumptions about what constitutes value. A BBC article entitled "Nature loss 'dwarfs bank crisis'" cites a study commissioned by the EU that tallies the annual losses from deforestation alone at between $2 trillion and $5 trillion.[20] The rhetorical shift toward economic language is meant to

highlight the limits of current economic thinking, with the implica-
tion that nature must be taken into account, especially in a time
when a global economic recession tempts governments to limit their
spending on "luxuries" like the environment. By coding environmental messages in an economic grammar, environmentalists are
able to speak a language that politicians understand at the same
time as exposing the myopia of an economic system that externalizes most environmental costs.

As such, the economic turn is useful for narrowing the longstanding rift between capitalism and nature that has separated
environmental and social justice issues, to the advantage of corporations who deploy a divide-and-conquer technique in order to
rationalize lax environmental standards.[21] Where once it was most
common for corporations to frame the issue as a choice between
jobs or the environment, as was the case with logging companies
claiming we either have owls or jobs,[22] many are now calling for
"green jobs."[23] One of the most outspoken proponents of green
jobs and the synthesis of capitalism and nature is Anthony Van
Jones, an activist and entrepreneur who wrote *The Green Collar
Economy*, in which he outlines a possible joint path to solving the
economic and environmental crisis.[24] The Introduction, by Robert
F. Kennedy Jr, compares decarbonizing our economy with eliminating the slave trade. When the British Parliament debated abolishing
the trade, slaves were a key source of energy and labour, and critics
believed the economy would crash if the trade was eliminated.
However, argues Kennedy, this was not the case: "creativity and
productivity surged. Entrepreneurs seeking new sources of energy
launched the industrial revolution and inaugurated an era of the
greatest wealth production in human history."[25] The same, he
argues, will be the case for carbon. The moral road, Kennedy tells
us, is also the best road for capitalism.

The economic turn that underpins *The Green-Collar Economy*
is the backbone of the discourse of green capitalism. The turn shifts
the debate in a few interesting ways, all of which seem beneficial
and to some degree necessary. By attempting to reconcile labour
and the environment, and offering "one solution [that] can fix our
two biggest problems," Van Jones positions himself as a utopian

bridge. He tries to interweave morality, government regulation, an open market, and entrepreneurship to create an environmental justice platform. He argues that framing the issue as a debate between economic growth and a green future is to offer "a false choice."[26] Many environmental economists agree.[27] Anthony Giddens, for instance, argues that "the other side of danger is opportunity"[28] and that "no approach based mainly on deprivation is going to work."[29] The utopian bridge between capitalism and nature, and between greed and altruism, seems to transform the dangers of climate change into an opportunity for renewed growth. Kate Soper makes a similar argument: "[We need to] go beyond the Leftism that remains transfixed by the apocalyptic sublime of the absolute and unrepresentable 'other' to capitalist modernity. We have, in short, to be prepared to track the surfacing of desires for otherness on the ground this side of the precipitous face of such radical social change, even at the cost of finding them in the wrong places, desired by the wrong people, and contaminated by all the banality and political confusion and ordinariness of the everyday consumer culture out of which they will (since from where else?) be emerging."[30] In other words, the locus of radical change may not reside where we think it should, or where we might want it to.

I discuss Hawken, Daly, and Van Jones in more detail when considering the techno-utopian mode. For now, I want to emphasize the appeal to "realism" and gradualism as it relates to the production of hope and a politics of the possible. In an article arguing for a new green modernity, Beck takes a stance against the kinds of apocalyptic arguments and horror statistics typical of many forms of environmentalism: "In the name of indisputable facts portraying a bleak future for humanity, green politics has succeeded in de-politicizing political passions to the point of leaving citizens nothing but gloomy asceticism, a terror of violating nature and an indifference towards the modernization of modernity."[31] Lester Brown makes a similar point, adding that "restructuring the global economy according to the principles of ecology represents the greatest investment opportunity in history."[32]

Rhetorically this is a very appealing position. It helps explain the popularity of the green capitalism narrative as a variant of Francis

Fukuyama's 1992 claim that we have reached "the end of history" and that liberal democracy and capitalism represent the apex of society.[33] Since the environmental crisis can, as I later argue, signal a fundamental flaw in capitalism and its ability to internalize the crisis in any meaningful way,[34] the appeal to reconciliation is crucial for maintaining capitalist hegemony by conflating economics with capitalism. This have-your-cake-and-eat-it-too attitude is precisely why the term "sustainable development" is so popular. Its inherent vagueness allows it to function as common ground for competing ideologies, ironically transforming nature into a justification for its own (ab)use. To speak of investment and hope, rather than renunciation and apocalypse allows green capitalism to contain what is meant by sustainability, in ways that favour growth and allow it to recode climate change as another example of creative destruction[35] and the need for technological innovation.[36]

In addition to facilitating a neoliberal grammar of markets, other popular/populist narratives can be drawn upon to shore up the end-of-history appeal of green capitalism. Much as Barbara Kingsolver did with her "edible patriotism," Van Jones frames the task in nationalistic language, comparing the decarbonization of the economy to the Manhattan Project and the Apollo mission,[37] feats of technological heroism that were equally ideological victories in the fight against communism and the ascent of American hegemony. U.S. reliance on oil is thus positioned as an anchor keeping a once-glorious nation from maintaining its rightful place as an economic superpower. Van Jones also invokes the spirit of "wartime mobilization,"[38] arguing that a green-collar economy is a way for the United States to regain moral and economic leadership in the world. His whole book appeals to reviving the "true" spirit of the American dream in the face of a shifting world economy that is seeing U.S. economic hegemony slip.

The book's jingoistic optimism encourages a sense of possibility and transformation, a crucial attitude in the global North at least, since addressing climate change would inevitably mean giving up certain kinds of mobility and consumption patterns. In addition to providing consumers with satisfying alternatives to wasteful and honorific consumption, ethical and green consumerism can help assuage some of the dissatisfaction people are feeling in the hurried pace typical of fast capitalism. Moreover, in a time of deep economic crisis following the financial collapse of 2008/09, it is important to frame the environmental crisis such that it won't immediately be rejected by politicians, economists, and a public that has largely bought into the idea that it is the economy, and not nature, that makes the world go round.

The failure of the 2009 Copenhagen Climate Change Conference to provide a roadmap beyond the Kyoto Protocol shows just how tenuous the coalition between sustainability and development really is. Although many countries, including the United States, have pledged to reduce emissions, the targets and dates are not binding, and controversy over how to include developing economies – especially China and India – in future talks remains a huge stumbling block to the implementation of binding emissions targets and cuts. Many of the low-hanging fruit of eco-efficiency have already been picked,[39] and future investments will therefore yield less profit, thereby challenging the order of priority of nature and capitalism as deficits balloon and profits deflate. Without a means of addressing the need to constantly grow either through a process of creative destruction or through competition, it is unlikely that capitalism will be able to deal with the demands of the environmental crisis. The momentum of green capitalism has slowed down in recent years as belts tighten and the rhetoric of economic sustainability overtakes ecological sustainability, especially as Italy and Greece have fallen into solvency crises and claim they can no longer afford climate change initiatives. Barack Obama's reluctance to bring up climate change during the 2012 election campaign was due to a belief that the population was simply too concerned with economic growth to listen to arguments about the price of energy or carbon taxes. While necessary, the economic turn seems like a risky strategy.

THE ECONOMIC TURN: SETTING THE STAGE

The economic turn can be broken down along an ideological spectrum for the purpose of considering how a range of positions imagine and prioritize the relationships between capitalism, nature, and value. As mentioned above, the problem with the economic turn is that, in an attempt to evaluate nature through conventional means such as GDP and growth, other values tend to be pushed aside. In Figure 1, rather than describing viable and self-contained relationships, I show the value accorded to them as examples of certain discourses and ideological positions. My interest is to understand the values associated with each position, in relation to making our economy greener. I say "economy" because I would like to keep that concept separate from capitalism, which is just one system among many of allocating resources. The chart represents some key ideological positions and responses, focusing on the production of value and the prioritization of nature and culture in relation to the green economy. To clarify, "the greening of capitalism" refers to the process by which the environmental crisis is challenging capitalism to consider the value of nature in new ways. This re-evaluation is a necessary precondition for continued accumulation, in the sense that even if capitalism does not formally recognize the limits of nature, it must constantly accommodate to those limits in a variety of ways, including price increases, new technologies, energy systems, and the basic mechanism of supply and demand. What are contested, as I hope the chart reveals, are the vastly different responses and futures possible according to the choice of approach to these problems. The environmental crisis can just as easily sustain capitalism as it can challenge its obsession with growth and offer an alternative economic arrangement.

Following Jane Bennett's assertion that "the cultural narratives that we use help to shape the world in which we will have to live,"[40] the idea that we can green capitalism is a powerful (meta)narrative capable of reinvigorating ecopolitics by suggesting a familiar path rooted in familiar economic ideas. The addition of the descriptor "green" to the discourse enables the term to enfold some important "alternative value practices to capitalism,"[41] practices that are central to the identity and coherence of the politics of the pantry. Concepts such as conviviality, mutual aid, the shared table, and human-scale face-to-face economies are otherwise difficult to accommodate within capitalism. In considering the role of value struggles in resisting capitalist modes of production, Massimo De Angelis looks at the "hegemonic redefinition of discourse" as a process of enclosure.[42] Nature, economy, ecology, sustainability, green, even economics – all these are terms whose definitions are highly variable and contestable. For De Angelis, "the politics of alternatives is ultimately a politics of value, that is a politics of establishing what the value *is* that connects individuals and wholes."[43]

Green capitalism, on the far left of the continuum, refers to the most commercial and most profit-driven form of this accommodation within capitalism; it focuses on consumerism and is often associated with "greenwashing." Since capitalism is the dominant social and economic force shaping human history at this time, I am lumping all responses/modes under the broad process called the *greening of capitalism*, a process that I view as fundamentally open and contestable. *Green capitalism*, on the other hand, is much more crystallized and represents the dominant interests of neoliberalism as an attempt to maintain the primacy of the free market, private property rights, free trade, and entrepreneurial freedom. The chart in Figure 1 serves a largely heuristic purpose that is intentionally at odds with the language that informs the rest of the book, the language of embroilments and imbroglios,[44] of nature-culture hybrids,[45] assemblages,[46] networks,[47] and webs. Each mode – ecological modernization, techno-utopianism, and apocalypticism – tells a different story and suggests a series of practices that seek to address the environmental crisis from specific loci of power/knowledge, and with a particular set of instruments and ideological biases.

Broadly speaking, ecological modernizers are about institutions, techno-utopians about evolution, and the apocalyptics about revolution. Ecological modernizers believe that the environmental crisis is essentially a market failure and that by internalizing it through accurate price signals, we can address issues like climate change without abandoning growth or profit. Techno-utopians begin the shift away from an economic grammar of markets and money, and frame the debate instead in terms of morality and scientific objectivity. The apocalyptic mode, on the other hand, embodies the Malthusian belief that humans have vastly overstepped the carrying capacity of the earth. Applying pressure with horror statistics and guilt, this mode is concerned with finding alternatives to capitalist values and pushing us toward a vastly different economic arrangement. My use of the continuum is meant to suggest the permeability of the modalities, while at the same time singling out ideological positions and their material consequences.

To reiterate, the chart is not meant to unite the book, but rather, to suggest how terms like "sustainability," "value," and "growth" become key sites for the struggle over the trajectory of current and future solutions. In his influential book on ecological modernization, Maarten Hajer reminds us: "[story-lines] not only help to construct a problem, [but] they also play an important role in the creation of a social and moral order in a given domain. Story-lines are devices through which actors are positioned, and through which specific ideas of 'blame' and 'responsibility,' and 'urgency' and 'responsible behavior' are attributed."[48] The way we tell this story of capitalism and nature has radical consequences, especially in terms of speaking for and listening to nature. Christopher Manes points out that for the most part, "Nature is silent in our [Western] culture."[49] Since nature can only be imagined by humans through tools such as language, narrative, and metaphor, the question of the deployment of discourse, cultural ecologies,[50] literature, and metaphor is crucial to understanding the effects of the shift toward a "green" form of capitalism. Lawrence Buell argues that "the environmental crisis involves a crisis of the imagination the amelioration of which depends on finding better ways of imagining nature and humanity's relation to it."[51] By making nature speak in an economic language, rendering "services" and "resources," ecology becomes subsumed by economy.

I am concerned, therefore, not only with the historical context of these modes, but also with their role in maintaining certain kinds of logics, trajectories, lines of flight, momentums, and stories. These stories matter because they set the course of public investment and the direction of policy. Especially in an economic climate where austerity justifies a crisis mentality of limited options and "prudent" financial investment, counter-narratives are more important than ever. Who gets to decide the future we can or cannot afford? What values will be plugged into the equations that transform risk into opportunity? Without compelling narratives that simultaneously challenge the system and provide alternatives, the current economic crisis can and will result in an even deeper neoliberal agenda fundamentally incompatible with the planet's survival. And let me be blunt: survival is what's at stake – the survival of humanity and the systems upon which it depends. This is a crucial moment in history where capitalism's contradictions and excesses are plainly visible, and in such moments of danger, power must retrench or give up ground. Language is important because it can crystallize and naturalize certain modes of understanding the world. As De Angelis points out, capitalism is a "social force that aspires to colonise the whole of life practices,"[52] a force that in the process seeks to impose economic values as the *single measure* of all things.

It is precisely for this reason that I spend so many pages discussing green economics before examining how alternative food movements are negotiating the realm of value and practice within the structural constraints of capitalism. For while locavores and the sustainable food movement have captured the public's attention and offer very real and useful solutions to making agriculture more resilient and sustainable, they are still largely part of a middle- and upper-class movement that must realize its own history and the limits or costs imposed upon it by the useful, and necessary, language of economics. This book is written as a hybrid text: its celebration of local food is tempered within a broader discussion of the greening of capitalism, precisely so that academics, practitioners, and local eaters can understand the extent to which local food is an aspect of a much bigger structural problem relating to capitalism and the emergence of a new economic system. I want to celebrate local food in order to save it from the "success" of organics – to challenge those who are interested in the issues and seduced by the pleasures of the table to make connections between what they eat and the broader perspective. Food can become a powerful educational tool, a kind of gateway drug into radical politics, alternative social values, globalization, and permaculture.

Figure 1 delineates a spectrum of value in order to illustrate that value systems involve constant struggle, negotiation, and most important, are always unfinished. The future is fundamentally

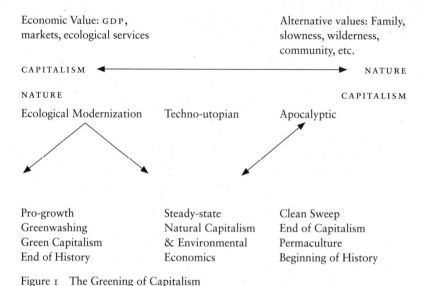

Economic Value: GDP,   Alternative values: Family,
markets, ecological services   slowness, wilderness,
                                                        community, etc.

CAPITALISM ◄──────────────────────────────► NATURE

NATURE   CAPITALISM

Ecological Modernization   Techno-utopian   Apocalyptic

Pro-growth   Steady-state   Clean Sweep
Greenwashing   Natural Capitalism   End of Capitalism
Green Capitalism   & Environmental   Permaculture
End of History   Economics   Beginning of History

Figure 1   The Greening of Capitalism

open, and the continuum is meant to suggest a schematic for understanding how the question of sustainability can be answered in different ways and with dramatically different results. The spectrum
helps visualize the extent to which economic logic shapes the
imagined and actual solutions to environmental problems, by
emphasizing how imbricated value and practice, imagination, and
action truly are.

ECOLOGICAL MODERNIZATION: MARKETIZING NATURE AND NATURALIZING MARKETS

Maarten Hajer's theoretical account of ecological modernization in
The Politics of Environmental Discourse can be extended into a
consideration of current configurations of capitalism and nature.
Hajer identifies 1972 as a turning point for ecological modernization. It was the year in which the Club of Rome's "Limits to
Growth" and the UN Conference on the Human Environment in
Stockholm[53] helped shift the dominant approach to the environmental crisis. Prior to 1972 the approach had been to develop
departments and legislative frameworks that compartmentalized
the environment into air, soil, water, and sound, and to subsequently

hand out pollution permits in order to regulate the market.[54] Pollution was "not generally recognized as a structural problem," and as such, was subservient to industry.[55] Ecological modernization changed the idea that pollution was something that could be dealt with after the fact, with end-of-pipe technologies like chimneys, drains, and water-processing plants. Hajer documents how this earlier approach was largely replaced in the 1980s by policy-focused ecological modernization.[56] He defines ecological modernization as "the discourse that recognizes the structural character of the environmental problematique but none the less assumes that existing political, economic, and social institutions can internalize the care for the environment."[57] This requires that pollution can be monetized and internalized in a positive-sum game that requires universal participation.[58] In these terms, the environmental crisis becomes an issue of proper management and a "strategy of political accommodation of the radical environmentalist critique of the 1970s."[59]

Of the positions I have identified along the continuum between nature and capitalism (Fig. 1), "ecological modernization" is the closest to capitalism in terms of its reliance on the economic grammar of markets, profit, throughput, efficiency, and wealth generation. As the chart shows, I further divide ecological modernization into two sub-categories: green capitalism and environmental economics, which share important similarities and a desire to value nature within an economic framework, but which represent a significant divergence. In the context of valuing nature economically, "ecological economics" has used terms like "natural capital" as a "means to control the discourse of sustainable development."[60] The major distinction between ecological modernization and ecological economics is the former's emphasis on growth versus the emphasis of steady-state economics,[61] a difference that is both discursive and material.

"Environmental economics" can be seen as an attempt to beat capitalists at their own game, revealing the limitations of treating nature as a resource and garbage dump and of discounting future generations in favour of immediate profits. However, it also illustrates the danger of using economic language. Despite the serious critiques proposed by ecological economics that target growth, their challenge is easily contained within the overarching logic of capitalist value and displaced by profit-seeking activity. Natural capitalism and ecological modernization – two names for the same movement – can therefore be understood as an attempt to rewrite capitalist valuation practices from within by broadening the scope of what is being valued. One of the key appeals of local and organic food is precisely this dimension of working from within the system, and the rhetoric of voting with one's dollar helps defuse any claims that the system is inflexible or cannot adapt to both social and environmental pressure.

Ecological modernization is characterized by a profound schism over the goal and function of economic systems as they relate to the historically given condition of capitalism as a dominant world system. It is thus crucial to examine the rhetorical strategies and metaphors of ecological modernization, for the struggle to appropriate terms like "sustainability," "green," and "ecology" is perhaps most acute in this modality. Both natural and green capitalism accept the basic language of market economics and are therefore circumscribed by the imperative discourse of capitalism. Ecological modernization is the purest example of the economic turn. It reveals some of the pitfalls of adopting the language of capitalism as a strategic tool to create discourse coalitions among environmentalists, policy makers, economists, and a public that has largely bought into the idea that the health of the economy is more important than the health of the planet. These pitfalls become even more acute as the protracted economic crisis threatens to monopolize the attention and priorities of politicians. While ecological modernization promises to bridge capitalism and nature, it does so in an unbalanced way, with synthesis possible only under favourable conditions of economic growth.

Organic food is an example of how ecological modernization internalizes and incorporates critique into meagre accommodations, greenwashing, and the establishment of new markets that prioritize growth and consumerism above all else. Like covering a landfill with a park and then capturing the underlying methane and calling it green energy, the change is largely cosmetic, and what lies beneath will one day emerge to reveal a toxic legacy.

Although environmental economics[62] contains many different analyses of the relationship between capitalism and nature, and relies on divergent and competing discursive fields and methodologies,[63] the underlying critique of a growth-based economic system has remained consistent throughout the discipline's history. In the late 1960s and early 1970s, Herman Daly, Kenneth Boulding, and Nicolas Georgescu-Roegen suggested that "economics should focus more on the material and energy flows and search theoretical tools from mechanistic and evolutionary systems theory,"[64] a direction that led to the development of ecological economics in the 1970s. In one of the earliest and most influential texts of the discipline, "The Economics of the Coming Spaceship Earth" (1966), Kenneth Boulding compares two idealized economic systems: a cowboy economy that is fully open and a spaceman economy that is closed. In the article, Boulding criticized neoclassical economics for being "obsessed with ... income-flow concepts to the exclusion ... of capital-stock concepts."[65]

A common rhetorical strategy of ecological modernists is the metaphor of natural capital, a polysemic term that invokes notions of an active rather than passive nature which produces value and generates wealth. The term also suggests a dynamic relationship between economy and ecology, and creates a powerful discursive coalition between otherwise disparate actors. While some, like Maria Åkerman, are critical of the reductionism of ecological economics as it attempts to monetize the intrinsic value of nature,[66] Åkerman recognizes that as a "linguistic device, a fluid object" it has provided a "common ground of communication for actors coming from different social worlds, acting in different contexts, involved in heterogeneous practices and having different goals."[67] It is for this reason that Herman Daly and Joshua Farley emphasize a common root with neoclassical economics, while at the same time pointing out the limitations of ecological economics and thus framing it as an arboreal branching rather than a radical split.[68]

Unlike the apocalyptic mode, ecological economics is careful not to alienate the general public with strong rhetorical and revolutionary demands. Rather, Daly and Farley carefully position themselves as reformists who are trying to cure the "economic autism" of neoclassical economic systems through a "necessary evolution of conventional economic thought."[69] They believe that markets have their utility, but not that markets can reveal all desires, goals, and means, or that they should be followed exclusively. In a sense, they are trying to move capitalism from the far left of the spectrum, toward the right, where other values can begin to exert a force on the way capitalism measures worth.

Ecological economics declares itself a transdisciplinary science that tries to address the limitations of ecology, which tends to treat ecosystems as separate from humans, and also the limitations of capitalism, which tends to ignore natural services in order to sustain the demands of unrestrained growth. Ecological economists call for an end to growth, measured as throughput (quantitative: resources in and waste out), but not to development, which is qualitative and involves "realization of potential, evolution towards an improved, but not larger, structure or system."[70] They are careful to define sustainable development as "qualitative improvement in the ability to satisfy wants (needs and desires) without quantitative increase in throughput beyond environmental carrying capacity."[71] That being so, they propose an alternative model to growth based on a steady-state economy, which would be capable of maintaining "constant stocks of wealth and people at levels that are sufficient for a long and good life. The throughput by which these stocks are maintained should be low rather than high, and always within the regenerative and absorptive capacity of the ecosystem."[72] This is one of the most radical critiques of capitalism offered by environmental economics, but it also reveals why the idea of a Trojan horse within capitalism simply will not work. By attacking growth, that engine of capital's restless movement and its *raison d'être*, environmental economics demands a shift that is too radical for its modest proposal. Moreover, it is easily contained by appeals to sustainable development and green growth, which on the surface appear to value nature. Ecological modernists have a strong "belief in the possibility of decoupling economic growth from negative environmental consequences" and a confidence that "society in its present form need not be changed, as pressures from customers, environmental groups, legislators, etc. will force organizations to take environmental responsibility and come up with technological solutions."[73]

One of the most popular figures of environmental economics is Paul Hawken, author of *Natural Capitalism* and *The Ecology of Commerce*. Hawken has made many appearances on popular documentaries such as *The 11th Hour* and *The Corporation*, and is the author of hundreds of popular articles and books about environmental economics. He optimistically argues that "the world stands on the threshold of basic changes in the conditions of business. Companies that ignore the message of natural capitalism do so at their peril."[74] Like Stern, Hawken emphasizes the investment potential of redesigning the world along a radically more sustainable path. Spurred by the prospect of massive gains in efficiency, Hawken believes we will be able to transform the industrial metabolism so that it mirrors natural cycles. For example, using developments in biomimicry, which takes nature as a model in the development of new materials and industrial techniques, he argues that we can produce material goods that are significantly less resource-intensive and toxic. Whereas the first industrial revolution accumulated material capital at the cost of natural capital, and because we have destroyed so much of the true basis of wealth, capitalism will face limits to prosperity based on resource scarcity.[75] Thus, markets must invest in conservation in order to grow. By factoring the depletion of natural capital into the cost of production, businesses will find new ways to extract and use what they need without damaging the environment.

Hawken's model assumes that the market, with some tweaks and internalizations, will react and conform to the undeniable logic of natural capitalism once a critical mass has been achieved. As with Stern's argument, the environmental crisis can be understood as a market failure and also as an immense business opportunity. By internalizing all sources of material value, Hawken claims, we can fully account for damage to the environment and harness the incredible power of the market to allocate resources to solve the environmental crisis.[76] In a strange way, the economic autism of capitalism can be understood as an issue of information, echoing the consciousness-raising campaigns of many mainstream environment-alists, and suggesting that markets simply need the right signals.

As I have already mentioned, the danger of adopting economic language lies in the ability of that language to over-determine, dir-ect, and incorporate critique. As an example of how effectively rad-ical propositions like environmental economics are translated into neoliberal contexts, let us consider organic food. Today's organic food is a response to a consumer- and producer-driven movement that has emerged as part of a broader environmental consciousness and anxiety about toxicity, health, and the deleterious effects of industrial agriculture. Advertisers have cleverly tapped into this anxiety, with green marketing appearing on everything from pizza boxes to designer yogurts and probiotic breads. Despite consumer willingness to pay premiums for green products, the lack of trans-parency and reliable information can easily lead to cynicism, as the words "natural," "green," and "eco-" appear on products that clearly do not embrace the ideals they conjure up. The current state of organic food is an arena where marketing, consumer activism, and profit have interacted in fascinating ways (which chapters 2 and 3 attempt to unravel) but for now, I want to focus on the rela-tionship between the market and the goals and ideals of the organic food movement as an alternative value practice. As Julie Guthman points out, even though the organic movement has never formally articulated an anti-capitalist stance, "it has gained coherence and momentum through the shared awareness that the undesirable aspects of mass food production are at least in part the result of profit-driven agricultural industrialization."[77]

Early back-to-the-land communes, small-scale producers, co-operative buying clubs that focused on direct marketing, Com-munity Supported Agriculture (CSA), and other alternative forms of ownership and production all challenged an industrial food sys-tem that was based on vertical integration and the dominance of a handful of huge, multinational producers. For many involved in the original counter-cultural movement, the fact that Wal-Mart now carries organic food would invalidate any gains they had made. I can now go into my local supermarket's organic section and buy

Organic Batter Blaster, a pancake/waffle batter in a pressurized can that can be squirted into a pan or waffle maker. The status of such a product as "certified organic" reveals the effects of market forces and consumer demand on what began as a movement with strong anti-capitalist and utopian tendencies. The popularity of organics is a market success story, but represents a failure of the system to accommodate any radical change, and as such, can be read as a cautionary tale of how green capitalism and environmental economics can easily merge into various hegemonic configurations of ecological modernization. That is, organic food participates in a larger greening of capitalism that reveals how the system is capable of monetizing a movement by emphasizing choice and ethical consumption above values such as the preservation of nature, co-operative organization, and small-scale production.

The vulnerability of consumers to the values of ecological modernization comes in part from the powerful narratives marshalled by organic and local food movements. Michael Pollan, for example, argues that organic food companies have realized how lucrative the stories told by organics can be. Organic food is the fastest-growing sector of the food industry, and many companies are using what Pollan refers to as the "supermarket pastoral"[78] to sell their products. Organics offer a rich pastoral narrative of heroic family farmers fighting in the name of mother nature by standing against Goliath corporations interested only in the bottom line. The narrative gratifies our deepest nostalgia for connection with the earth and a taste for authentic experiences. It offers a "return to a utopian past with the positive aspects of modernity intact"[79] and, as Leo Marx puts it, a "landscape of reconciliation"[80] which, in the context of industrial organic, serves to support rather than challenge the system.

Thus we see companies like Kraft and General Mills buying up organic farms and mass-producing food on an industrial scale that is dependent on energy-intensive transportation networks. Like conventional agriculture, industrial organic slips into a botanical treadmill of production[81] that relies heavily on off-farm inputs and monocultures.[82] Pollan criticizes industrial organic as "a venerable ideal hollowed out, reduced to a sentimental conceit printed on the side of a milk carton."[83] Similarly, Laura DeLind points out that "the codification and commercialization of organic has helped to catalyze a 'second generation' response to food system issues – the local food movement."[84] By adopting the logic of ecological modernization, organic food became entrenched in the industrial monocropping model. Spurred by books such as *The 100-Mile Diet*, *The Omnivore's Dilemma*, and *Animal, Vegetable, Miracle*, the local food movement has thus proposed a move beyond organic, a move concerned not so much with labels and accreditation[85] as with helping foster local distribution networks based on direct marketing and models of farmer-consumer co-production. Chapters 2 and 3 examine these developments in greater detail, especially in terms of the relationship between storied food, advertising, and the embodied knowledge acquired from CSAs, gardening, and cooking. One of the most compelling aspects of the local food movement is the potential of forms of embodied knowledge to resist commodification and thus to avoid the path that organic has taken. But for now, lets focus on the relationship between nature and capitalism, between economic arguments and more personal, environmental, and socio-political ones.[86]

As an attempt to introduce alternative value systems into capitalism, organic food has largely failed. For this reason, I consider organic food in the ecological modernization category; the appeal to consumerism and voting with one's dollars has largely evacuated organics of any of its revolutionary momentum. Considering the fate of organics, DeLind argues that we need "ways of thinking and feeling about local food that cannot be easily appropriated and/or disappeared by the reductionist rationality of the marketplace and that can balance and reframe an economic orientation with more ecological and cultural understandings of people in place."[87] The arguments of the ecological-modernist paradigm fail precisely in their inability to move beyond the rationality of the market and the economic grammar of yield, consumer demand, ethical consumption, and neoliberal subjectivity.[88] Alternative food movements have attempted to push beyond this value system, only to become the frontline of capitalism's attempt to colonize new sources of value.

Once again, what I want to emphasize here is the oppositional dichotomy between the market as a means of addressing and accommodating demands for sustainably and ethically produced goods, and the history of co-opting those demands into a neoliberal logic. The ecological modernist mode is characterized by its promise to provide sustainability, growth, and *profit within the framework of the current system*. It is impelled by the undeniable power and appeal of the narrative of the citizen-consumer hybrid that changes the world one dollar at a time, and the "realistic" approach of environmental economics to changing the system from within. And yet, as the example of organic food illustrates, the entrance of companies such as General Mills, ConAgra, and ADM into organic farming has resulted in a fundamentally altered industry[89] that relies almost exclusively on off-farm inputs and which emphasizes individual health and consumer choice, rather than the environmental benefits of its products.[90]

It is for this reason that I lump organics and ecological capitalism within the discourse of ecological modernization. As a strategy of accommodation, ecological modernization is able to colonize the alternative models of ecological economics by emphasizing the economy over ecology, transforming an otherwise radical critique into basic pollution controls, consumer labelling laws, and an emphasis on free choice. The economic turn can thus be seen as a necessary evil, which allows for communication between disparate actors but comes at a substantial price. The ability of alternative/local food movements to effect real and lasting change is dependent on the influence of non-economic values in steering the course of the future of food.

TECHNO-UTOPIANISM, OR HOW I STOPPED WORRYING AND LEARNED TO LOVE THE FLOW CHART

Environmental problems are often difficult to grasp in terms of cause and effect, and scale. It is hard for many people to understand how small decisions such as the car they drive or the food they eat can have any appreciable effect on the environment.

Invocations to "think global and act local," complicate things further, as a desire to do good on the level of the community can spiral
out into a perpetual game of NIMBYism (not in my back yard), or
stall in the arena of international negotiations as a similar strategy
plays out between nations. This game of hot potato often ends with
wealthy communities/countries with political clout passing the
buck to impoverished areas within their country or beyond, where
the absence of environmental regulations and the existence of populations with no political voice allow a local pollution problem
to be solved by pushing it out of sight and out of mind.[91] Global
warming is the quintessential problem of scale, and is different
from other kinds of pollution because we rarely experience it
directly. Even storms such as Hurricane Sandy or Katrina with clear
connections to climate change cannot be "proven" as such on the
level of matters of fact. With respect to global warming, we are
"wholly dependent on the research and monitoring work of scientists to track the progress of warming and map its consequences."[92]
Because of this, global warming is a different kind of crisis, one
that must be mediated by various parties and institutions to make
the information comprehensible to the public. In the case of climate
change, involving hugely complex data and thousands of computer-
generated climactic scenarios, the normal presence of uncertainty is
easily construed as justifying inaction.

The 2009 "climategate" controversy, in which a group of Russian
hackers downloaded and disseminated personal emails from the
University of East Anglia's climate research unit, is an excellent
example of the way scientific data, media, and politics can mix.
The controversy touched off a storm of accusations of interference
with the peer-review process, scientific withholding, collusion, and
peer exclusion, and the right-wing media have treated it as evidence of a conspiracy to misrepresent the severity of the global-
warming crisis. Although an independent British commission has
exonerated the scientists,[93] the controversy is a clear illustration of
how powerfully the politics of representation can shift the terms of
a debate. For ecological modernists, it is crucial to represent climate change and the environmental crisis in terms of free choice,

markets, and capitalist logic in order to create a shared vocabulary that can address the joint ecological and economic crisis.

Addressing and representing risk and uncertainty in science as they relate to policy issues and public perception is perhaps the quintessential difficulty of contemporary ecopolitics. How is it possible to respond to the prospect of a future crisis that is by its very nature unknowable? How do we make environmental issues more urgent, more pertinent to our everyday lives, without slipping into discussions of individual choice and consumer activism? How can we account for the future? The techno-utopian mode tries to move beyond economic arguments by emphasizing the moral character of the environmental crisis, while at the same time focusing on translating science into a discourse of futurity and responsibility. By moving away from the language of markets and money, techno-utopianism frames the debate in terms of morality and scientific objectivity, with a blend of moral outrage, trust in scientific leadership beyond politics,[94] and a utopian faith in technology.

The growing awareness of environmental destruction has led many people to be receptive to environmental messages, whether shown by the rise in popularity of hybrid cars, CFL light bulbs, or organic food. Despite its materiality, however, the environmental crisis does not necessarily manifest in objective or concrete ways. As Timothy Luke reminds us, all toxicity and risks associated with the environmental crisis are "social acts of political interpretation."[95] Toxins are "socially produced, and the process of evaluating their costs and benefits frequently uses scientific evidence in disinformative ways."[96] All parties involved inevitably manipulate this riskscape for their benefit, whether in the hope of maintaining economic growth, increasing investment in alternative energy, forming stronger local economies, or resisting capitalism. Environmentalism is big business and many people hold stakes in various imagined futures.

For such reasons, discourses about risk, toxicity, and culpability are difficult to navigate, especially when it comes to complex scientific theories. Even as the rhetorical tone of the debate becomes more and more apocalyptic, people will continue to struggle and make choices that align with their worldviews. The emphasis on science-based policy, exemplified by the Bali and Copenhagen round of climate talks, amplifies this tension, as members of the public realize they must make pro-active decisions about their personal relationship to the causes and effects of climate change, while at the same time abdicating decision-making responsibility to specialists and scientists who supposedly have our best interests in mind. The climate of risk is exacerbated by various levels of expertise and specialization. Giddens's reminder is apt: "we are all laypeople in respect of the vast majority of the expert systems which intrude on our daily activities."[97] Precisely because so many environmental issues demanding expertise straddle the boundary between different scales of personal, local, national, and international risks and opportunities, responsibility is easily passed along, and the scale and scope of response are not always clear. An issue within a local watershed can reverberate around the world, and small decisions made every day by consumers can magnify exponentially.

For Ulrich Beck, "[the] central concept is not 'crisis' but 'new global risk.' Risks are, essentially, man-made, incalculable, uninsurable threats and catastrophes which are *anticipated* but which often remain invisible and therefore depend on how they become defined and contested in 'knowledge.'"[98] The risks relating to food are entangled on a number of scales, and respond to many seen and unseen forces. From food security and individual hunger, to systems of unequal development and the politics of starvation, concepts of futurity, morality, duty, and responsibility are part of a larger discourse of the green economy. The techno-utopian mode works to translate uncertainty and risk into the moral language of responsibility and futurity. Carbon capture and storage, geo-engineering, the hydrogen economy, and visions of high tech eco-cities such as Masdar, are all illustrations of the techno-utopian blend of science, morality, and faith in reason. Let us consider two specific examples.

The first, Al Gore's *An Inconvenient Truth* uses a mixture of moral argument and scientific expertise to address risk and uncertainty by establishing the impartial status of the scientific-manager as wise leader. The second example is vertical farming, a futuristic solution to urban sustainability and local eating that epitomizes the techno-utopian faith in progress, scientific ingenuity, and technological developments as key prerequisites of social and environmental justice.

Because many environmental problems are long in scope, complicated to understand, and preclude everyday knowledge, the role of a translator such as Gore is becoming increasingly important. Since most of us are laypeople in relation to many of these systems, it is equally important to examine the process of translation as filtration and distillation. What assumptions, ideologies, and systems of power/knowledge are contained within techno-utopianism? What rhetorical strategies and metaphors are used? And how do they shape the broader debate about the role of capitalism and ecology in steering the human response to climate change, peak oil, and the future of food?

Since the environmental movement of the 1970s prompted a wave of regulation that was supposed to prevent the environmental crisis from devastating the world, many environmentalists have come to lament a widespread lack of political will and the extent of corporate cronyism behind the basic environmental laws in place today. *An Inconvenient Truth* deals with this anxiety directly, taking on the oil lobby and the climate-change deniers and skeptics who have invested heavily in sowing seeds of public doubt by claiming that global warming is scientifically unproven. Although Gore is not the first to criticize the excessive media coverage of climate skeptics like Bjørn Lomborg and the American Petroleum Institute, *An Inconvenient Truth* was immensely successful in appealing to a lay public ill-equipped to understand the phenomenally complex science of global warming and thus held hostage to newspapers and other popular media capable of translating the data. In the movie Gore frequently points out how climate-change deniers try to "reposition global warming as theory rather than fact."[99] He argues that even though there is almost universal scientific consensus that global warming exists and is caused by human activity, the media have given half their time to the climate deniers. For Gore, the solution lies in raising awareness of the facts and engendering faith in the leadership of impartial scientists. The movie attempts to move beyond politics by arguing for the truth status of climate change science, thereby shifting from a discourse of risk to one of crisis. The popularity of *An Inconvenient Truth* is largely related to Gore's ability to position himself as an interlocutor who can speak as a layperson and translate the science into a compelling narrative that balances the apocalyptic implications of climate change with hope that a better future is possible.

To that end, the central figure in *An Inconvenient Truth* is the flow chart or graph; at one point Gore explains how his attitude was transformed by a university professor who showed him a chart with CO_2 concentration and temperature in perfect correlation. For Gore, his moment of environmental awakening was directly linked to statistics and scientific data. He recreates this experience for the audience with a picture of the earth breathing in and out as the graph of temperature and CO_2 concentration marches steadily upward, invoking an unexpected mixture of awe and feelings of biophilia,[100] along with raw scientific data. The data are then linked to iconic images of polar bears and glaciers collapsing. His sense of amazement about the science is palpable as he declares, "the ice has stories to tell us."[101] In this sequence, Gore is trying to legitimate climate change science by showing us how it can give us the ability to read the book of nature. Nature is used to support the data, which in a strange way come first, and offer an objective view unclouded by politics.

The ocean temperature graphs, for example, come before Gore's discussion of Hurricane Katrina and the destruction caused by warmer ocean temperatures. The movie functions as a visual politics of technocratic management, fostering a trust in data and science-based policy that Gore claims is absolutely necessary if people are to harness their moral outrage in productive ways. Thus the rather dramatic and now infamous hockey-stick graph of CO_2 concentrations rising off the charts, as he explains how scientists brave the Antarctic cold to bring us a record of the past, is meant to visually represent an objective form of moral outrage: "this is not a political issue, so much as a moral issue."[102] By emphasizing that "scientists have an independent obligation to respect and present the truth as they see it,"[103] Gore transforms the audience into the "technical-political object of management and government,"[104] while at the same time claiming to transform that government with moral legitimacy. In this blend of "objective" data, moral outrage, apolitical rage, and faith in technological progress, Gore exemplifies the techno-utopian modality.

Overall, the movie is as much about Gore as it is about climate change. Gore focuses on his own journey to expose the truth and enlighten the public to the dangers of climate change, a journey that echoes the heroic endeavours of the scientists who brave Antarctic conditions to bring the public the truth. He weaves together his own quest with iconic images of the imperilled earth, including the earthrise photo with which he begins and ends the movie. But it is the ending that is particularly illustrative of the system of moral technocracy that Gore supports. As he discusses why he was compelled to take his message to the people, he recollects that it was because his early exposure to climate science gave him a window into the future: science literally leads to responsibility. As he opens up to the audience, the camera pans out from a grainy, black and white image of Gore standing in front of an image of Katrina. The outline of his body is the window into the future – white, privileged, consumerist, sponsored by Apple, wearing a suit, and jetting around the world to spread the word. His silhouette cuts through the hurricane, as if taming it, rendering its eye more human, manageable, and digital. The eye of the storm and the eye from space interplay through a technocratic subjectivity of scientific facts, data, and consensus on the one hand, and political failure, moral abjectness, and ignorance on the other. Gore becomes a translation matrix, a means by which to channel the data into the realm of politics and policy in a seamless and graphically slick package. His is a Mac version of climate change: he stands in front of the storm, transformed into an image, reduced to a PowerPoint presentation.

Despite the power of Gore's appeal, the movie is remarkably deficient in imagining what an alternative future means, making a brief series of suggestions at the end of the film that involve changing light bulbs, driving less, buying offset credits, and supporting politicians who are aware of the issues. Gore assures us that "when the warnings are accurate and based on sound science, then we as human beings, whatever country we live in, have to find a way to make sure the warnings are heard and responded to."[105] Thankfully, he says, "humanity already possesses the fundamental scientific, technical, and industrial know-how to solve the carbon and climate problems."[106] Like the ecological modernists, Gore assures us that "if we do the right thing we will create a lot of new wealth and jobs, because doing the right thing will move us forward."[107] He ends the movie saying: "we have everything we need save political will. But in America, political will is a renewable resource."[108] He thus transforms the insecurity cultivated throughout the movie into some rather weak shifts in personal behaviour and a trust in the objective truth of climate science. Morality is once again reunited with capitalism, and the future promises to be a slightly greener version of today.

Giddens argues that "fateful moments are threatening for the protective cocoon which defends the individual's ontological security, because the 'business as usual' attitude that is so important to that cocoon is inevitably broken through."[109] *An Inconvenient Truth* neuters this fateful moment by limiting the argument to an emotional and visual rationalization of the science behind climate change, translating scientific data into an emotional technocracy. In the process, the movie ignores the underlying and systemic roots of the problem and allows the individual to avoid feeling the ontological insecurity that is necessary for stimulating the kinds of changes suggested by the scope of the problem. By making the changes seem like technical design solutions, the ontological disruption of global warming as a fateful moment becomes a reaffirmation of the role of capitalist techno-science in solving the environmental problematique. The mixture of moral appeals, scientific (un)certainty, and consumer activism creates fertile ground for green governmentality, as "the economics and ecologies of risk ... create tremendous new opportunities for cadres of educated professionals to work productively as better resource managers."[110] The wise technocrat is a central figure in the techno-utopian modality, and convincing the audience to trust the science is a crucial move in establishing a form of green governmentality capable of deflecting the anxiety of navigating an uncertain and risky future. Although Gore does much to challenge the climate-change deniers, the movie's main function is to engender trust in the objective scientist by making an impassioned plea for separating politics from science.

Discussions about how humanity will feed the future, as populations continue to grow and climate change transforms the nature of agriculture, have a long history of relying on similar techno-utopian narratives about science ultimately releasing nature's true cornucopia. The idea of the vertical farm, a skyscraper that produces its own energy, collects rain water, and grows local and organic food year round, has captured the imagination of many. Dr Dickson Despommier's radical proposal for simultaneously addressing climate change and food security has attracted a lot of attention, both positive and negative. The Columbia University professor of Health and Microbiology manages a website on the topic and has published *The Vertical Farm: Feeding the World in the 21st Century*. Although there is no working model of such a farm, its potential has occasioned many articles in major periodicals, and a documentary funded by the musician Sting is planned to follow the construction of the first vertical farm in China. I am less interested in debating the possibility of such a project than I am about the way the concept frames questions of sustainability, technology, capitalism, and nature. The idea of a vertical farm is perhaps more compelling than the reality; it promises to unite town and country, science and nature, and to banish hunger at the same time as addressing poverty and land degradation.

A similar project, called Sundrop Farms, is currently being tested in the Australian desert. Using parabolic solar panels and advanced technology to desalinate water and grow food in the desert, the inventors have enacted a "miracle" which they claim "can supply billions with healthy, cheap food, help save the planet and make a fortune?"[111] Armed with a faith in the seemingly politically neutral scientist-entrepreneur, these types of projects promise to solve our most pressing issues and turn a profit at the same time. Seamlessly bridging the gap between ecological modernizers, with their faith in markets, and apocalyptic warnings, with their insistence that

humanity is on a path toward destruction, they promise to fulfill
the old-testament invocation to make the desert flower.

Despommier argues that agriculture is among humanity's most
ecologically destructive activities, and cites evidence that almost all
areas currently under cultivation show significant signs of degradation.[112] The idea of the vertical farm offers a utopian reconciliation
of science and technology that combines Malthusian fear of over-
population outpacing food production with horror statistics of the
effects of agriculture on biodiversity, soil erosion, water, and climate. Vertical farming evokes a seductive vision: it "promises to
eliminate external natural processes as confounding elements in
the production of food, since crops will be grown indoors under
carefully selected and well-monitored conditions, [e]nsuring an
optimal growth rate for each species of plant and animal year
round."[113] From the disciplining of nature's vagaries to the promise of solving hunger and climate change and eliminating the use of
herbicides and pesticides, the vertical farm embraces the vision of
a sanitized modernist aesthetic of scientific control, streamlining,
and faith in reason, while at the same time maintaining external
nature as a pure, binary opposite. Despommier makes an optimistic argument: "The best reason to consider converting most food
production to vertical farming is the promise of restoring ecosystem services and functions. There is good reason to believe that
an almost full recovery of many of the world's endangered terrestrial ecosystems will occur simply by abandoning a given area of
encroachment and allowing the land to 'cure' itself ... One vertical
farm with an architectural footprint of one square city block and
rising up to 30 stories (approximately 3 million square feet) could
provide enough nutrition (2,000 calories/day/person) to comfort-
ably accommodate the needs of 10,000 people employing technologies currently available."[114]

The vertical farm would literally take the dirt out of farming,
moving plants indoors into a realm of pure management and biological control, tapping into a longstanding modernist desire to
overcome nature. Science becomes almost magical, producing a
miracle of cornucopian abundance by simulating nature directly.
Drawing on examples of technological fairs, expos and Disneyland,

Alexander Wilson argues that the Western, rationalist approach too often responds to scarcity and crisis as if they were "technical problems that could be solved with 'objective' research, planning and administration."[115]

Warren Belasco examines the history of similar proposals for agriculture, ranging from meals in a pill and algae burgers, to artificial meat grown in laboratories. In the 1930s, food security issues were often perceived through the curative lens of science, technology, and business. Many futurists saw agriculture as horribly wasteful and believed that the food of the future would be grown in laboratories, with steaks being formed from other steaks, and microbes and yeasts providing other foodstuffs. The dream of a meal in a pill offered panaceic visions of a playground world: "the assertion that hyperindustrialized food production would enhance soil conservation and convert unsightly farms to decorous parks was a central tenet of technological utopians."[116] Futurists believed that technology would solve, rather than exacerbate, the problem of soil erosion and environmental degradation. Malthusian concerns specifically about food and population spurred huge funding grants for research into alternative food sources, especially algae and yeast.

For example, during the 1950s in the United States, many people believed that chlorella[117] could feed the world. Scientists and the media envisioned a future of tubes filled with algae in warm sunny places, needing almost no labour but having the capacity to banish hunger from the world.[118] The algae turned out to be hugely expensive and difficult to produce, and still did not taste good or live up to the laboratory conversion rates. It was deemed too expensive to sell as animal feed or as cheap burgers, but Japanese companies were able to market it in high-end health food stores by promoting its ability to control weight, prevent cancer, and boost immune system functions.[119] Belasco remarks that algae's "actual fate as a food source shows how, in the absence of an explicit, well-funded public commitment specifically to feeding the poor, new food research may drift towards high-end markets."[120]

The idea of the vertical farm recycles this much older vision of a modernist future, while at the same time tapping into a desire for local and organic produce and an increasing concern with carbon footprints. Stan Cox and David Van Tassel have criticized Despommier in the same vein as Belasco, accusing the vertical farm concept of trading on unrealistic technological fantasies and extending the logic of industrial agriculture – literally – to absurd heights.[121] They disagree with the fundamental math, suggesting that stacking plants vertically would require enormous amounts of energy and that "just to meet a year's U.S. wheat production with vertical farming would, for lighting alone, require eight times as much electricity as all U.S. utilities generate in an entire year."[122] They advocate instead permaculture systems based on diverse perennial crops that establish "deep, long-lived roots to protect the soil, manage water, nutrients efficiently, and help restore the belowground ecosystems that agriculture has destroyed."[123]

As with *An Inconvenient Truth*, what is missing in Despommier's vision is an analysis of power and distribution. Who would build, own, and operate these farms? To what extent would the produce grown within them compete with and displace rural farmers? He acknowledges that "at present the abundance of cash crops is more than sufficient to meet the nutritional needs of the world's human population, [and that] delivering them to world markets is driven largely by economics, not biological need."[124] Despite this, vertical farms offer a solution based on increased production, rather than on the politics of distribution. If current trends in genetically modified food and agriculture are any indication, vertical farms would not solve the problem by simply producing more food. Vandana Shiva has written extensively on the deleterious effects of bioprospecting and industrial farming on agriculture in the global South, especially on the ownership of seeds and the treadmill of production that occurs once farmers are enticed into industrial methods.[125] Inevitably, these kinds of capital-intensive proposals end up dispossessing the rural poor of their land and sending them to live as disposable populations within vast urban slums.[126] Despommier's own analysis points toward economics, rather than ecology, as the primary source of starvation. Unless these vertical farming buildings were to become common property, which would be hard to conceive of since their manufacture and operation would be a highly technical and capital-intensive affair, then the politics of fair distribution would by no means be assured.

Without a strong critique of the inequities foundational to capitalism, various techno-utopian dreams are doomed to replicate conditions of scarcity amplified by the ecological and economic injustice already present, conditions that are sure to increase as population growth strains the regenerative capacity of the earth. If it is true that we are producing enough calories today and people nevertheless exist in a state of food insecurity, it seems likely that, given the momentum of capitalism, this insecurity will increase as scarcity becomes less an economic issue and more a result of the physical limitations of nature. While it is important to maintain a sense that a better future is possible, the combination of moral appeals, emotional technocracy, and green governmentality tends to foreclose the possibility of radical action, and instead slips closer to the meagre accommodations of green capitalism. The utopianism of techno-utopianism actually represents a failure of imagination, a failure to think differently or to venture beyond the entrenched ideology of growth and development. It is in fact an anti-utopia, in the sense that it becomes trapped in an end-of-history limbo where the logic and trajectory of the entrenched system are imprinted onto a faith that technological advancements will usher in a cornucopia of abundance.

APOCALYPTIC NARRATIVES:
FAT KIDS AND THE END OF FOOD

Apocalyptic narratives about food, oil, obesity, and the death of the family farm are examples of the interconnected discourse of oil, climate change, and agriculture, and articulations of value practices that offer alternatives to capitalism. Within the context of the continuum of responses to the question of how we can value nature, this mode is the furthest from capitalism, and underlying many of its critiques is a deep cynicism about the ability of capitalism to account for nature in any meaningful way. Whereas ecological modernists try to value nature by providing an estimated cost that completely accounts for the full impact of a product or service, and techno-utopianists argue for technological solutions based on a moral economy of progress and technological advancements that will release nature's true cornucopia, the apocalyptic modality relies on alternative value practices such as spirituality, community, and slowness as means of averting ecological collapse. Those espousing the apocalyptic modality believe that change must be deep and profound: a major shift in culture is necessary – not just advances in technology and market mechanisms – if we are to prevent eco-apocalypse.

Although some of the texts I discuss here do not conform to the formal definition of apocalypse as pertaining to the end of the world, they share a number of features: an invocation of a sense of doom, binary conceptions of good and evil, and a reliance on the persuasive power of a looming catastrophe or crisis ranging from the end of capitalism to the end of the world. The apocalyptic modality can be understood as a prioritization of alternative values above and beyond capitalism. For example, David Suzuki argues that "economics itself is an invention that makes no ecological sense."[127] The apocalyptic modality suggests that the rift between capitalism and nature may be too deep to bridge.

Along the continuum of capitalism and nature, apocalypticism makes the greatest demands that humanity move from seeing the economy as a source of value, to valuing a presumably more authentic base in nature. Neil Evernden suggests that "we are not *in* an environmental crisis, but *are* the environmental crisis," in the sense that our way of knowing and being in the world is the problem.[128] Historically, various environmentalisms have tried to offer different visions of value and worth rooted in nature. For example, deep ecology, often connected with Henry Thoreau, Wendell Berry, Edward Abbey, and Gary Snyder, is associated "with a valuation of wild and rural spaces, self-sufficiency, a sense of place, and local knowledge and sometimes with an alternative spirituality."[129] Deep ecologists appeal to the idea of biocentric equality, whereby "all organisms and entities in the ecosphere, as parts of the interrelated whole, are equal in intrinsic worth."[130] Departing from the modern scientific discourse of objectivity and mechanistic assumptions regarding nature, deep ecologists take the principles of the universal right to self-realization and biocentric equality as their *modus oper-andi*. They often position themselves as the true or real environmentalists, using pejoratives like reformist, weak, and shallow to categorize more anthropocentric environmentalisms that focus on conservation, recycling, or green consumerism. Deep ecologists view nature as a victim of modernization, but also as its salvation.[131] They value wilderness in particular, and their glorification of nature, solitude, and wildness has strongly influenced environmental movements and literary critics within the U.S. context.[132]

There is a fundamental tension between modernity as progress, the dominant narrative of green capitalism, and modernity as regress, the dominant narrative of the apocalyptic mode. The tension between enchantment and disenchantment – between fantasy and realism, poetry and science – goes to the heart of environmental realpolitik. It also reveals the extent to which the environmental crisis is a crisis of our mental ecologies. How can we save a planet from ourselves? How could we move beyond the intractability of the present and usher in a future where alternatives to the course of modernity can emerge? What would be the characteristics of this new world?

Many of the texts I have discussed so far express at least some degree of apocalyptic dread. Whether in lamenting the corporatization of food, the reduction of biodiversity, the degradation of soil, or the decline of the family farm and the family dinner, the apocalyptic modality is concerned with finding a way out of the current historical moment. The urgency of averting this apocalypse is the impetus for changing the food system and for the rage that impels members of apocalyptically inspired alternative food movements to envision another world. As Imre Szeman points out, "the discourse of eco-apocalypse understands itself as a pedagogic one, a genre of disaster designed to modify behavior and transform the social."[133]

Bill McKibben, for example, embraces the environmental crisis as a lesson that, if approached correctly and with reason, can transform the world in positive ways by helping dethrone the capitalist economy and its attendant assumptions about progress, wealth, technology, and development. In his *Deep Economy*, McKibben makes an impassioned plea that local and small is beautiful, and that once basic security has been met, we must avoid the pitfalls of pursuing wealth endlessly for the sake of itself. *Deep Economy* is filled with statistics, examples and, above all, hope that another future is possible, a future that is fundamentally different from capitalism in its value system. McKibben suggests that the social, economic, political, and environmental problems we face today are avoidable if we can learn to pursue happiness and small-scale community-based economic systems, and re-learn how to take pleasure in family, community, and nature.

Two common threads in the apocalypticism of storied food are dependency on oil and the problem of obesity. They are illustrated by several publications and visual media, such as Jamie Oliver's television series *School Dinners*, the documentary *A Crude Awakening*, two separate books with identical titles by Paul Roberts and Thomas Pawlick called *The End of Food*, and Michael Pollan's *The Omnivore's Dilemma*.[134] As mentioned earlier, the apocalyptic theme is a dominant approach to the idea of crisis that runs throughout storied food, and through environmentalism in general. Lawrence Buell has said that "apocalypse is the single most powerful master metaphor that the contemporary environmental imagination has at its disposal."[135]

How, then, does the apocalyptic imaginary complement, reject, or amend the neoliberal notion that we are at the end of history? The apocalyptic mode seems to try to address all aspects. By imagining the end of capitalism through ecological collapse, this mode is, counter-intuitively, utopian in its vision of an alternative way of being. It is both enchanting and disenchanting in the sense that it assumes an "image of modernity as disenchanted, that is to say, as a place of dearth and alienation (when compared to a golden age of community and cosmological coherence),"[136] while also encouraging affective attachments to the world through the enchantment of everyday life. In the case of many of these authors, looking backward to sustainable farming practices rooted in traditional techniques, artisanal labour, and heritage seeds provides a narrative that is hopeful about the future, and yet extremely cognizant of the structural limitations impeding that vision. (It is for this reason that I place apocalypticism at the far right of Figure 1.)

The tension between regressive nostalgia for the pastoralism of a simple past and a more progressive utopian desire for a better future is not easy to resolve (and is considered more fully in chapter 2). It points to a major difficulty of apocalypticism: the need to communicate the scope and scale of the environmental crisis in a way that acknowledges the problems and barriers while avoiding the very real problem of envisioning a system so totally different that the only way out is the apocalyptic clean sweep. Once again, the stories we tell have a profound effect in shaping the world we create. Just like the dual poles that structure many environmental critiques, the utopian impulse for a better world, when tempered by the inevitable necessity for an apocalyptic clean sweep leads to material and ideological effects that can produce a profound feeling of paralysis and despair. These story-lines shape policy, individual and institutional responses, and generally affect our capacity to imagine alternatives on a very basic level. As was the case with my students, the apocalypse is simply a given: a sign of the times.

Discussions of the obesity crisis and peak oil share many elements, but obesity is perhaps the most controversial and yet most easily accessible narrative of storied food, precisely because it taps into a common anxiety about an uncontrolled body, whether individual or planetary. Especially when it comes to obesity, the sense of crisis manifests in moral panic and the rhetoric of ballooning healthcare costs,[137] while discussions of peak oil revolve around excessive and unequal consumption. Both evoke aspects of individual responsibility and addiction. Put another way, they are concerned with the status of the subject in relation to advertising, consumption, ecological decline, and agency.

The end of food is a common thematic in apocalyptic narratives. Many of the texts I have already mentioned share the fundamental assumption that something has gone horribly wrong with agriculture. A common refrain is that, despite the apparent success of modern agriculture in providing mountains of cheap calories with fewer people working the land, the true costs are multiplying in the form of a system of production and distribution heavily reliant on oil. Revealing this hidden world of externalities is one of the key goals of storied food, especially within the commodity biography.

Many commentators point out that vertical integration in the food industry has brought the spread of deadly and endemic pathogens,[138] a seriously degraded land base,[139] and a decrease in the varieties of vegetables and animals – and a resulting vulnerability to climate change.[140] Paul Roberts argues that "to an important degree, the success of the modern food sector has been its ability to make food behave like any other consumer product."[141] The paradox, according to Roberts, is that although the modern food industry is economic, "food itself is fundamentally not an economic phenomenon."[142] We have had to alter the food we eat, breeding less nutritious but more standardized varieties to accommodate the system, and as a result have left ourselves vulnerable to pathogens, obesity, chemical contamination, and a general loss of skills and knowledge. Prioritizing the economic over the biological has led to a fundamental distortion of the entire food system, forcing organic nature and the biocultural systems that are part of it into an economic derangement that cannot be sustained. Roberts's book reads like a horror show that catalogues in great detail the failures and problems of modern agriculture and the reasons that he sees the system collapsing under the weight of its own success. Most of the argument comes down to the effects of capitalism, especially on the meat industry and convenience foods. The desire for profit, requirements for long distance transport, and the seduction of cheap food have transformed what was once a solar economy into an economy saturated by oil.[143]

Pawlick's *The End of Food* focuses more directly on what has happened to food itself as it has become an economic artifact. Pawlick begins by tracing the nutritional vacuity of a modern hybrid tomato compared to an heirloom variety: "Higher in fat, higher in sodium, lower in calcium, potassium, Vitamin A, and Vitamin C, losing iron, phosphorous, niacin and thiamine, today's tomato looks as if it is almost calculated to lack whatever nutritionists recommend."[144] The demand for plant varieties that can withstand mechanical harvest (in order to avoid having to pay farm workers a living wage), and which ripen uniformly and can successfully travel long distances has created conditions in which the economics of the industry trump all other concerns, including nutrition, taste, sustainability, and labour relations. Pawlick argues that the end of food is the point where nutritional content declines and toxicity increases so much that food does more harm than good.[145] For Pawlick and many of the texts in the apocalyptic genre, capitalism and oil are to blame.

Dale Pfeiffer's book *Eating Fossil Fuel* looks at the extent of modern agriculture's reliance on hydrocarbons. According to Pfeiffer's analysis, the fecundity of the ironically named "green revolution" is rooted in the development of fossil-fuel–based fertilizers and pesticides and the use of hydrocarbon-fuelled irrigation.[146] Monocultures cultivated by industrial agriculture are possible only when whole ecosystems are essentially sterilized and then reinvigorated with the most basic nutrients required for life: phosphates, nitrogen, and potassium.[147] This linear, reductionistic model has made unprecedented short-term gains in yield, but at great costs. In the United States, 400 gallons of oil are used annually to feed each citizen, and even more to transport, process, cook, and distribute the food. Shockingly, that number is increasing, while farm production is falling.[148] Soil can only take so much before it becomes sterile, and we only have so much oil. A pound of processed breakfast cereal made from wheat uses thirty-two times the amount of energy needed to make a pound of flour; and the manufacture of just the can used to contain pop consumes ten times the energy contained in the drink.[149] Seen in this light, oil is responsible for masking soil degradation, through nutrient substitution with fertilizers, while at the same time providing the *illusion of abundance* and allowing the global population to rapidly increase. Subtract oil from the equation and we are left with a seriously degraded and in some cases sterilized land base incapable of supporting the very population that oil made possible.[150]

The apocalyptic genre is almost overburdened by these kinds of statistics, deployed in a shock-and-awe tactic that is meant to invert the techno-utopian teleology of progress with a sense of impending collapse – to reveal the distortions generated by capitalism by suggesting that our attempt to rush ahead is really just the futile running in place of the Red Queen in *Alice in Wonderland*. Jared Diamond's *Collapse*, Alan Weisman's *The World Without Us*, and

James Kunstler's novel *The World Made by Hand* are just a few examples of bestselling books that marshal apocalypse for pedagogical purposes. The list of such publications is virtually endless. Environmentalists have long relied on the apocalyptic implications of ecological collapse to justify urgent action, and for good reason. Rachel Carson's *Silent Spring* and *The Population Bomb* by Paul Elrich both present visions of a world in crisis, and their message is to a certain extent necessary. And yet, this approach has obviously not worked very well; as with alarming statistics of global poverty, it is easy to become numbed by the sheer scale they imply. What can one possibly do in the face of such a problem? How can one person make a difference? Something different is needed before we can be inspired to action. As Jane Bennett reminds us, "one must be enamored with existence and occasionally even enchanted in the face of it in order to be capable of donating some of one's scarce mortal resources to the service of others."[151]

A good example of the work that apocalyptic dread accomplishes is the documentary *A Crude Awakening*, a film that tries to show how deeply reliant modern humans are on petrochemicals. Portraying oil as the secret mover of modern history, it predicts that the end of oil will be the end of history. The movie uses a lot of old footage from the 1950s which boasts of the endless quantity of oil still left in the United States, and envisions a future of phenomenal wealth and technology that will liberate humans from toil and sweat. It turns the progressivist narrative of history on its head by suggesting that modern-day peak-oil deniers and techno-utopians who envision a hydrogen economy smoothly replacing hydrocarbons, are equally ludicrous. The film allows for no hope: oil is such a rare and energy-dense source of fuel that we can never replace it in any way that would allow contemporary humans to continue as they are. As with James Kunstler's *A Long Emergency*, the only way to save the planet and humanity is seen to be the apocalyptic clean sweep of peak oil. The apocalypse becomes the means for reharmonizing humanity with nature.

In considering such an eco-apocalypse, Szeman suggests: "There is a sense in which disaster is all but welcome: the end of oil might well be a case of capitalism digging its own grave, since without oil, current configurations of capital are impossible."[152] This is particularly true for theories of ecosocialism that embrace the clean sweep that will come when capitalism faces the environmental crisis and is eliminated in favour of a more just, sustainable, and diverse system that may emerge in its place.[153] In Joel Kovel's view, given that "capital tends to degrade the conditions of its own production" and "must expand without end in order to exist," the only conclusion is that this "combination makes an ever-growing ecological crisis an iron necessity so long as capital rules, no matter what measures are taken to tidy up one corner or another."[154] As one dominant strain of the apocalyptic mode, ecosocialism sees capitalism as fundamentally anti-ecological and asserts that the only solution is to abandon its structures and start anew.[155]

There are two major camps in the debate over the future of food. Techno-utopians see the food crisis as a sign that we need a new round of technological innovation to boost productivity – namely transgenetic crops that can adapt to harsher climates, or high-tech forms of agriculture such as the vertical farm. Apocalyptics, on the other hand, interpret the same crisis as a sign that industrial agriculture has "nearly exhausted the underlying system's restorative capacities."[156] They see the promise of transgenetic crops as simply an extension of the very mentality responsible for our current situation, and argue that the only solution is a new, sustainable agriculture that is conscious of natural limits and treats nature like a co-producer rather than a sponge for inputs. "Beyond organic" advocates in this camp wish to abandon the economic logic of agribusiness and use traditional methods, technology, and new research to create "consciously designed landscapes which mimic the patterns and relationships found in nature."[157] The new system, they say, must go even further and foster human communities by reestablishing agriculture and food at the centre of the community. Farming "needs to be redefined in terms of biological, ecological and social principles ... and not the purely chemical and physical principles that industrial agriculture is now based on."[158] Rhetorically speaking, the apocalyptic mode is meant as a kind of slap in the face, deploying horror to shock us into a search for alternatives.

For Pollan, the apocalyptic is manifest in the congruence of oil and obesity. In *The Omnivore's Dilemma*, corn is the root of all evil, the villain of the story. Whether as an example of the rise of agribusiness and industrial farming reliant on huge amounts of oil, or in its much maligned form as high-fructose corn syrup (HFCS), corn has become a central player in arguments declaring the end of food and the primary culprit in the obesity crisis facing North America. Corn links the obesity and agricultural crises within a larger narrative of capitalism and nature, and forms the central nodal point for considering how food, economics, and peak oil are becoming enmeshed in the locavore movement. Much of *The Omnivore's Dilemma* tells the story of *Zea mays* and its domination of "more of the earth's surface than virtually any other domesticated species, our own included."[159] Pollan argues that "corn is the protocapitalist plant."[160] It is the ideal commodity: it takes well to intensive production, can be broken down and reassembled into countless products, and has allowed Americans to eat enormous amounts of meat because cheap, subsidized corn provides the bulk of animal feed.[161] In storied food, corn often embodies apocalyptic dread:[162] as one of the commodities most responsible for the development of the current agribusiness model, it has provided the mountains of cheap calories required to satisfy our sugar and meat addictions, and made fast food possible. In terms of oil, corn is the perfect sponge: "every bushel of industrial corn requires the equivalent of between ¼ and ½ of a gallon of oil to grow, or around 50 gallons per acre."[163] Corn has become a kind of stand-in for oil in a lot of storied food: it is the vehicle for humans to eat petrochemicals, and the means of shifting from a solar-based agricultural system to a system saturated in oil.

After elaborating on the consequences of intensive monocropping and discussing farm policy, Pollan turns to junk food and obesity, especially to corn's most evil manifestation: high-fructose corn syrup. Pollan argues that the entire food system is skewed toward the production of cheap calories, and because corn is so easily converted into an array of junk foods, it has become much cheaper to fill up on chocolate and pop than on broccoli. For Pollan, this makes for an obvious conclusion: especially when a corn-based diet feeds the poor, it is inevitable that people will eat too much and get fat.[164] Arguing that people are unequipped to deal with the surfeit of calories, Pollan appeals to a problematic hybrid of biological determinism and a cultural industry thesis[165] that portrays an ignorant public caught up in an advertising machine. Marketing targeted to children, in combination with low costs and an evolutionary preference for sweets, has co-opted our "thrifty gene," which allows us to eat more when presented with surplus so that in times of plenty we can store energy for use in times of scarcity. Biologically, it is a very useful adaptation that many animals have. Many contemporary humans, however, are now presented with such large portions at such cheap prices that it is hard to keep our calories in check: "our bodies are storing fat against a famine that never comes."[166] Junk food and the obesity crisis can thus act as an apocalyptic counterpoint to the "real" food Pollan encourages people to eat.[167]

Julie Guthman finds this argument very flawed, suggesting that as a discourse, "obesity has achieved the status of an infectious disease."[168] While Guthman is sympathetic to Pollan's goal of transforming the food system, she argues that, by evoking obesity, "Pollan turns our gaze, perhaps inadvertently, from an ethically suspect farm policy to the fat body."[169] She contends that the science of obesity research is so tied into moral arguments, and so poorly understood, that it can no longer be taken at face value.[170] In addition to stigmatizing the fat body, she claims, the discourse of obesity transforms the bulk of the population into dupes: bottomless pits for the various incarnations of corn that lifelong advertising has made impossible to resist. Guthman rejects Pollan's argument that we are wired by evolution to respond to sweets and fats, making us hopelessly attracted to fast food. She believes that this argument interprets the obese body as something abject, immoral, and in fact, unnatural: a product of an omnipotent corporate environment. Fat people are therefore singled out as being "short of subjectivity,"[171] and the apocalyptic narrative is thus an intervention, a means of fleshing out that lack. The fat body, Guthman says, becomes the epitome of the subject caught within the advertising food machine, without free will, eating itself to death: an artifact of hyper-consumption that reveals our own complicity and suggests we are all just a few burgers away from losing control. On the basis that it divides the world into obese victims and super-subjects such as Pollan, who can resist the power of the advertising regime, Guthman rejects obesity as a critical discourse.[172]

We can also see how the emphasis on obesity displaces other concerns in *Jamie Oliver's Food Revolution* (2010), which takes Oliver's "School Dinners" model to America, and in turn abjectifies the fat body by mobilizing the panic related to obesity in order to make better television. He chose to film in Huntington, Virginia, because it is the "fattest town" in America and therefore the world. The obese body is used as a visual metaphor for all that is wrong with the global food system, especially in affluent countries that have abandoned traditional food cultures. I agree with Guthman that, as a rhetorical strategy, the minimizing of agency on the part of the obese is very troubling. However, while Guthman is right about the dangers of reducing agency to biology, her argument isolates the theme of obesity at the expense of the other elements of these apocalyptic narratives. Kelly Brownell, for example, understands obesity as the product of a toxic, obesigenic environment "in which food and agricultural companies produce too many calories, particularly in meat and highly processed foods."[173] In this view, obesity is understood as a social issue and not a simple matter of personal choice or even genetics. For Pollan, obesity is but one example of the many effects of modern agriculture, and in recent books and articles, he has focused more on farm policy and ecological literacy.[174] Moreover, for Pollan and Oliver, obesity itself is actually a policy issue. Rather than discussing personal responsibility, they are both critical of school systems that try to save money by feeding children cheap food, and a federal farm policy that subsidizes corn and soy and thereby makes junk food the most affordable way to eat. In this case, the most compelling apocalyptic discourses are rooted in the confluence of obesity and a farm system awash in petrochemicals, suggesting that individuals are less to blame than a structural economic policy.

Jamie's School Dinners takes up the link between individual bodies and public policy by examining the privatization of the school lunch program in Britain. The series begins with an account of the British school meals system, which involves the usual cast of actors: budget-cutting bureaucrats obsessed with saving money, unscrupulous corporations shilling processed junk, and ignorant parents slipping fries and chips to their children through the school gates after Oliver tries to take over the lunch program. The show is an experiment: Oliver wants to take over a London borough and serve twenty thousand children healthy school lunches that fit within the governments allotment of 37 pence per portion. According to Graham Sharp, "in 1980 under Margaret Thatcher's brand of neoliberalism, the government released local authorities from the obligation of minimum nutritional standards and the requirement to spend a minimum amount of money."[175] Oliver hopes to reverse this by using the government's own discourses of health to shame it into spending more money on education, food, and staff in order to address what he sees as a national embarrassment. While the series is fascinating for a number of reasons, what I am interested in here is the way that public and private, class, subjectivity, and taste rub against each other. School dinners in Britain are a significant site of class struggle. In some areas, the school dinner is the primary meal of the day, and many children qualify for free or subsidized meals. *School Dinners* begins in Oliver's home, where he feeds his own children a plate of vegetables and organic chicken that he figures costs £3.50 a portion. His own experience of running a restaurant is equally discordant. While a school dinner is allowed 37 pence a portion, Oliver is accustomed to using a ball of buffalo mozzarella, costing as much as seven school dinners, as a garnish. This tension manifests throughout the show.

Jamie's School Dinners is perhaps Oliver's most activist documentary. From being a lifestyle expert, he transforms himself into a moral entrepreneur.[176] Oliver launches a scathing critique of the privatization of school dinners and the accompanying deskilling of staff because of the elimination of cooking from scratch. He focuses on teaching the kitchen staff how to cook rather than merely reheat, in an effort to reverse the effects of cost-cutting economic logic within the schools that, as in the fast food industry, reduces labour to the most basic tasks. Most of the "cooks" are used to opening up packages and warming up the contents. Children are served an abundance of highly processed and unhealthy foods and their taste buds have become tuned to industrial food. Like many other texts in the apocalyptic genre, Oliver's relies on horror statistics as a way of shaming the government into action. He turns the government's own bureaucracy and emphasis on health against various ministers, feeding them what the children eat, and showing them the results.

Oliver visits doctors in wards where children have stopped passing stools for months at a time because of the lack of fibre in their diet and the large quantities of sugar, refined flour, and fat they eat. He shows local hospitals that hold constipation clinics because some of the children are literally vomiting stool. Many of these kids eat no other vegetable than French fries, and because the school dinner is often the primary meal of the day, the home offers very little respite. *School Dinners* explores the tension between class, taste, and obesity in some fascinating, and I would argue, productive ways. Rather than privatizing responsibility, he makes the discourse of obesity highly public on the show, exposing causes and effects as rooted in class politics and a government that, in the name of money, has given up on a generation of children. Joanne Hollows and Steve Jones point out that "although many features of the Jamie brand – his laddishness, sense of fun, childlike enthusiasm and Italianicity – have remained firmly in place, his TV series have progressively moved from a recipe and lifestyle format to an engagement with social and cultural issues."[177]

For Oliver, this meant a multifaceted campaign addressing structural issues such as government funding, and also cultural issues such as parental support and cooking skills. The first school meal program he takes over does not proceed as planned. His meals come in way over budget, and the children, having spent years accustomed to tempting junk food, simply do not eat what he offers. Oliver soon shifts tactics and starts younger, trying to work with elementary-age children and taking a much more integrated approach that encourages the kids to cook and take part in the culture of food. Much in line with the taste education of Slow Food, Oliver takes the children to a farm, educates them about ingredients, and tries to get them all engaged in the entire process. Taste education isn't a matter of distinction or manners; it involves developing a palate capable of interpreting what it experiences in terms of a "situated pleasure"[178] – a pleasure based on knowledge and fully aware of various narratives of production and consumption, of the desire and violence that link eater and eaten, producer and consumer. Taste education creates an active and engaged subject who is very different from the victim of obesity that Guthman describes. It "attempts to situate food in what it sees as more authentic, enriched and convivial contexts where the aim is how best to savour and enhance pleasure, rather than gain a momentary 'fix' from food."[179] In essence, taste education attempts to move outside the kind of economic reductionism that reduces food to fuel, and focuses instead on community, conviviality, the shared table, and healthy living through the development of skills.

The public and the private further coalesce as Oliver enters the homes of some of the children who are particularly recalcitrant. He teaches the parents basic recipes and talks about the need to eliminate processed foods from their diets. Despite its appeal to an obesity crisis, *Jamie's School Dinners* does not reinforce the concept that abject obese bodies lack agency. The emphasis on taste education, government policy, and parental support acknowledges the multiple scales of the issue and avoids privatizing discourses. As Hollows and Jones argue, "his mission is to democratize skills and knowledge rather than reinstate the authority of expert knowledge."[180] By the end of the show, Oliver is able to convince the British Government to spend £280 million over the span of three years to improve school dinners. In 2006 junk food and highly processed meats were banned from British schools in favour of freshly cooked meats and vegetables. While the culture of junk food prevails, as demonstrated by the now infamous – maybe exaggerated – incidents of parents sneaking chips to their children through school rails repeatedly shown during the program, the government has at least admitted the need to spend more time and money on school meals. Perhaps more important, the program has shown how the discourse of obesity can work in productive ways, and that we must move beyond seeing economics as the only measure of success.

Oliver has garnered a lot of attention for his various campaigns, some of which is positive, and some of which criticizes his model of moral entrepreneurship as a variation of the "discourse of broken Britain" and an "anti-statism that is central, if not limited to, contemporary Conservatism."[181] Hollows and Jones are critical of the way that shows like *Ministry of Food* make their point through Jamie, who is able to marshal moral concern as a form of capital: "The source of the obesity epidemic is made visible through Natasha and Claire's choice of commodities, in their kebabs and crisps. By devaluing the cultural practices of Rotherham's working class, the show also enables the middle-class viewer to experience their own cultural worth: identification with Jamie's authority offers a respectable distance from 'the problem,' and his fans are reassured that they, with their rocket [arugula] and parmesan, are not contributing to the nation's troubles."[182] While this is true on one level, the full story is more complicated. As mentioned in my discussion of *School Dinners* and *Food Revolution*, Oliver also makes considerable strides toward a systemic evaluation and critique of neoliberal policies that offload responsibilities on parents and school boards forced to make do with their paltry budgets. Moreover, by approaching the family and school as a site of taste education, Oliver is working on the level of embodied knowledge and skills that are crucial to retuning bodies toward sustainable food systems.

As Michael Carolan points out, "when bodies become tuned to a grip on food through alternative sources, Global Food ceases to be as attractive."[183] Oliver's emphasis on teaching children about the culture of food from field to fork goes a long way to making this possible, as does his laddish charm and pastoral appeal within *Jamie at Home*. His shows walk a fine line between reality TV and activist documentary, often in a way that makes me uneasy. While I tend to agree with Hollows and Jones that Oliver participates in some regressive narratives about individual responsibility that echo neoliberal ideologies, we need to consider some of the other strains and ideas circulating within these shows. Chapter 2 attempts exactly this by breaking storied food down into sub-genres.

What attracts me most in Oliver's approach is his emphasis on empowerment through skills building. A show like *Jamie's Ministry of Food*, in particular, has a mission to teach basic recipes as a means of getting people back in the kitchen and cooking together as a family. *Ministry of Food* takes aim at the role of convenience food and the elimination of cooking skills from an entire generation. Carolan makes a crucial distinction between embodied knowledge and representational or portable knowledge that sheds a positive light on Oliver's campaign. Embodied knowledge is at play when "food production [is] known literally – firsthand."[184] Portable knowledge fixes information in space and time: it travels well by communicating information in words, pictures, and diagrams to convey information. For many, this form of abstract, authoritative knowledge "lies at the heart of conventional agriculture with its emphasis upon highly transportable knowledge, such as feed charts for livestock and standardized NPK (nitrogen, phosphorous, potassium) application rates."[185] Both forms of knowledge are important, but each carries with it certain skills, assumptions, and approaches to understanding the food system. In Vandana Shiva's view, "dominant scientific knowledge … breeds a monoculture of the mind by making space for local alternatives disappear."[186] On the macro level, this manifests in a one-size-fits-all approach of high-input global agriculture. On the micro level, we witness the loss of cooking and growing skills that is at the heart of the "real food" revolution advocated by storied food. Both emerge from the same distinction between embodied and portable knowledge and the subsequent deskilling.

In many ways, the distinction between embodied and disembodied knowledge can be summarized in the difference between following a recipe and learning a technique. When I first started to make sourdough I depended on recipes. Having never really made bread, I studied books and websites and eventually found a recipe I could use – so many cups of flour, this much time, these steps. These are the kinds of recommendations we are used to, and this model of theoretical knowledge underpins the entire green revolution in agriculture. It is also, for the most part, how policy makers approach the environmental crisis under both the techno-utopian and ecological modernization mode. It involves a technocratic form of knowledge that travels well and its virtue comes from its portability and the ease with which it can be applied across a wide variety of circumstances. Models such as these are comforting because they yield good enough results. What is missing, however, and what I believe is crucial for addressing the environmental crisis and adapting to climate change, is a profound shift away from this form of top-down, technocratic, disembodied form of knowledge. We need forms of tactile, somatic, situated knowledge that are sensitive to local conditions, individual desires and communities, and which can encourage people to shift toward a different model of pleasure, value, and ethics that can account for nature outside the narrow terms of the economy.

Making sourdough bread is an example of the type of knowledge I mean: you quickly realize when you start that every time you make it, the ratios are different. Since sourdough is a wild food, you need to be attentive to the delicate balance of yeast and lacto-bacteria, which operate in different temporalities. Humidity, temperature, and the texture of the flour can all dramatically alter the flavour, loft, and quality of the final product. If I simply follow a recipe, rather than feel for texture and stretch, and if I use a timer for the "proper" rise, then I risk having a dense brick of unpalatable bread. Sourdough takes skill and patience and a willingness to engage with the bread on its own terms. It takes embodied knowledge that is learned *in situ*. Oliver often focuses on this type of knowledge in shows like *Jamie at Home*, or in his suggestion to "pass it on" as a model for *Ministry of Food* and *Food Revolution*. In *Ministry of Food*, he funds a teaching kitchen in order to empower people with new skills. After they learn a set of recipes and techniques, he asks them to teach two other friends, who will also teach two other friends, and thus initiate a chain reaction. Oliver is working on multiple scales and levels, often at cross-purposes, and perhaps not always aware of the contradictions, but nonetheless to great effect. My next chapter, by focusing on storied food as a literary genre, illustrates the way shows and texts like these can be understood in relation to a broader politics of the pantry. It is crucial to tease out the varied purposes, assumptions, and ideologies at work in these very complex texts, which in most cases have very lofty goals to inspire action and, as in Oliver's case, change entire government programs. It is much too easy to simply celebrate or denounce – something deeper is going on here.

Many of these texts share a focus on alternative value practice that can help reorient the subject toward a form of sustainability that is more localized and recognizes limits. The techno-utopian knowledge of the environmental crisis, predicated on the scientific "god trick"[187] of disembodied knowledge, large institutions, and one-size-fits-all solutions, is inadequate on its own to deal with the problems we are facing today; and one could argue that this type of knowledge is at the heart of the problem. Climate change will strain the ability of every individual, community, nation, and ecosystem to adapt, and the answers must be plural and attentive to local variation, while at the same time acknowledging the global nature of the problem. Knowledge gleaned through the senses, the sensuous knowledge that is made available through the embodiments celebrated by local and Slow Food, is a road toward developing a new epistemological foundation for addressing the environmental crisis. The true power of embodied food politics is its ability to provide an alternative way of engaging with and knowing the world, a kind of parallel course to business as usual. Embodied knowledge "too exuberant to be confined within representations has lost its currency, no longer existing on an equal plane with objective knowledge."[188] Storied food, which draws on sensual experiences and celebrates taste, touch, and the ephemeral, can help situate bodies in places and enchant, alongside darker apocalyptic discourses. Alternative food practices can therefore help people realize what it is that disappears in global food, things that are often invisible at the point of consumption (environmental costs, soil fertility, future generations) while at the same time, helping them crave a different world.

The next chapter considers storied food with the express aim of discovering how narratives imagine questions of agency, responsibility, the relationship between scale and scope, individuals, and the system. As we look through the unprecedented proliferation of

popular food literature as a genre, we will get a sense of the numerous ideas at work, so as to distil a common goal, or perhaps more
important, to discern the next step. For, as with many of the texts I
explored above, the very plurality that they celebrate can lead to a
disintegration of purpose or a historical amnesia that makes any
suggestions seem anemic and hopelessly romantic. By looking at
them together and breaking storied food into a number of sub-
genres, we will get a better sense of what is going on. Having
situated the politics of the pantry within a broader history of
environmentalism and the emergence of a compelling but problematic form of consumer-based activism, we can now move on to
considering what these stories can do, or at least, what they imagine
is possible.

2

Storied Food and the Transparent Meal:
Writing the Foodshed

One of the most direct and profound interactions between ecology and economy occurs in the realm of agriculture. Whether in the role of subsidies in maintaining certain kinds of production-consumption arrangements, the decline of the family farm, the rise of agribusiness, or the effects of nitrogen and pesticide run-off on the environment, agriculture is a hybrid of economy and ecology. In any given year, farm policy or technological innovation can have just as great an effect on world grain harvests and crop yield as the weather. Moreover, food production accounts for a considerable portion of humanity's ecological footprint, contributing 12 percent of greenhouse gasses, 38 percent of water pollution, and 45 percent of all terrestrial habitat alteration.[1] As the human population balloons and global warming shifts climactic zones, the question of how we will feed ourselves will become more central. As I argued in the previous chapter, although modern technology has released what appears to be a cornucopia of cheap food, the techno-utopian dream of food abundance is slowly being replaced by a profound anxiety about what the future of food holds. The critique increasingly launched at conventional agriculture, that it has "incurred substantial direct and indirect costs and may represent a Faustian bargain,"[2] challenges the conventional notion that only intensified production can feed the world.[3]

While many North Americans take relatively abundant and cheap food for granted, for most of human history, and for many people in today's world, scarcity is closer to the reality. Imagine someone from the nineteenth century walking through a modern supermarket, with its brightly lit shelves overflowing with the bounty of the entire world. A typical U.S. supermarket contains 45,000 items,[4] many of which have travelled around the world several times before arriving for our consumptive pleasure. And yet, that abundance is maintained by a shockingly small genetic diversity. Of those 45,000 products, a quarter contain corn.[5] It is estimated that 30,000 vegetable varieties, and 33 percent of livestock breeds have become extinct in the last century.[6] Not only does this represent the destruction of a significant cultural heritage, since most of these plants and animals are also intimately tied into traditional ways of life, but as global warming shifts the climactic contours and conditions of bioregions around the world, our collective survival depends on the ability of agriculture to adapt, and the means of doing so lies in the seeds we sow.[7] Industrial agriculture has – very literally – shaped the food we eat in the name of economics: by breeding cultivars to become more economically useful, focusing on their yield, uniform ripening, visual uniformity, and ability to withstand transport, many modern-day agricultural producers have sacrificed taste, nutrition, disease resistance, and adaptability.[8] Corn, rice, soy, and wheat now provide most of our calories, and much of that is limited to a small group of cultivars, many of which are quite sensitive to heat and cold.

Like many other authors questioning the vitality of the industrial food system, Warren Belasco asks: "Is the banquet over?"[9] Will our grandchildren have the same access to food that many of us enjoy? In the United States today, there are two million prisoners, but only 960,000 farmers,[10] a statistic that reveals the effect of the profound shift in labour and technology that has taken place in modern forms of industrial agriculture. Farmers today are perhaps more efficient than they have ever been, and yet that efficiency has come at a profound cost, not least of which has been a deskilling and loss of sensual knowledge related to sustainable agriculture. Those lost cultivars and animals were embedded in cultures and practices that are rapidly disappearing, and beyond their genetic diversity, we are also losing forms of knowledge and practice that require living bodies to remember them.

Most North Americans know farming only through advertisements, nostalgic memories, or literature rather than through direct, embodied experience. For most of us, agriculture implies an economic arrangement more than an interaction with the natural and social world. Labels and advertisements have replaced sensorial experience as the prime means for determining quality and anticipating pleasure, and food is engaged with mainly through commodity chains and over-the-counter exchanges. Acquiring food means swiping a credit card at a discount supermarket or, at best, handing over money at a local farmers' market. Marketing practices have occluded many of the underlying significations of food in North American culture. Even what we think of as sustainable or ethical consumption draws on economic practices that remain, largely, within the parameters of green capitalism.

With fewer of us having direct experiences of what farm life actually entails, we have become increasingly reliant on stories surrounding food, as the recent decade's explosion of writing and film about food attests. In this chapter I look more directly at food politics and the emergence of vibrant food communities as alternative value practices to capitalism, specifically at the ways in which struggles around food and various food stories and practices are emerging, converging, and diverging from the trajectory of green capitalism.

There are currently many forms of politics emerging from food, and they often work at cross-purposes. The ways various movements imagine themselves, the kinds of stories they tell, and the political possibilities that arise from food narratives are equally capable of either challenging or protecting capitalism. These movements and stories are wildly diverse in the way they participate in the broader struggle of reimagining what the ultimate purpose of the economy should be. Whereas "green capitalism" tends to remain locked within the logic of markets, growth, and profit, the "green economy" takes many forms. Green capitalism is a disciplinary mechanism of the market which has emerged as capitalism struggles with the environmental crisis – an attempt to naturalize the market as a means of regulating all social and biological systems. The values we have come to associate with food are often created by the novelty that marketers draw on in an attempt to capture more of our food dollars. And yet, the proliferation of community-supported agriculture (CSA) programs, farmers' markets, community gardens, and heritage seeds can be seen as an attempt to create "alternative modes of co-production [that are] predicated on making visible what capital's value practices keeps invisible."[11] In other words, while the politics of the pantry offers lucrative opportunities for green consumerism, it also represents a key locus of struggle over the very definition of the good life and the role of capitalism in shaping the future. Chapters 2 and 3 are not roadmaps to a sustainable future, but rather considerations of existing alternative food movements and their narratives in relationship to the world, and the diverse – and often messy – ways in which theory and practice manifest.

The politics of the pantry is affected by many forces, ideologies, desires, and conflicting goals. The profound transformations that organic food has undergone as it has become mainstream and industrialized provide important examples of the ways in which discourses of sustainability, choice, citizenship, consumption, and alternatives become caught up in larger narratives of capitalism and nature. It is precisely because I believe that food matters, that it has the potential to connect people to issues of climate change, peak oil, and the green economy in embodied, material, and accessible ways, that I engage in this study of alternative food movements. It is also for this reason that I have written myself into the process, trying to avoid the seductive path of negative academic criticism, and focusing instead on some of the enabling aspects of storied food as part of an utopian imaginary.

In its inaugural issue, the *Journal of Environmental Humanities* posed a key question that animates my consideration of storied food. "An important tension is emerging between, on the one hand, the common focus of the humanities on critique and an 'unsettling' of dominant narratives, and on the other, the dire need for all peoples to be constructively involved in helping to shape better possibilities in these dark times. The [field of] environmental humanities is necessarily, therefore, an effort to inhabit a difficult space of simultaneous critique and action. And so, we are required to re-imagine the proper questions and approaches of our fields. How can our accumulated knowledge and practice, built up over centuries, be refashioned to meet these new challenges, and to productively rethink 'the human' in more than human terms?"[12] It is this difficult space of critique and action that I am attempting to occupy as I try to synthesize a wide variety of theories into a complex middle ground that acknowledges the power of utopian, romantic narratives while also pointing out their flaws and gaps. Ultimately, I think this is precisely the space of possibility – but also the impossible space of contradiction – which attracts so many people to the politics of the pantry.

Jane Bennett's concept of enchantment[13] offers a provocative model for examining some of the ways in which food can invigorate my largely disenchanting tale of capitalism from the previous chapter. While chapter 1 painted a rather typical image of modernity as disenchanted, I now look to food as a site of real-life enchantment that can foster forms of situated, embodied knowledge capable of providing moments of freedom, however fleeting. Such moments are crucial for imagining and putting into practice what Massimo De Angelis calls the "beginning of history," or (in less enchanting terms) the "overcoming of a mode of social co-production that is emanating antagonism."[14] De Angelis's beginning of history is about conceiving other possible worlds on the borderlines of capitalism, by thinking like a weed and poking around the edges. Despite some very real concerns with class politics and gender,[15] storied food and the practices it entails can offer moments of possibility within the realm of the everyday. My analysis may at times seem too ludic, as if I am naïvely celebrating alternative food practices as unproblematically good; food politics, especially various forms of localism, cannot solve the problem of sustainability. Especially in the wealthy West, gourmet food, farmers' markets, home cuisine, and gardening are typically bourgeois pursuits and cannot (and should not) be offered up as a kind of pan-political movement capable of uniting the world at a mythic shared table. Food is a way in, but only one way, and the movement is by necessity fragmented and to a certain extent should remain so. It is precisely in the polyvalence of food that much of its vitality and energy emerges. In comparison to other more conventional bourgeois engagements with nature, such as getting back to the wilderness, the act of growing food, I believe, represents a more honest effort to work through the contradictions of late capitalist naturecultures.

My analysis focuses on the attraction of food politics to a very Western, affluent, and writerly audience. As such, it contains many gaps, largely because I cannot address everything that food touches upon, but also because I am trying to speak from my own subject-position and understand what it is that has attracted me to this movement. As a thirty-two-year-old white male who immigrated to Canada from Ukraine at the age of four, I view the world through specific lenses tied up in cultural identity, class, leisure, and pleasure; but I also approach it as an academic with a commitment to political critique and environmental sustainability. Food narratives and practices relate to enchantment and the pleasures of the everyday; they are also part of a larger project of resisting the discursive – and actual – enclosure of various lifeworlds by neoliberalism. For the purpose of this chapter, after beginning with a genealogy of the genre, I luxuriate in the stories with a critical but sympathetic reading that foregrounds the intent and potential of storied food. In a sense, I want to explore the tension between writing the food-shed and living in the foodshed, between politics in theory and the embedded entanglements of lived experience.

STORIED FOOD: LIFTING THE VEIL

What to eat? It seems like a simple question, but a quick glance at bookshelves and the media reveals scores of literary works, movies, TV shows, documentaries, and blogs devoted to this seemingly simple, mundane and everyday act that most human beings accomplish several times a day. Why this resurgence in interest? Why this nostalgic pining for simpler times when, at least in the West, technology and a hugely elaborate division of labour has ostensibly liberated many of us from the toil of soil and kitchen? Why do contemporary humans feel the need to get expert advice on this topic? What could be simpler than deciding what's for dinner?

Choosing what to eat is no simple matter. Taken seriously, it is an exceedingly complex question that goes to the heart of issues of social and environmental justice, sustainability, animal rights, globalization, the purpose of economics, and the future of capitalism as an organizational logic for human activities. Food represents a discursive constellation of power and knowledge that draws on numerous disciplines and ways of knowing. The struggle over food narratives is linked to competing notions of progress, the good life, pleasure, class, gender, and – most important for my purposes – sustainability. The previous chapter situated the sustainable food movement within a broad environmental movement, and further, within a struggle over the values of economics. I considered how capitalism can or cannot value nature and, in focusing on economic policy and its relationship to social movements and narrative, showed how story-lines assign blame and responsibility, and impose trajectories and momentums that shape the very conditions for environmentalism in this century. Terms such as "sustainable," "natural," "green," and "organic" are fundamentally open, and the way we define them has profound implications for the macro-level of economic and environmental policy, as well as for the micro-level of life politics, consumer activism, and sustainable consumption.

In what follows, I look at the Slow Food[16] and locavore movement, and discuss popular texts such as Alisa Smith and J.B. MacKinnon's *The 100-Mile Diet*, Gary Paul Nabhan's *Coming Home to Eat*, Michael Pollan's *The Omnivore's Dilemma* and *In Defense of Food*, Barbara Kingsolver's *Animal, Vegetable, Miracle*, and Erik Schlosser's *Fast Food Nation* as representatives of a genre concerned with tracing food's convoluted path through the modern industrial foodshed. This path, frequently obscured and intentionally obfuscated, is the pipeline of industrial agriculture. A supermarket is one link in an anonymous, placeless foodchain that provides the consumer out-of-season fruits and vegetables, and limitless packaged and frozen foods containing hundreds of ingredients, many of which can hardly be considered food-like. Supermarket food is purely a commodity: exchangeable and storyless, and essentially untraceable. The chicken in its plastic foam tomb, the package of breakfast cereal, the gleaming waxy apple all bear the marks of commodification. Their story has become subsumed in a brand, obliterated in the process of getting them to market. Although food perhaps represents the ultimate use-value, exchange has transformed it to the extent that we now consume many things past generations would hardly recognize as edible: things that have been bred, selected, and transformed into an idealized form that approximates food, but is at once more beautiful and terrible. Food has become an idea, born of the desire for efficiency and above all else, low cost: it has become something that sustains and, increasingly, destroys.

The concept of storied food is about creating *readable narratives of the foodshed* which have the potential to reveal the social mystery of capitalism in a lived, material way, and as such, help create the conditions for sustainability. Many of the books and films in this genre represent the struggle against a system designed to make it difficult to trace the path. The chain of meaning can be obscured, as in the case of a frozen burrito, or it can be revealed, more or less honestly, as in the case of a farmers' market stall. In the process, questions of agency, economics, politics, and ethics become enmeshed in the cultural production of food. Crucially, the meaning of food is always mediated by culture, whether through traditions passed along by generations of cooks and eaters, or through the comfort marketing of Quaker Oats and Aunt Jemima. Most examples of the genre of storied food see the industrial foodshed as characterized by a broken semiotic chain: it is exceedingly difficult to know the story behind a package of cereal, whose ingredients are by their nature commodified at every level, right down to the genome. One box of processed dry cereal is identical to the next because the entire trajectory, from seed to plant, to milling, to transportation, to marketing, and finally to consumption, is rendered anonymous, subsumed in a brand, an idea.

Place too is erased from this path, as are the labour of the farm worker, the pesticide burden of farming, the huge amount of energy used to process the food, the addition of vitamins and minerals required to qualify the product as food, and the environmental

costs of the entire affair. The whole process is opaque by design. In
the case of factory-farmed meat, the pastoral image of the family
farm is a necessary conceit, for to reveal the torturous conditions
and degradation involved in Intensive Livestock Operations (ILO)
would turn many away from the products.[17] The central concern
of storied food is thus to peel back the plastic and reconnect people
with the "agricultural act" associated with eating.[18] The goal is thus
largely educational, revealing what is concealed in the hopes of raising consciousness and changing everyday habits of the audience.

Michael Pollan's bestseller *The Omnivore's Dilemma* (2006) is
one of the path-breaking books in this genre, although Upton
Sinclair's *The Jungle* (1906), which revealed the hellish conditions
of Chicago's meatpacking industry, was perhaps the first modern
example. Both texts share the impulse to reveal what is concealed,
to make transparent what is hidden from view. They try to reconnect the material with the sign, food with culture. While Pollan's
text was by no means the first, it was significant for its impact and
timing. It tapped into – and expressed – the growing anxiety that
something is wrong with the way we eat. Its premise is simple: a
natural history of four differently sourced meals that seeks to trace
the hidden costs, connections, and pathways of the modern food
system. Pollan's goal is to demonstrate that eating is a transaction,
a form of exchange that allows energy to flow and thus either produces or resists entropy. By tracing an industrial, an organic, an
industrial organic, and finally a foraged meal, Pollan uses his jour-
nalistic talent to examine a food system from beginning to end,
accounting for it completely: "from a plant, or a group of plants,
photosynthesizing calories in the sun, all the way to a meal at the
dinner end of the food chain."[19]

Eventually, Pollan's narrative culminates in a "perfect meal" –
"one that's been fully paid for, that leaves no debt outstanding."[20]
This meal has been foraged, hunted, and grown entirely by Pollan,
and represents the ultimate goal of storied food, the transparent
meal in which the entire foodchain is revealed and accounted for. It
is a meal that can be eaten in full consciousness and in full conscience.
In this revelation, it becomes possible to tell a story, to understand

the foodshed in a perfect, albeit fleeting, moment of clarity. This perfection later becomes the ideal to which all other meals aspire, and the basis for Pollan's critique of commodification.

The genre of storied food can be divided into four types which illustrate the work these narratives do: the Commodity Biography, the Nostalgic Pastoral, the Utopian Pastoral, and the Foodshed Memoir. This distinction between types of narrative allows us to tease out what each of them enables or disables. What do they hope to accomplish? What genres do they draw on? What assumptions do they make? How do they conceptualize the environmental crisis? How are they situated in relationship to capitalism? Although many of the books, documentaries, films, and television shows I examine here share traits of each type, considering them in turn will help demonstrate some of the limits and possibilities of the strategies, techniques, rhetoric, and assumptions of each. By exploring these categories, I hope to provide a tentative map of contemporary alternative food movements and the growing body of literature surrounding them. In a broad sense, this chapter is about writing the foodshed, and thus focuses on pedagogy, taste education, and the desire to trace and reveal as a key moment of eco-literacy. The next chapter focuses more on power, ideology, and the political implications of these food narratives and movements as contextualized in my own attempts to inhabit my local foodshed. However, it is precisely in the entanglement of narrative and practice that storied food emerges as an alternative value practice to capitalism.

THE COMMODITY BIOGRAPHY: THE SOCIAL MYSTERY OF THE TWINKIE

If you have ever picked up a box of cereal or a package of cookies and stared haplessly at the ingredients, twisting your tongue over the mysterious multi-syllabic additives and furrowing your brow at how the best-before date extends into the next decade, then you have come face to face with the modern industrial foodshed. Much of the food we eat today is assembled: engineered from a clever combination of soy, corn, and edible petroleum products, to generate mouth-feel, scent profiles, and texture; stabilized, sterilized, and irradiated so as to ward off bacteria; and designed to manipulate evolutionary preferences for sugar, salt, and fat. In many ways, the production of modern food has more in common with the automobile industry than with the pastoral image of agriculture many people still hold in their imaginations.

In recent years, a renewed interest has arisen in understanding where our food comes from. The popularity of the 100-mile diet, eat-local campaigns, farmers' markets, and the organic movement speaks to a desire to know the story of food, to meet the people who grow it, or to participate directly in the lifecycle by growing food yourself. There are far too many books, documentaries, and television shows in this genre to discuss comprehensively, but a handful are paradigmatic and/or popular: Robert Kenner's documentary film *Food Inc.*, Jamie Oliver's *Jamie's Fowl Dinners*, and, again, Pollan's *The Omnivore's Dilemma*.[21] Their common purpose is to reveal the ways in which modern food production systematically conceals environmental damage, health effects, and the exploitation of animals, farmers, and labourers. Jonathan Morris describes the commodity biography as a text that "should be able to demonstrate how the relationship between consumers and producers (understood in the widest sense) around the globe has been mediated – both materially and metaphorically – through the product itself."[22] Within the genre of storied food, the commodity biography is thus primarily concerned with educating audiences to a hidden world, usually through some combination of statistics, shock tactics, and guilt. In many respects – such as the emphasis on commodification, consumer-label laws, standardized accreditation, and appeals to consumer rights, choice, and full-cost accounting – the commodity biography draws on the ideology of ecological modernization. By suggesting that knowledge is power, the genre hopes people will make the right decisions and accept the need to pay more for their food once they know its story.

Kenner's documentary *Food Inc.* is a perfect example of the commodity biography. It begins with a menacing Tim Burtonesque soundtrack that sets a mood for the shock and revelation to come. The camera pans over a series of agricultural stereotypes: a vast field of grain, a cowboy rancher rustling in a herd, and a red barn surrounded by a faded fence. From actual landscapes and people, to packaging utilizing the same images, the movie immediately establishes a visual metaphor. The connection between image and world, sign and signified has been broken. Pollan features as the voice-over: "The way we eat has changed more in the last fifty years than in the previous ten thousand. But the image that is used to sell the food is still the imagery of agrarian America."[23] The mood and music reinforce a sense that something is awry, that the viewer doesn't know the entire story. Pollan remarks that most of what we get in the supermarket is an illusion, the mere idea of food, not food itself – a hyper-real artifact of industry that increasingly bears no connection to nature. There are no seasons in the supermarket: a tomato is available any time of the year, picked green, gassed to ripen it, and shipped halfway around the world. It is the idea of tomato, what Pollan calls the "notional tomato."[24] And yet, the images used to sell the food remain pastoral.

As Pollan puts it, a deliberate veil is created by the "spinning of a pastoral fantasy" because "the industry doesn't want you to know the truth about what you're eating, because if you knew, you might not want to eat it."[25] And so the movie follows the foodshed backward from the shrink-wrapped package, to the processors, the farmers, and finally to the companies that provide the seeds: tracing an industrial ecology in its entirety. The images quickly became an anti-pastoral inversion of the opening scene: the machine has invaded the garden[26] and we watch a sinister fleet of combines harvest a field, while in the background factories belch smoke into a post-apocalyptic sky. A lone man in a business suit carrying a briefcase walks across the field, suggesting that the power of business over the farm is in the hands of a disproportionate few. The film sets out to reveal what Schlosser calls "the world deliberately hidden from us."[27]

The pedagogical aim of *Food Inc.* is to inform viewers, through the use of alternating images of the farm, industrial slaughterhouses, huge chicken warehouses, farmers who have no control over their land or animals, and numerous other deliberately concealed aspects of the industry, that knowledge will set them free.

The commodity biography tells the story of production by piecing together the fragmented lifeworlds and labours involved in food's transformation: it literally reassembles the food system piece by piece. It assumes a reader or viewer who is unaware by design and, echoing the cultural industry thesis of Max Horkheimer and Theodor Adorno, seeks to awaken that audience through criticism – by pushing through the fog of false consciousness with a process of demystification.

The commodity biography's primary concern is to move from image to reality, and this move usually begins with investigating the colonizing effects of capitalism on nature and culture. Like many aspects of our economy, the food system is a vastly complex network of seed producers, chemical manufacturers, growers, processors, transporters, and vendors. Many components of this system are vertically integrated with the result that, in the United States, a dozen companies control most of what Americans eat.[28] For example, Cargill and ADM control a third of all corn grown, and are involved in every step of the process, making Cargill the biggest privately held corporation in the world.[29] With most agricultural production in the hands of a few large companies that farm according to brutally Taylorist principles of efficiency and yield, the days of the small family farm are pretty much gone. *Food Inc.* demystifies the pastoral imagery used to conceal the worst abuses of the system by showing images of systemic brutality toward animals, and recounting stories of family farmers cast in David vs. Goliath roles. The commodity biography is thus primarily educational, seeking to illuminate the reader/viewer who is trapped behind the pastoral veil and social mystery of the commodity.

Jamie's Fowl Dinners (2008) employs similar tactics in order to reveal the whole story of the chicken and the egg. Hosted by Oliver, this ninety-minute special challenges many of the expectations of the cooking-show genre. Staged as a gala dinner, the show is a vehicle through which Oliver brings forward the true story of cheap food in the hopes that the truth will convince people not to eat battery-cage chickens and eggs. From the opening credits, the announcer asks: "Will they change what they buy when Jamie tells them the truth about fowl dinners?" The audience, consisting of self-avowed junk food addicts, organic foodies, "average" people, and executives of food-processing and distribution companies, is placed in the middle of the story. The stage surrounds a typical white linen service – a gala dinner complete with silverware, waiters, and expectant diners. All around them are various stages and screens, each relating to an aspect of the chickens' life.

For the first course, the waiters present silver dinner cloches, which, when lifted, reveal a dozen little chicks. The audience is immediately filled with doe-eyed empathy for the cute little birds as they spread out over the table in a tumble of yellow fluff, collapsing the typical distinction between consumption and production. Oliver asks the guests to sort the chickens by sex (indicated by their colour), and place the male ones in the box provided. The story is about to begin. To the audience's horror, Oliver takes the male chickens to a pair of white-coated men standing next to a clear plexiglass box unfortunately named the dispatching chamber. The rationality and efficiency of science take on the sinister logic of economics. In the egg industry, male chicks are economically useless, as they do not produce eggs and are not used for meat. So every male chick is either gassed or tossed alive into a giant blender, where they are minced for livestock feed or pet food. The announcer warns the audience that they will be witnessing every aspect of the production process and may find some of it disturbing. The chicks are placed in the chamber and a mixture of carbon dioxide and monoxide is pumped in while the audience watches as the birds gasp for air and die.

Symbolically and literally, as the cloche is raised, the veil between consumer and product, life and death, nature and culture is temporarily lifted, and Oliver peels back the layers of mystification that usually protect the industrial eater. He reveals the story of the food they are about to consume, and thereby fosters a process of co-production that suggests that consumers participate in the production and destruction of a lifeworld every time they buy something. While the tactic is brutal and in-your-face, the goal is to demystify the commodity, while at the same time offering an alternative mode of production in the form of organic and sustainable agriculture.

As Kenner did in *Food Inc.*, Oliver oscillates between pastoral and industrial imagery throughout the show. From death they move on to life, showing what a wild chicken looks like and explaining that this is a bird that can live for ten years. In contrast, "modern chickens are living machines, not a real bird at all."[30] They lay up to three hundred eggs a year, and reach slaughter weight in thirty-eight days. Oliver suggests that the male chicks are perhaps the lucky ones because they don't have to live such mechanized and commodified lives. But supermarkets have pushed the industry toward producing more and more inexpensive ingredients, especially for processed foods, which rely on liquid eggs and mechanically reclaimed meat (MRM) for binding agents and cheap fillers.[31] Once again, Oliver's guests are shocked when he shows them what a battery-cage looks like and asks if they would still buy the eggs if this image was on the package. As *Food Inc.* did, Oliver points to the role of pastoral imagery in concealing the truth. The show tries to cut through the commodity nexus by revealing the brutality of economic calculus. In this sense, the show moves in the direction of the apocalyptic mode, as it rejects economic value as a measure of worth. Oliver repeatedly emphasizes that the drive to save a few pence, to provide cheap meat, is at the heart of the problem. In the process, the hen becomes a cog in the machine, as close to life colonized by capitalism as possible. The film reinforces the machine-in-the-garden metaphor as Oliver walks through a large egg-processing facility that looks like something out of *The Matrix* – thousands of chickens, all shoved into cages without enough room to spread their wings, pecking at corn from a mechanized conveyor-belt, and laying eggs that are immediately rolled away.

Commodity biographies work on the premise that respect and responsibility are only possible with accurate information. Because so much of the production process remains out of sight and out of mind, it is difficult for the average consumer to demand better conditions for chickens: consumers buy eggs, not a lifeworld, and it is this disconnect that the commodity biography seeks to bridge. Oliver tries to show the true costs of the system: cheap unnourishing food that tastes bad, wretched and sickly birds, an obese population, farmers who have little control over their lives and are forced to comply with supermarket demands, and a huge environmental debt. In the process, consumption and production are linked.

Oliver's program then returns to the conventional cooking-show format he is known for, but with another twist. This time he makes a number of dishes for the audience to compare. Some with boxed liquid eggs, MRM, and battery-cage chickens, and others with the finest organic, free-range birds and eggs money can buy. He wants to illustrate that this food is even better-tasting and yet still affordable when it is home-cooked. Commodity biographies use the narrative impulse, the desire to lift the veil and see behind the curtain, to channel guilt into action. They succeed by removing some structural mystifications in order to foster more ethical and sustainable modes of co-production. For Massimo De Angelis, "the basic precondition for the constitution of alternative modes of co-production is predicated on making visible what capital's value practices keep invisible."[32] This is precisely what the best food narratives accomplish. They reveal a social mystery while at the same time imagining a new world – although in the case of many food narratives, that world is decidedly old-fashioned.

In the end, "authentic" pastoral imagery is used to revive the sense of consumer power. Both *Food Inc.* and *Jamie's Fowl Dinners* rely on this somewhat ironic return to the pastoral, which can be read in a number of ways. At best, the commodity biography helps foster a sense of co-production. In the case of the two documentaries I cite, this co-operative sense comes from the consumer's choice to support a farmer who treats animals and land with respect. For Oliver, this means free-range and organic farming of birds. But this is the point where the apocalyptic mode becomes subsumed by ecological modernization and the promise of green capitalism. As an antidote to the anxiety produced by his in-your-face approach, Oliver offers a pastoral farm scene that shows what a chicken's life can be. In a situation with no resemblance to the horror of the industrial shed, these birds play in the dappled sunlight of shade trees and roam about pecking the dirt in search of grubs and other delicious morsels.

Although Oliver encourages everyone to buy these kinds of chickens and eggs, he realizes not everyone can spend the money, since the birds cost up to three times as much. As a middle ground, he supports the Royal Society for the Prevention of Cruelty to Animals' Freedom Food Standard, which recommends open-concept barns with roosts, natural light, and an overall more stimulating environment for the chickens, and only costs an additional pound per bird. The RSPCA establishes and monitors a number of standards, which include maximum animal density, availability of shade, and other elements related to animal welfare. It is not perfect, but Oliver realizes he needs to get people in the door and address the real concerns of class and accessibility. As with many certification schemas, the consumer must trust the organization that sets standards according to "the limit of what is achievable, in terms of an animal husbandry and commercial viability."[33] While Oliver is clearly not fully satisfied with the standard and its ambiguity, he nonetheless supports its recommendations as an alternative to factory farming and as a means of assuring a basic level of animal welfare for those concerned but unwilling or unable to afford organic birds.

The Slow Food movement, which Oliver supports, also directs its attention to ethical consumption, food communities, and co-production. This focus is significant because it brings the world of consumption and production together, and allows for the enfranchisement of, for example, small producers from the global South. It also begins to peel away the layers of alienation engendered by the consumption of mass-produced commodities. Slow Food's Terra Madre awards support traditional modes of production by offering access to funds and marketing, and making connections with affluent consumers in the West. Although the awards are often small, they help from a pedagogical standpoint by linking producers and consumers across continents, and highlighting traditional practices around the world, thereby making their survival more likely. The movement also helps attract young people to farming by making it economically viable.

The Ark of Taste, another initiative of Slow Food,[34] likewise has the objective of saving endangered plants and animals, along with the communities that produce them. In both cases, Slow Food emphasizes that consumption is always in itself a creative act of production, in that every time we eat we choose to support certain practices and lifeworlds. While Slow Food has been criticized for being an elitist dinner club for lefties, the concept of co-production is crucial in articulating a counter-globalization position that respects local traditions and modes of production without slipping into cultural xenophobia or petty nationalism. Both of the latter are troubling, and are potentially regressive aspects of the celebration of local food, which I explore more extensively later in this chapter. Carlo Petrini, the movement's founder, identifies Slow Food and events like the Terra Madre awards as instances of community building that promote a "virtuous globalization."[35] Slow Food's primary concern is to foster an awareness of the connections that bind us to distant others, encouraging the creation of what Wendy Parkins and Geoffrey Craig refer to as "ethical cosmopolitanism."[36] Its counter-globalization stance recognizes and puts into lived practice the ecological injunction that everything is interrelated. The model of the Ark of Taste is a complex interplay of capitalist naturecultures, ecotourism, gourmet taste, ecologies, cultures, and economics that takes account of the role that capitalism plays in maintaining and destroying certain lifeworlds. The first step in the process of fostering these networks is the commodity biography, which, by emphasizing the underlying conditions of production and attempting to tell the stories hidden from us, allows consumers and producers to enter into a kind of community, even if it takes place over considerable distances and is nonetheless mediated by money.

However, as with ecological modernization, the commodity biography can easily be folded back into capitalist modes of production through the emphasis on codification and standards. As Julie Guthman has pointed out, "the drive for regulatory legislation effectively subsumed much of the organic movement into an organic industry."[37] As a result of the requirement for standards and consumer labelling laws, organic food has become a lucrative arm of green capitalism, thriving on the "sentiment that shopping creates possibilities for consumers to 'change the world.'"[38] Because of this, the organic industry has followed a largely industrial path, substituting botanical inputs for artificial ones, but nonetheless maintaining the production and distribution systems of large-scale mono-cropping.[39]

Both *Jamie's Fowl Dinners* and *Food Inc.* end with a call for labelling laws and stricter standards, and an invitation to consumers to spend more time and money on food. Oliver tries to connect money with welfare: "the more you pay for your eggs, the better the quality of life for the hen."[40] Although both works try to expose and thereby escape the commodity nexus, they are easily reintegrated into the system they challenge. Because their suggestions are largely focused on consumption – go to a farmers' market, demand accurate labelling, and buy fair trade – the knowledge of the practices they expose is easily contained by ethical or green products that offer escape. Label shopping acquires a redemptive and cathartic function that purges any guilt associated with the newly acquired knowledge. As Laura DeLind observes in her analysis of the organic industry, "when seduced by the charms of convenience and commodification, the addition of an ubiquitous organic label certifying an organic product's authenticity will absolve the consumer of any further need to think about the agrifood system."[41] Whether or not the local food movement will succumb to the same pressures organics did, depends largely on how narrative and practice are reconciled within the political and ecological imaginary of its practitioners.

PASTORAL NARRATIVES: FAILING THE RECOVERY?

In my earlier treatment of apocalypticism, I mentioned attempts to represent value in nature outside the logic of capitalism. For the alternative food movement, these attempts often involve the use of pastoral imagery. Whether this means using the supermarket pastoral to evoke a product's imagined connections with a simpler life, or the back-to-the-land experiments of Kingsolver's *Animal, Vegetable, Miracle* and Nabhan's *Coming Home to Eat*, storied food has a complicated relationship to pastoral metaphors and imagery. While many food narratives are critical of the supermarket pastoral and the way it conceals a corporate food system through images of harmony and rural bliss, those same narratives often rely on nostalgia for an ostensibly authentic form of pastoralism in the form of organic farming, farmers' markets, and so-called real food. The tension between the authentic and the simulated is a central problematic in arguments for and against the reform of the current food system. Many of the texts promoting storied food are guides meant to cut through the confusion, and books like Pollan's *Food Rules* function as translation matrices, helping readers decode the significance of additives and ingredients, and providing an overall picture of the industrial food system. Pastoral imagery plays a major role in storied food, both as a metaphor and as a material reality in the actual lifeworlds invoked, lived, and written about. I am interested in the work that pastoralism accomplishes, especially as a rhetorical device to bridge the narrative text or image with the material world. Specifically, how do narratives of fall and recovery function in storied food? What role does romantic idealization play in them? What, if any, is its pedagogical value? What are the effects of the multi-faceted use of pastoral imagery and aesthetic appeals to nostalgic narratives of harmony, ecological purity, and capital "N" Nature?

Evidence of the origins of pastoralism can be found as far back as Virgil's *Eclogues* and the early Christian ethic of care. The term generally refers to an idealized conception of nature that laments the loss of the simple life associated with a shepherd and his flock. According to Leo Marx, whose book *The Machine in the Garden* examines pastoralism within the American context, the pastoral tradition has valued a cultivated, rural, and peaceful "middle landscape"[42] between wilderness and civilization. Such a "middlescape" eschews both "the violent uncertainties of nature" and "the repressions entailed by a complex civilization."[43] The pastoral life invokes concepts of simplicity, spiritual wealth, connection to the cosmos, and material self-sufficiency. It does not regard nature per se as "sweet and pure," but admires "improved nature, a landscape that is a made thing, a fusion of work and spontaneous process."[44] In the American context, the pastoral was exemplified by Thomas Jefferson's vision of an agrarian America inhabited by the yeoman farmer: "self-sufficient and frugal, he lives off the land and is not dependent on others for his livelihood; he is also independent of urban society and its corrupt ambition and acquisitiveness. He thus has the virtue, simplicity of wants, and independent character necessary for self-governing citizenship in a democratic, egalitarian society of small property holders."[45]

For Marx, pastoralism is trapped either in pessimism or in individualism. Its visions of harmony and simplicity are implicated in the have-your-cake-and-eat-it-too attitude to nature and industry, a sentiment that underpins the appeal of green capitalism. In a sense, it requires a subject who has temporarily fled civilization and can thus claim a privileged position in relation to nature as a more authentic base of experience, without actually giving up the very industry that made this escape possible. Issues of social inequity, patriarchy, and class tend to be disregarded or swept aside in the appeal to values conveniently outside of history.[46] Green capitalism trades on a similar fantasy, seeking a reconciliation of growth, profit, and greed with the idea of sustainability. In both cases, the privilege of class, the implied infrastructure allowing access to the landscape, and the social arrangements of ownership and labour all tend to disappear behind the appearance of Nature constructed as pure and untrammelled. Ultimately, Marx rejects pastoralism as "a rhetorical formula rather than a conception of society, and an increasingly transparent and jejune expression of the [American] national preference for having it both ways. In this sentimental guise the pastoral ideal remained of service long after the machine's appearance in the landscape. It enabled the nation to continue defining its purpose as the pursuit of rural happiness while devoting itself to productivity, wealth, and power."[47]

In his classic work *The Country and the City*, Raymond Williams rejects the pastoral on grounds similar to those of Marx, arguing that from its inception in Greek poetry, pastoralism was always about a receding golden age of harmony beating on the present with the stick of "the good old days."[48] The Arcadia of the golden age is always receding in memory while at the same time being projected into a future utopia, a mythical memory, a precarious retro-future that imagines a world that was once whole and now stands broken. For Williams, this narrative usually serves a conservative politics and thus must be treated as suspect. For example, the tension in classical pastoralism between pleasure and loss, harvest and labour, and summer and winter had disappeared by the

Renaissance, which celebrates the "happy rural retreat"[49] and takes root in the country house and estate.[50] For Williams, the pastoral relies on erasures and hidden labour, such as the case of Sir Philip Sidney's *Arcadia*, which was written in a park "made by enclosing a whole village and evicting the tenants."[51] The Edenic imagery of the country home as a feature of a natural order that has returned to the grace of nature, where food appears as feast and labouring is no longer required, can only occur by making the labourers part of the natural landscape/order.[52] The appeal of the golden age, according to Williams, is rooted in the shift of values from a feudal and post-feudal way of life as a total system with "reciprocal social and economic relations"[53] to the alienated organizational order of capitalist agriculture. For most, "it was a substitution of one form of domination for another: the mystified feudal order replaced by a mystified agrarian capitalist order, with just enough continuity, in titles and in symbols of authority, in successive compositions of a 'natural order,' to confuse and control."[54]

Pastoralism is often accused of sentimentalism and of succumbing to a romantic idealization of nature hidden behind pseudo-scientific notions of harmony and balance.[55] For Timothy Morton, the idealization of nature has prevented us from recognizing our role within ecology: "the dreamy quality of immersion in nature is what keeps us separate from it." Morton argues that "to contemplate deep green ideas deeply is to let go of the idea of Nature, the one thing that maintains an aesthetic distance between us and them, us and it, us and 'over there.'"[56] Like William Cronon, who advocates abandoning the idea of wilderness, Morton is highly critical of the idea of Nature and the ideological baggage it carries.[57] Many theorists now focus on the social entanglements of nature and use the language of networks, webs, rhizomes, and cyborgs as a way out of the quagmire of binary logic.[58]

What interests me here is the appeal to authenticity and the real beneath the concept of the natural and the pastoral within these romantic notions of Nature. Pastoralism has indeed been guilty of various erasures and I do not want to gloss over them. In the case of green capitalism, the myth of the pastoral is a central dynamic in the struggle over terms like "sustainable," "renewable," "green," and "ecological." Some ecocritics, aware of many of the problems of pastoralism, have nonetheless tried to salvage it. Lawrence Buell identifies pastoralism broadly as an anti-urban desire to return to a more authentic "natural" state, although this state is profoundly shaped by cultural norms. "Historically, pastoral has sometimes activated green consciousness [and] sometimes euphemized land appropriation."[59] Although the pastoral is often dismissed as a "willful retreat from social and political responsibility,"[60] Buell contends that despite its contradictions and ideological baggage, the pastoral can function "as a bridge, crude but serviceable, from anthropocentric to specifically ecocentric concerns."[61] For example, Buell points out the intended function of the pastoral imagery at the beginning of Rachel Carson's *Silent Spring*: "This pastoral inset trades strongly on the old dream of the simple life but it is hardly a simple nostalgia piece, since it was intended and was perceived to be a direct challenge to the chemical industry. To read it as a regressive fantasy is to read it the same way the pesticide industry's defenders want us to read it."[62]

Along similar lines, anthropologist Virginia Nazarea examines the function of nostalgia in Seed Savers Exchange (sse), a non-profit organization that aims to preserve and cultivate heirloom varieties of plants. "Unlike conventional understandings of nostalgia, which are fixated upon previous experience (and their 'authentic' recreation), sse made the past something that could always-already be experienced. Home thus becomes not something that one returns to but something that one dwells within and creates. sse helps to make this ever-changing milieu of sensuous experience possible."[63] It is clear that nostalgia cannot simply be dismissed as automatically regressive; nor can the pastoral be reduced to an imagined retreat from modernity. The work that such ideas do is significant and, given the near omnipresence and appeal of pastoralism in so many texts within the storied food imaginary, it should not be rejected on theoretical grounds.

Are we in fact romanticizing the present if we reject the past as a model, by relegating the desire for more "authentic" and convivial social relations to mere nostalgia? Or is the contrary perhaps the case? In rejecting the narrative of progress associated with techno-utopianism, is it possible that the romantic turn toward pastoralism upsets an equally romantic conception of technology and progress that uncritically maps the present onto the future? Perhaps it is techno-utopianism that is romantic about the present and the future, and pastoralism that provides a radical glimpse into a viable alternative value system? De Angelis, in discussing the beginning of history, rejects the idea that we have arrived at a moment of ideological unity (the end of history) and that the current system simply needs to be extrapolated to everyone. Instead, he looks at different modes of temporality in terms of value creation. In particular, he speaks of circular time, as a temporality associated with natural cycles and a return home, and therefore with normalization and a process of solidifying values through repetition in everyday life. In contrast to phase time, which involves the emergence of new ideas and practices, circular time manifests in the repetitive rhythms of the mundane and everyday. Green capitalism operates on all these times, but is particularly intent on returning phase time into the circular time of capitalist accumulation: in other words, subsuming novelty into habit. This is precisely the locus of the violence inherent in green capitalism, and also the impasse of the imagination that the politics of the pantry must face. It also helps explain why the pastoral, as a representation of circular return to an imagined past, can help in the process of value and norm creation outside the typical circuits of capitalist value. When something new emerges, it must become part of the everyday and thus part of our mundane habits in order to stick. This is why the focus on skills building, conviviality, labour, and community that I explore in discussing the utopian pastoral mode can help make space for other temporalities associated with more natural rhythms that can root our lives in lived practices resistant to the enclosure of common spaces associated with green capitalism. Because capitalism thrives off enclosing any space of alterity, it is crucial to resist these enclosures in a variety of ways.

While I am sympathetic to the danger of some of the erasures committed by romantic concepts of the pastoral, I am also attracted by the romantic turn. Indeed, I think its appeal to a different temporality, to a more authentic connection to community and nature,

underpins the entire sustainable food movement; and to reject
the romantic as regressive nostalgia is to miss a crucial source of
energy and a powerful narrative that is already being marshalled
by marketers. Jane Bennett suggests that we must allow ourselves
to "become temporarily infected by discredited philosophies of
nature."[64] It is important, she says, to practice moments of "meth-
odological naïveté"[65] rather than critique, in order to cultivate a
sense of the world that is receptive to the actions of non-human
agents, assemblages, and something "other" which can impel people to see the world as filled with forces, trajectories, propensities
and tendencies of their own.[66] For Bennett, "the image of dead or
thoroughly instrumentalized matter feeds human hubris and our
earth-destroying fantasies of conquest and consumption."[67] Capitalism in particular acts as a kind of magic capable of bringing life
to a dead world, transforming wood into Marx's dancing tables.
For Bennett, and for many other ecocritics, the worldview that
reduces nature to inanimate stuff is fundamentally at odds with the
more generous, ethical, and ecologically respectful view that we
need in order to address the environmental crisis. Bennett argues
that this approach requires that we love the world and see it as
fundamentally enchanting.

While many things have the ability to enchant and challenge this
form of instrumentalization – as my childhood experiences with
McDonald's, recounted in the Introduction, suggest – the pastoral
within storied food must be approached with generosity, if only
because it is a powerful narrative that can become attached to
regressive fantasies of escape into a mythic past, and be used as a
veil for covering some of the most brutal aspects of industrial food
production. As part of a larger genre of storied food that is foundationally concerned with revealing the truth behind the label, pastoralism does not necessarily lead toward a regressive politics. It is
possible to rehabilitate pastoralism as a worldview that can open
up actual and imagined places, and has the potential to encourage
the cultivation of a slow and mindful inhabitation of the world. By
trading on the discredited philosophy of pastoralism, I hope to
show how elements of the desire for a simple life, however tainted,
are a crucial component in moving from text to world. When it

comes to practices like urban homesteading, backyard chicken coops, and community gardening, the pastoral can function as a serviceable bridge between the urban and rural.

I therefore propose two strains of pastoralism within storied food. The first is a traditional nostalgic pastoral narrative that tends toward a Christian, conservative, romantic notion of wholeness rooted in the Jeffersonian yeoman farmer and an escape from the city. It relies on a narrative of fall and recovery, sin and redemption, and reinforces the town-country split. It is best represented by Barbara Kingolver's *Animal, Vegetable, Miracle* and the works of Wendell Berry. The second, utopian pastoralism, is much more urban and less romantic, and is exemplified in the very popular British cooking shows *Jamie at Home* and the *River Cottage* series, and *The Urban Homestead: Your Guide to Self-sufficient Living in the Heart of the City.* I hope to make the case for the emergence of an urban pastoralism that is tied into surviving the threat of peak oil and regaining home skills like gardening, pickling, bread making, and cooking. Although both strains of the pastoral imaginary overlap in places, the distinction is crucial to understanding how practices of inhabiting the foodshed and the politics of the pantry emerge from the pedagogical impulse of these works. Since both nostalgic and utopian pastoralism have clear ecoliteracy goals, it is important to tease out some of the history and ideological momentum they embody.

NOSTALGIC PASTORALISM

Barbara Kingsolver's *Animal, Vegetable, Miracle* is the 2007 best-seller that chronicles her family's attempt to live a more authentic, local life on their Kentucky farm after fleeing the city life of Tucson, Arizona: "We wanted to live in a place that could feed us: where rain falls, crops grow, and drinking water bubbles right up out of the ground."[68] From the onset, the book takes the format of what Susie O'Brien refers to as a "pedagogical memoir."[69] Kingsolver's family journey is twofold: "We were about to begin the adventure of realigning our lives with our foodchain."[70] This realignment takes place on the private level: her family has left the city to live what they regard as the good life and reconnect to family roots and nature, following the rather typical downsizing narrative of the cosmopolitan urbanite seeking a simpler, back-to-the-land life in the country. Carl Honoré's *In Praise of Slow* examines this trend in the twenty-first century; but, as Raymond Williams has pointed out in *The Country and the City*, there is a long history of rural escape, especially as tied into a gentleman's countryside that conveniently erases the actual labour on the land.

And yet as a memoir, Kingsolver's transformation is a public act, and one concerned with labour – a demonstration of an alternative value practice and way of life that cannot be easily subsumed into a narrative of ecological modernization. She blends an apocalyptic focus on horror statistics and crises with a nostalgic return to a more authentic home. She often makes statements such as: "if every U.S. citizen ate just one meal a week (any meal) composed of locally and organically raised meats and produce, we would reduce our country's oil consumption by over 1.1 million barrels of oil every week."[71] The personal and the political are reconciled through the act of eating, and the crisis of peak oil is brought down to the level of individual choice. Kingsolver recounts a pastoral narrative of fall and recovery: we have left the land and become an industrial people who have lost any connection to nature. She laments that "for modern kids who intuitively believe in the spontaneous generation of fruits and vegetables in the produce section, trying to get their minds around the slow speciation of the plant kingdom may be a stretch."[72] The book is filled with recipes, suggestions, DIY tips, and stories of plants, especially old varieties, and it generally celebrates rurality as a more authentic way of life.

Like Kingsolver, Wendell Berry celebrates an organic society, one literally rooted in the soil and made whole through a realignment with nature. Berry is without a doubt America's pre-eminent pastoralist and voice for rural values, having written countless essay collections, novels, and poetry volumes celebrating rural living in Kentucky. Julie Guthman identifies his oeuvre as one of the strongest voices in "contemporary agrarian populism" with its "concern with corporate power, the role of big science in agro-industrialization, and the implicit links between the social organization of farming and ecological outcomes."[73] Berry embraces the Jeffersonian ideal of the freeholder, "one who works his own land and nothing more."[74] Agrarian populism looks toward "a purer American vision of a society founded on the order of nature."[75]

In the same way that apocalypticism seeks to root society in a more authentic form of nature, nostalgic pastoralism embraces an idealized agrarian order as the basis for a more democratic and authentic society. Both Kingsolver and Berry understand this ideal to be fundamentally rooted in small-scale sustainable farming, and such an understanding rewrites the notion of modernity as progress. Kingsolver makes a connection, for example, between the green revolution and the munitions industry's need to find a use for ammonium nitrate after the Second World War. In the course of its popularization as a fertilizer, a system of violence was extended to the farmer's field with devastating results. For Kingsolver, that violence permeates society: "the next explosions were yields on Midwestern corn and soybean fields,"[76] inaugurating a process that has made the current system possible.

In his book *Just Food*, James McWilliams echoes Guthman in arguing that many of the misconceptions surrounding food boil down to "the misleading allure of a lost golden age of food production – a golden age of ecological purity, in which the earth was in balance, humans collectively respected the environment, biodiversity flourished, family farms nurtured morality, and ecological harmony prevailed."[77] Furthermore, "the perpetuation of this myth is a cheap but powerful rhetorical strategy to burden the modern environmentalist with a false standard of pastoral innocence."[78] Both Berry and Kingsolver tend to mystify our relationship with the global in favour of a harmony rooted in honest labour on the land. They rely heavily on a vision of romantic wholeness to inflect and justify their political and social projects, inferring that nature and ecology transcend ideology. However, as Slavoj Zizek points out, ecology is never innocent, and "the very gesture of stepping out of ideology pulls us back into it."[79] For Kingsolver, local food just makes sense, and in the same way that techno-utopianists try to move beyond politics by focusing on facts, Kingsolver marshals a series of scandalous statistics about ignorant children who cannot identify where their food comes from,[80] the ecological insanity of transporting food across the world, [81] and the role of food cultures in rooting a people in nature.[82] Food transcends ideology in the sense that it roots humanity in a deeper, more authentic, organic relationship with the earth and thus with other people through an "edible patriotism."[83]

Guthman and McWilliams make a good case that pastoral narratives are dangerous in their reliance on purity, authenticity, and nature as a good beyond politics. The invocation of edible patriotism,[84] organicism, and other dubious appeals to nationality and locality are troubling because of the easy way in which they become wrapped up in other, often regressive narratives. For example, Kingsolver makes a sweeping claim: "Shopping at the hardware store owned by a family living in town. Buying locally raised tomatoes in the summer, and locally baked bread. Cooking meals at home. These are all acts of love for a place."[85] But what exactly does this mean? Are all local hardware stores good? What if they have a racist hiring policy? What if the local baker uses white flour that has been bleached until it has no nutritional value? What if you are a terrible cook – is that still loving to your family? Home is a complicated site that is filled with comfort, memory, security, escape, but also with violence, fear, commodification, and a retreat from the political. Nostalgic pastoral narratives rely on a kind of knee-jerk, Manichean worldview whereby local and small are always good and global, and big is always bad. While the appeal to pastoralism is meant to reveal a fundamental dependence of humanity on nature, the emphasis on a particular form of rurality has the effect of erasing certain class and gender histories in a way that can lead to very regressive and conservative politics.

Guthman rejects agrarian populism as a deeply conservative vision that in many ways supports the very institutions of private property that have led to the agricultural crisis. She argues that agrarian populism "places tremendous value on farmer independence rather than collective action."[86] It is also "deeply suspicious of state intervention, does not question the individuation of markets, and, most fundamentally, remains a defense of private property."[87] Ownership and stewardship are linked in a version of the tragedy of the commons: you wouldn't destroy your own land, and thus for Berry, "the household is the last bastion against cultural estrangement."[88] The desire for a more authentic form of life resonates in troubling ways with similar appeals to individualism, private property, and freedom within neoliberalism.

In the process, so much is left out. What of those with no place in the home or at the mythic shared table? Sandor Katz warns, for example, against the hetero-normativity of the family farm ideal of agrarian mythology, which historically, has excluded many people.[89] As a homosexual Jew with HIV living in a commune in rural Tennessee, he has first-hand experience of the power of community not only to include, but to exclude. We must remember, too, that housewives of the 1950s celebrated the introduction of frozen meals as a liberation from the daily drudgery of housework. As Lynn McIntyre and Krista Rondeau point out, "a shift in food acquisition practices that emphasizes local, in-season, home-produced foods will require significant work by a household's primary food provider, typically the woman."[90] On an even broader ecopolitical level, it is important to consider the consequences of discourses of locality as they relate to global environmental issues that simply cannot and should not be dealt with on a local level. How, for example, can global warming be addressed locally? While the appeal to home-cooked meals, scenes of gentle farmers tilling the land with respect, and equally happy animals frolicking in green meadows can provide a powerful critique of modernity, we must also ask: what kind of politics do these texts envision? And for the purpose of this book, what kind of economic system do they envision? What relationship between economy and ecology do they endorse?

Nostalgic pastoralism is predicated on escape: falling into a romantic conception of nature, and seeking redemption and atonement by extracting oneself from the evils of society. Trading on images of rural harmony, the subject falls into the anti-modern position that Bruno Latour criticizes, a position that tends to create "pretty ghettoes"[91] that allow him or her to re-create and experiment with pastoral harmony without giving up the comforts of industrial civilization. As Bauman argues, escape is the only available substitute for utopia today. We seek refuge in our private utopias, gated communities, and s u v s, the very opposite of what the utopian drive ideally should accomplish as a collective wish-fulfillment fantasy.[92] In respect to storied food, this can take the form of the life experiment, whereby a person undertakes to transform his or her life, by a stratagem such as adopting a 100-mile diet, giving up certain foods, or, more generally, embracing a lived philosophy. The last section of this chapter deals with the transformation of the everyday, which demands individualism and the acceptance of a kind of hardship, although community is its first refrain. For nostalgic pastoralism, there is no room for the city. Authenticity involves "casting off ... all things modern in order to enable one to become a true subject of nature's will."[93]

One gets a sense in reading Kingsolver and Berry that their experiences with bucolic bliss have saved their souls, and that they have managed to find an authentic mode of being in a postmodern world. But how can interested readers do the same? How can they cross the great divide between urban and rural, simulation and the real, and commodity and life? And what about people who like city life and would never want to actually live in the country? Do these texts serve a purpose for them? Do they offer anything more than a literary adventure, a form of virtual ecotourism and escape fantasy? How is their appeal to authenticity any different than the marketing campaigns of so many companies that promise authentic, natural ingredients, and various other blandishments of the supermarket pastoral? Michael Pollan's *Food Rules* and *In Defense of Food* offer a simple heuristic: if your grandmother wouldn't recognize it as food, don't eat it. The tension between real and fake manifests very strongly in storied food. Within the commodity biography, we see this in the distinction between artificial and real food, the supermarket pastoral and the real deal. Most of the texts don't seem particularly concerned, as if grandma is a category of truth in and of herself, appealing to common sense and thus ignoring the complex process of signification, class, taste, and history behind food practices. Even the search for the transparent meal raises the question: what is the status of representation in storied food? How does one move from being a victim caught up in the machinations of the food complex toward the stance of a critical consumer hero consciously participating in modes of co-production that sustain rather than destroy nature? This is not to deny the value of the desire for pastoral spaces, but rather to complicate its acceptance and thus protect it from regressive narratives.

By considering the regressive ideologies that attach themselves to pastoralism, we may be able to work through to some of the more progressive elements. By giving our attention to skills building, we can make it possible, I believe, for utopian pastoralism to function as a rhetorical bridge from text to world in a way that balances town and country, asceticism and pleasure, and utopia and dystopia. The narrative of utopian pastoralism, understood as a project of imagining a better future, and an alternative value practice rooted in hope, is less nostalgic and more forward-looking. It is less a pining for an imagined past than the mobilization of affect with the goal of producing places that can sustain humans and non-humans alike. It is about teaching people the arts of the urban homestead, and thus focuses more on alienation and labour then on recreating a pastoral Eden. It is less a narrative of escape than one of common good based on a desire to become part of a community that has some measure of control over its future. It is therefore best understood as a strategy of commoning that runs in opposition to the individualism of neoliberalism and more regressive forms of agrarian populism.

UTOPIAN PASTORALISM

Political theorists of revolutionary change have always struggled with the question: how do we get from here to there? How do we move from one socio-economic order to another? Massimo De Angelis, in his book *The Beginning of History*, considers how to move beyond the view that capitalism represents the end of history. He tries to lift the "soporific veil"[94] of everyday attempts to naturalize the market which conceive of capitalism as a totalizing force with no outside, and which, as in the case of ecological modernization, functions by internalizing and colonizing alternatives through a process of accommodation and shallow reform. By addressing autonomous zones and practices, fields of relations, commons, conviviality, and gifts that exceed the logic of capitalism, De Angelis begins to theorize the possibility of alternative value practices that challenge the social antagonism endemic to capitalist modes of production. He calls this process the beginning of history, a new future in which, rather than fighting directly against capitalism on behalf of a particular system, "[struggles] for the conditions making up a context of human interaction in which value practices that are alternatives to those of capital can flourish and prosper."[95] By looking at capitalism as a subsystem of a larger system of social co-operation, through such relationships as family kinship, community, gift exchanges, or friendship,[96] De Angelis tries to avoid the kind of reification of capitalism that sees all resistance as futile. Since capitalism aspires to be a whole, to colonize all lifeworlds, it is crucial to acknowledge the presence of "temporary space-time commons"[97] in order to "see more clearly how things are related, so that on our return into the midst of the scenery, we can measure ourselves and others, our relations of co-production, and the values that give meaning to our actions more thoughtfully."[98]

Food politics represents the locus of one of these alternative practices that De Angelis theorizes, and even in its provisionality and in the tension between resisting capitalism and reinforcing it, food can provide glimpses into the "beginning of history" in a way that is immediately accessible and appealing to many people. It is thus important to consider pastoralism in a different light, as a practice grounded in the everyday that tries to foster what Susan McManus calls "utopian agency." McManus argues that the utopian challenge to think differently "seeks to open spaces of alterity and critique; its alterity seeks to alter, to intervene within the configuration of the present by revealing new and different possibilities, not to legitimate the world as it is already given, already known, already ordered."[99] Once again, we must return to the question of how we get from here to there, or how to cross what Fredric Jameson defines as the "the space of the utopian leap" or "the gap between our empirical present and the utopian arrangements of [an] imaginary future."[100] I would like to consider this space as it relates to food politics, precisely because the manifestations of this gap offer key arguments against alternative food movements. Whether it is the claim that organic cannot feed the world and that it is only for the elite, or the spectre of Malthusian depopulation and its programs of rational state planning and enforced vegetarianism,[101] the accusations of impossibility continue to haunt the movement and discredit it as utopian in the pejorative sense of being impossible, dreamy, or doomed to failure.

In his later works, Leo Marx "departs from his earlier view of pastoralism as antipolitical and sees it instead as offering a radical challenge to late capitalism. Such a challenge would draw on *pastoralism's utopian energies as well as its substantive values*."[102] Many critics have argued that the inability of environmentalism to deal with working landscapes dooms the movement to failure.[103] This is one reason that I consider the pastoral middle-scape, as a representation of a working landscape, in terms of its ability to focus on the negotiation between humans and nature, rather than a celebration of its radical otherness. Insofar as it inhabits discredited philosophies, utopian pastoralism can begin to open a space of possibilities that registers actual landscapes and modes of life, while at the same time imagining a better world. It can function in the dual sense of utopia, both as a critical diagnosis of the root of all evil and as a collective wish-fulfilment fantasy. Whereas the nostalgic pastoral searches for an authentic self, the utopian pastoral is much more interested in unalienated labour, although humanist appeals to the real are nonetheless present.

The utopian pastoral is about fostering skills that break down the everyday mystifications and divisions of labour characteristic of capitalism, and it can thus be read as an attempt to produce a more complete, but not necessarily "authentic," human being. Experiences of DIY enchantment and hands-in-the-dirt pleasure can enchant with micro-utopian glimpses of what is possible, and thus perhaps educate the body in forms of agency that can help resist the economic turn. The space of the utopian leap is best inhabited by a discredited philosophy such as romanticism for a number of reasons. The first is that there is something very seductive about the desire for local control embedded in the romantic narrative. Marketers know this, and the local food movement does as well, and it is probably rooted in the general experience of negative globalization, as power has shifted from the nation-state to the transnational corporation. As Bauman points out, "the real powers that shape the conditions under which we all act these days flow in *global* space, while our institutions of political action remain by and large tied to the ground; they are, as before, *local*."[104] The desire for local control, for a form of agency rooted in the soil and in local communities, speaks to this, and romantic conceptions of nature, although they are deeply problematic, feed on this desire.

Let us dwell for a moment on alienation and lack of skills. Anthony Giddens argues that "the deskilling of day-to-day life is an alienating and fragmenting phenomenon so far as the self is concerned."[105] In terms of food, this deskilling[106] manifests in a number of ways, ranging from a broad inability to even recognize a fruit or vegetable in its unprocessed form, to the inability to grow your own food, to an increasing reliance on processed foods and take-out. According to many studies, in the developed world "up to half of consumer expenditure on food and drink is now spent eating out."[107] Because food is an inelastic product – we can only eat so much – processors know that convenience is a major selling point, and dollar per dollar, much more is made on a box of corn flakes than on a cob of corn. The marketing of convenience, the deskilling of basic cooking ability, and poverty have all contributed to the over-consumption of processed foods that are high in sodium, fat, and sugar.

Today, one of the fastest-growing food trends is in portable snacks that can be eaten with one hand and yield no mess, because 19 percent of meals in America are eaten in a car.[108] Many of the texts within storied food lament the effects of this deskilling, ranging from the loss of the shared table as the centre of family life[109] to a profound disconnection from nature,[110] the rising obesity crisis,[111] the reduction of agricultural biodiversity,[112] the corporatization of food,[113] and global warming,[114] just to name a few. Overall, there is a sense that capitalism has colonized eating, degrading it from its original contexts of home and hearth and source of culture, to something more vulgar and utilitarian.

The series *Jamie at Home* is an excellent example of utopian pastoralism. Filmed at his country home in Essex, the show oozes pastoral appeal. Each episode is organized around a seasonal ingredient from Oliver's elaborate, walled kitchen garden, which he uses to demonstrate various recipes from field to fork. The meal is always accompanied by a brief history of the plant and suggestions of how to grow it, with an emphasis on small urban places. For example, in the episode on potatoes, Oliver shows the audience how to grow a sack of potatoes on a balcony in a plastic bag filled with dirt, leaning against the wall. The whole show is rustic: from Oliver's casual dress, the ancient cutting boards and mismatched ceramic bowls and platters, his tendency to cook right in the garden on a stump over some coals, to the very style of his cooking; onions are left with stalks on them, garlic is unpeeled, food is haphazardly manhandled, and measurements are rarely taken. All of it speaks to the quality of the ingredients and a pastoral aesthetic of rugged, rough-and-ready cooking that epitomizes Slow Food: simple, yet elegant peasant food for an urban audience. Skills are what allow you to make it delicious and quick. He is always a bit messy, tossing things over his shoulder in the garden, and sometimes presenting food that looks slightly burned. Much of the fit and finish of a typical cooking show is intentionally absent.

The emphasis of the show is on cultivating skills by demystifying gourmet food. Oliver consciously abandons the figure of chef as auteur associated with the cooking-show genre, as he seems to almost bumble through the recipes. We get a sense that we are actually watching him in his home, and while this illusion is obviously crafted and scripted, the effect is important. For example, in the "Winter Salad" episode he slips while walking over the raised beds, and the wind is blowing so hard he can barely stand: it hardly seems like the right time to film a show, and one wonders why they didn't simply postpone until a more suitable day. The viewer's pleasure is tied into the transformation of space as private becomes public, and garden enters the kitchen. The dinner always starts in the garden, reinforcing that food comes from the earth, and revealing the foodshed while teaching old skills. In the episode on root vegetables, he teaches the audience how to clamp beets, which involves putting them in sand and covering them up so you can store them without refrigeration. Although this seems arcane, it results in tastier, crisper vegetables, and means a small closet can serve as a rudimentary root cellar. Another episode teaches basic skills involved in pickling and preserving. He often emphasizes what he calls "mothership recipes," techniques that translate into many different skills and allow you to cook a dinner from scratch very quickly, using a variety of ingredients on hand, and thus avoiding processed, so-called convenience foods.

For Alexander Wilson, the cognitive dissonance between the imagined landscapes of pastoralism and the actual landscapes of capitalist agriculture are maintained by sentimental and selectively nostalgic versions of country life. The only way around this is to bring food production "back to the city, especially the raising of fruit and vegetables, poultry and fish. These old skills need to be recovered and propagated."[115] Oliver trades on the fantasies of pastoral harmony while at all time insisting these are skills for city folks. His own persona embodies this tension. The country house participates in the fantasy of the happy rural seat, especially since the very wealthy Oliver spends most of his time at his London residence. However, his country home is also a working farm that provides most of the produce and eggs for his restaurant, Fifteen, which Oliver established as a school for disadvantaged youth who want a way into the culinary industry. In general, *Jamie at Home* embodies the Slow Food aesthetic and philosophy of uniting pleasure and politics. By celebrating the pleasure of food, Parkins and Craig argue, "self-artistry affects the ethical sensibility of individuals in their relations to others."[116] In other words, the slow arts are not merely cultural or individual; they respond to the subjectivity of a globalism imposed from above in a way that allows individuals to reposition themselves and resist in an everyday manner, transforming the mundane acts of cooking and eating into a political critique of the established global order. It helps tune bodies toward a different food experience and in the process, brings to light an ethical horizon of eating rooted in pleasure.

Both *River Cottage* and *Jamie at Home* are demonstrations of the Slow Food philosophy. In discussing *River Cottage*, Lyn Thomas points out that "both nostalgia and utopia are invoked in the scenes of local life, which in their depictions of seasonal celebrations, cricket matches, egg-rolling competitions, cider drinking, and the like suggest a harmonious community tradition rooted in the pastoral view of England as a nation of villages."[117] And while these idealized images can be problematic, they do suggest a new definition of the good life that helps disenchant the narrative of green capitalism by appealing to non-commodified alternative values. Kate Soper argues that "the chances of developing or reverting to a more ecologically sustainable use of resources ... are dependent on the emergence and embrace of new modes of thinking about human pleasure and self-realization, especially, in the first instance, on the part of the affluent global elites."[118] This combination of escape to the country and focus on teaching skills to urbanites helps bring the two together in a productive assemblage of pleasure and critique.

In a sense, Oliver's success can be attributed to his finding a balance between the various sub-genres of storied food I have identified and the way he is able to synthesize social responsibility and pleasure. He relies on the pastoral image to bring the audience home and to encourage them into the attitude that cooking can be fun and useful. The genteel countryside is present throughout *Jamie at Home*, and affords the viewer a number of pleasures: the pleasure of celebrity, the pleasure of home, an idealized country estate, a fantasy of escape, and also, a rewriting of home work as pleasure rather than drudgery. This part of Oliver's public persona is vital for seducing the viewer – and for providing the capital he needs for his more political projects, which end up costing him money. On a fundamental economic level, neither Fifteen nor Oliver's anti-obesity crusade could exist without their profitable pastoral counterpoint. Oliver seduces the viewer with the sensual experience of food as culture, food as comfort, and food as celebration. He embodies the tension and contradiction in Slow Food between pleasure and politics, and offers an alternative hedonism rooted in both nostalgia and utopianism.

As already mentioned, the pastoral is often dismissed as a retreat from the political. But this is only the case if one subscribes to a model of politics that eschews pleasure. However, as Jameson suggest, "utopia emerges at the moment of the suspension of the political,"[119] and in this moment of paralysis, a genuine freedom emerges. Within the context of enchantment, utopian pastoralism can be critical and aware of its own history, utilizing the enchantment of a harmonious world, however tenuous, and mobilizing pleasure into projects of ecoliteracy such as farm-to-school programs that focus on urban youth growing and preparing their own meals, or the One Pot Pledge, which tries to convince urbanites in the UK to plant even just one herb or vegetable in their window or on their balcony. These practices aim to reconnect the urban with the rural by making the city a vital part of food production, at the same time reminding people that food actually comes from the land. From the perspective of narrative, the utopian pastoral is important in its ability to "register actual physical environments as against idealized abstractions."[120] For storied food, narrative and practice are necessarily entangled, for when stories inhabit bodies, change emerges from desire rather that prescription. Unlike the case of the apocalyptic retreat into rugged individualism, within utopian pastoralism pleasure and knowledge unite. As Wendell Berry argues, "a significant part of the pleasure of eating is in one's accurate consciousness of the lives and the world from which food comes."[121]

Environmentalism is too often associated with apocalyptic messages, and as I have already argued, such messages can lead to a feeling of paralysis that reinforces the notion that we have reached the end of history. Conversely, they can buttress the construction of consoling fantasies of nostalgic pastoralism and lead to some rather regressive politics of entrenchment and escape that resonate with neoliberal modes of subjectivity. Pleasure is vital in (re)enchanting environmental politics in the twenty-first century. There must be something worth saving – a world we can love and enjoy. In her assessment of the local food movement as an outgrowth of organics, Laura DeLind argues that "without an emotional, a spiritual, and a physical glue to create loyalty, not to a product, but to layered sets of embodied relationships, local will have no holding power."[122] We need ways of making non-econometric arguments stick, and affective attachments can provide utopian moments of possibility that push upon the edges of capitalism. Following Bennett's idea of temporarily inhabiting discredited philosophies, the romantic elements of utopian pastoralism can function as a kind of utopian bridge. As Jameson points out, utopias always require enclaves; in their diagnostic function as identifying the root of all evil, they must also function as a collective wish-fulfillment fantasy that attracts us. They must therefore maintain a radical alterity as they pull us from the present into the future. The imagined harmony of the past helps to resist the wholesale liquidation of the future, as well as the collapse into the present that Jameson identifies as one of the central characteristics of neoliberalism. It is in this collective dreaming that utopias can invigorate a politics of the pantry and break away from the deadening prospect of history ending upon the pyre of neoliberalism. A self-conscious revitalization of the discredited, deeply pleasurable philosophy of pastoralism, with all its contradictions and layers, can provide such a moment, and thus begin to challenge the market-based grammar of the economic turn.

In order to do this, utopian pastoralism must resist nostalgic narratives of the real, and focus instead on authenticity as a form of "informed or situated pleasure."[123] This would allow for a crucial shift from narratives of Edenic fall and recovery so common in nostalgic pastoralism, to conceptualizations of pleasure as an ethical engagement with the current historical-ecological context – one that stimulates a utopian drive toward a new world, while remaining firmly planted in this one. In other words, this is not a utopia predicated on escape into an imagined past, but a utopia as collective wish fulfillment, critical diagnostic tool, and enclave. It is the possibility of a new world that impels advocates of Slow Food to preserve a dynamic cultural and ecological heritage. It is precisely in a desire to create a home, and not a return to an imagined past, that we can understand the emphasis on skills building. As in nature, where biodiversity is the best means for ensuring a future, in Slow Food, tradition and locality are a means of establishing the conditions for survival. Tradition becomes a precondition for the future in that it recognizes the continuity of the past and refuses to imagine the end of history and its concomitant entrapment in a perpetual now. In moving from text to world, storied food provides a form of narrative enchantment that encourages action and participation. It also moves between the private and the public, a tension I explore more carefully in the section on the foodshed memoir and in the following chapter.

The *River Cottage* series is another example of the utopian pastoral and its emphasis on building skills. The creator, Hugh Fearnley-Whittingstall, is a popular celebrity chef, real food[124] campaigner, author, journalist, and downshifting smallholder. The *River Cottage* series consists of a number of television shows and books that explore Fearnley-Whittingstall's attempt to simplify his life by becoming a smallholder in a gamekeeper's cottage in Dorset. Two separate series within the overall oeuvre, *Escape to River Cottage* (1999) and *River Cottage Treatment* (2006), focus particularly on educating an urban audience disconnected from the land. *Escape to River Cottage* chronicles the beginning of his journey and announces itself as a typical rural fantasy: "Like many city dwellers it's long been my dream to escape the urban sprawl, find a little place in the country and live off the fat of the land, thriving on whatever I can grow, gather or catch."[125]

Escape to River Cottage contains six episodes that track Fearnley-Whittingstall's first year on the farm, and while the setting is bucolic and very pastoral, the pastoral is not idealized, nor does it attempt to hide the actual labour on the land. It involves death, failed gardens, slugs and pests, struggle, heartache, and lots of work. One particularly difficult episode shows his struggle over killing his pigs, both of which had become part of his daily routine for months. He goes through the whole process, acknowledging that if he is to fill his pantry for the winter and pay back his neighbours for all their help, he needs some porcine currency. By revealing the whole life of the pigs and taking responsibility for their death, Fearnley-Whittingstall inhabits the foodshed in a way that can translate pastoralism into a lived reality. His pigs are more than just pork: he must take responsibility for their lives and deaths, and quality becomes more than just an economic calculus. It is a process of co-production, one that he hopes his audience will acknowledge and translate into a sense of responsibility and respect. After processing the pigs, curing his own ham and prosciutto, boiling the head to make headcheese, simmering the ears, and stuffing the stomach, Fearnley-Whittingstall throws a pig party to thank his neighbours and friends for their support. He uses every part of the pig, even transforming the most disgusting bits into gourmet food.

The show takes a more explicitly pedagogical turn with *The River Cottage Treatment*,[126] which tries to reform the lives of a bunch of self-defined junk food addicts who never cook from scratch and rely almost entirely on takeout and convenience foods. In the same vein as *Food Inc.*, *The River Cottage Treatment* focuses on the consequences of the supermarket pastoral, which in the case of meat, include the erasure of the animal's lifeworld from the process. The consumption of meat has become profoundly disconnected from the actual lives of the animals involved, and has allowed an industry to develop that only considers efficiency and cost. *The River Cottage Treatment* shows the audience and the fast-food junkies what eating a chicken really means. Fearnley-Whittingstall makes the group kill a chicken, clean it of feathers, gut it, and cook a lovely meal from scratch. As in the case of the commodity biography, the series attempts to reveal the hidden costs of industrial agriculture by demystifying the process. The series not only teaches participants about taking responsibility for a specific chicken's life, but also how to provide themselves with quality, humanely raised ingredients for less money than the prepared food they are used to, by making things from scratch. The campaign for real food relies on *the emotional resonance of care and stewardship that emerges from the pastoral imagery and experience as a way out of the malaise of being trapped in the commodity nexus.*

The people chosen for the series are all urbanites and will most likely remain so, and the show targets an urban audience that has little if any experience with elements of the agricultural lifecycle. Because such a small portion of the developed world is involved in farming, storied food is crucial to revealing what farm labour entails. Rather than maintaining the urban-rural split, the show helps to unite the two by bringing the audience and participants to the realization that every decision they make in the supermarket literally shapes the landscape around them. It helps foster a sense of co-production that moves away from the simplistic consumption-production bifurcation, and thus empowers the viewer to support alternative models of agriculture that are more humane, sustainable, and delicious.

While the utopian pastoral depends on the concept of authenticity and the real as an antidote to modern alienation, especially in its reliance on the rhetoric of downsizing and escaping the city, it does this by celebrating all aspects of the food chain and pointing out "the negative side-effects of affluent Western lifestyles."[127] By celebrating without idealizing, the utopian pastoral can move away from a politics of scarcity and sacrifice, while at the same time acknowledging the violence of nature and what it means to be a carnivore. It idealizes, but also reveals the muck and dirt and blood involved, creating a kind of perverse utopia of everyday life that emerges from the messy, tangled, and bloody world where categories blur and boundaries bleed into each other. Especially when it comes to killing an animal, *River Cottage* tries to push the audience beyond sentimentality and into *a practical ethics of stewardship that attempts to realign the gastronomic axis within a circuit of co-production that makes it possible for the city to help the country thrive.* By bringing the rural into the home of the viewers and reminding them that consumption is always an act of production, while at the same time empowering through an emphasis on skills, Oliver and Fearnley-Whittingstall help to create the possibility of ecological wisdom and enchantment in everyday life. While their ultimate suggestion is to buy organically raised birds and to cook from scratch – and thus can be read as nothing more than a commodity biography encouraging green consumerism – I believe their model goes further, precisely because of the paradigm of co-production that emerges, and the ways that authenticity becomes enmeshed in embodied forms of skills and pleasure.

Recent years have seen a whole series of new books that celebrate the home arts and try to teach people how to live sustainably. One volume in particular shows how the pastoral can function to unite the rural and the urban, rather than separate them. Kelly Coyne and Erik Knutzen's book *The Urban Homestead: Your Guide to Self-Sufficient Living in the Heart of the City* is a guide filled with tips on vermicomposting, backyard chicken coops, grey-water systems, rain-barrels, raised-bed gardening, canning, ecological pest control, and numerous other skills. What is most interesting to me, however, is the rhetoric of the urban homestead. The book moves away from the idea that one must escape to a small-holding somewhere in the country, and thus needs the capital to make this happen, and instead gives suggestions on how to become responsible and self-sufficient within a city. It celebrates cities like Shanghai and Havana whose citizens produce many of their vegetables and much of their meat within the city limits.

Growing your own food, even in small amounts, changes your relationship to food. It changes you from being just a consumer to being a producer and helps foster, in other aspects of your consumption, an awareness of what co-production means: "We do not accept that spending is our only form of power. There is more power in creating than in spending. We are producers, neighbours, and friends."[128] Co-production emphasizes precisely those practices and values that exceed capitalism, and thus participates in the beginning of history as an inhabiting of alternatives, however temporary or incomplete they may be. Coyne and Knutzen advocate turning your lawn into a garden, joining a community garden or CSA, or simply occupying empty space in the city: "to an urban homesteader, any empty place means an opportunity to grow food."[129] The emphasis on skills and ecological literacy helps the reader to move from text to world, from theory to action. Jane Bennett argues that "ethical political action on the part of humans seems to require not only a vigilant critique of existing institutions but also positive, even utopian alternatives."[130] The utopian pastoral attempts just such a dual outlook, inhabiting the future by looking to the past, and *transforming ethics into a process of place-making*.

LIFE NARRATIVES AND THE FOODSHED MEMOIR

In his book *Coming Home to Eat*, Gary Paul Nabhan asks a simple but profound question that goes to the heart of storied food: "What if each of us, day by day, fully fathomed where our food comes from, historically, ecologically, geographically, genetically? What would it be like if each of us recognized all the other lives connected to our own through the simple act of eating?"[131] Nabhan responds in terms of "coming into the foodshed,"[132] a process that is as much a literary act as it is a physical one. Responding to the feelings of alienation generated by globalization and a food system disconnected from land and community, *Coming Home to Eat* is about finding the narrative threads that connect us to the myriad lives that the simple and daily act of eating reveals. It is a memoir of his journey to eat locally from around his desert home in Arizona, and involves an "extended communion with [his] plant and animal neighbours, the native flora and fauna found within 250 miles of [his] home."[133] By shortening the narrative distance between the lives he is connected to within that gastronomic axis, Nabhan engages in a truly sensuous, embodied form of knowledge that offers one version of what it might mean to live sustainably.

Most of the texts I have explored in the previous section have something in common. The authors make a commitment at the beginning of the book to transform their lives in an attempt to realign themselves with the foodshed. For Pollan, this commitment involved hunting, foraging, and creating a perfect, transparent meal. Kingsolver takes the challenge a bit further and tries to produce most of her own food on her farm. Unlike Kingsolver who flees the desert in order to go somewhere that can feed her, Nabhan tries to inhabit his desert home fully and completely. In all cases, the authors transform their lives to realign themselves with their local environment in a way that is attentive and celebratory. Eating in local and embodied ways allows us to become the author of our story – to take control of our personal narrative and in the process to connect with the lifeworlds that eating brings us in proximity to.

The popular 100-mile diet campaign is perhaps the quintessential foodshed memoir, and has generated countless blogs and campaigns encouraging everyone to eat close to home. Spurred by a Vancouver couple, Alisa Smith and James MacKinnon, the 100-mile diet has rocketed in popularity, with countless groups and 100-mile clubs popping up around North America. The typical 100-mile blog chronicles the struggles and joys of discovering what your locality has to offer, and engages in nature writing as a technique of self-discovery and ecological subjectivity. Eating locally is more than an act of consumption; it is a way of recognizing the lives we are connected to through this daily, mundane act we take for granted. Coming home to eat means becoming conscious of the way our lives are connected through the gastronomic axis, and taking responsibility for the production of place and the transformations that occur as a result. While distance seems to be the major concern, actual miles and gallons of gas are less important than what happens to your everyday life as eating is politicized.

Like many other books in the genre, *The 100-Mile Diet* begins with an idyllic, transparent meal, gathered mostly from around Smith and MacKinnon's remote cabin, and eaten with friends. The couple asks: "Was there some way to carry this meal into the rest of our lives?"[134] Narratives of storied food often contain this kind of dawning awakening and realization of disconnection as a motivating force. The meal is emblematic of larger issues and a general dissatisfaction with the pace of the protagonists' everyday lives. MacKinnon and Smith begin with a sense that something is out of joint, that the world has "gone sideways"[135] and a recognition that treading lightly and with awareness is the only option. Their story is a journey of discovery that attempts to connect the private and everyday with broader global concerns such as agricultural diversity, economic systems, and public policy. The book functions as a counter-narrative of enchantment for those disillusioned by the promises and comforts of modernity. It offers a form of alternative hedonism rooted in a critique of consumer culture and a search for a more authentic form of unalienated labour. The choice of a 100-mile diet is meant to function as a daily reminder of how we relate to the world around us and the true costs and consequences of Western living. Their experiment is a way of embodying those reminders in the everyday: "We could continue to decipher every far-flung product that appeared on our supermarket shelves. Or we could start fresh. We could immerse ourselves in the here and now, and the simple pleasures of eating would become a form of knowing."[136]

There is something about food that makes the above step necessary. It is at once immensely personal and political; resolutely material and also abstract. And for this reason, it demands an engagement with the everyday. When I started thinking about this book – before I had read much of the literature discussed here, and before *The 100-Mile Diet* had been released – I felt it necessary

to transform my everyday life. Although I have always been concerned with the ethics of food, having been a vegetarian for over a
decade, I felt I needed to go further. So for the last few years I have
been actively coming into my own foodshed and reskilling in the
lost home arts. I have eaten a largely local diet, learned how to forage for wild edibles, extensively preserved the bounty of summer,
grown a large heritage garden, worked on an organic farm, and
participated in various CSAs. My experiences were difficult at
times, but immensely rewarding, and I describe them directly in the
coming chapter. But first I want to look specifically at the desire to
transform the everyday that underlies the genre. Until this point I
have focused mainly on stories in order to examine some of the
discourses, rhetorical strategies, and ideologies beneath the narratives. I have also tried to show how storied food functions less to
link narrative and practice together than to show how they are
already enmeshed and do – or could – reciprocally shape one another
in positive ways.

The critique that sees alternative and local food practices as
manifestations of a neoliberal logic is well founded on one level.
The local food movement is circumscribed by a powerful logic and
a system that shapes the very language and conditions of possibility. Likewise, the argument that states that Slow Food is only an
option for those with the time and money to practice it is also
equally correct and necessary. I am uncomfortable, however, with
the way that both these critiques tend to foreclose the question of
"what next?" If capitalism is such an iron system, organizing all
social and economic relations in a force field of exploitation and
greed, then resistance in any form is surely futile. Much of this
book has focused on breaking down the responses to the greening
of capitalism and storied food into distinct strains or genres. My
purpose was to disentangle their different arguments. Many of the
texts I have chosen, especially those of Pollan and Oliver, actually
contain all of the elements within them. Beyond mere heuristics,
the value of thinking about storied food in terms of genre is that it
can help to identify arguments and values that are regressive in and
of themselves, or which combine with forces or other ideologies
to become regressive. As in the case of the commodity biography,

which can lead to empowerment through knowledge but often ends in a call for labelling laws and consumer rights, we can see how easily stories are sold back to us. Likewise, pastoralism becomes a conceit on the side of a milk carton, and autobiographical elements tend to resonate with a broader neoliberal reduction to the individual and the body. In the form of advertisements, storied food can be directed to regressive ends. But this is not the whole story.

Where I differ from many other critics is that I do not regard these problems as an impasse. I see them rather as sites of struggle where the entity we call capitalism attempts to enclose a new source of value. As with any struggle between two unmatched foes, the losses on the part of the less powerful will tend to outnumber the wins; but as long as the fight goes on, there is always hope. And I think hope is the most difficult thing to maintain when facing off against a force as powerful and Protean as capitalism. Despite the growing evidence that capitalism is in fundamental contradiction with nature (apocalyptic mode), the emergence of green consumerism is a testament to the dynamism of the system. I have many problems with reducing agency to this form of consumer activism, but I still buy organic, drive a hybrid, and buy "green" products all the time. What the politics of the pantry offers is a glimpse into an excess that cannot be contained by the logic of the market: a utopian vision that can help shatter the current feeling that this is all we have left, that the only option is to keep on growing the economy until we all become rich and can solve climate change with some ingenious technological trick. As a diagnostic tool, the romantic and utopian longings for unalienated labour, authentic food, and "real" community can help identify the "root of all evil." The first step of any utopia is to banish this evil, to provide an apocalyptic clean sweep that allows the garden to flourish. For locavores, limiting the distance one's food travels accomplishes this task because in encourages the development of local, face-to-face economies. The utopian pastoralism of food offers a unique combination of practical hands-on training and a longing for a past that perhaps never was, but which nonetheless inspires a future that could be.

We must work through the political and economic for, as chapter 1 has shown, the value of food is literally up for grabs. Time, class, and gender relations are all very real limits that need to be addressed. It is my hope that by outlining a history of modern environmentalism alongside a periodization of capital as it struggles to address the environmental crisis, I have shown the very real structural limitations to the politics of the pantry. What I hope I have also done, in occupying a complex middle ground that refuses to reduce the politics of the pantry to a manifestation of neoliberalism, is to reveal the cultural, spiritual, and ideological dimensions of the environmental crisis. As much as we must change the material conditions of exploitation in order to become more just and sustainable, we must also change our habits of thought as well. This is precisely why I think we must dare to dwell in utopias even if they represent a problematic romantic turn. While the environmental crisis signals an apocalyptic rupture between capitalism and nature, let us remember that the desire for a clean sweep, for a world without us, is actually a desire for a fresh start. This utopian desire can pull us toward a better world by identifying core problematics and help us imagine what it would take to get from here to there. Rather than seeing the space of the utopian leap as abysmal and fundamentally impassable, let us think of it instead as a buffer against history. We cannot escape the conditions that have made us, but we can, for a moment, create enclaves where experiments such as the 100-mile diet give a glimpse of another world.

This is precisely why so many authors transform their lives with these sorts of lifestyle projects. In addition to providing a kind of authenticity, however questionable that may be, narratives of personal transformation play out the difficulties and possibilities of ethical glocalism and self-reflexive cosmopolitanism[137] in a way that allows readers to imagine themselves embedded in the same mechanisms without the feeling of helplessness that often comes with awareness of the ecological crisis. By focusing on the mundane, everyday enchantments of baking bread, gardening, and cooking, storied food appeals to categories of the real and authentic in order to bring the reader into a more direct and urgent relationship to the material. According to Giddens, building self-identity is a process of narrative formation that requires that individuals create and write their history and future.[138] In a sense, this is precisely what storied food is about – the desire to write oneself into the foodshed, into a life process that has been severed and fractured by capitalism. By transforming a subject's everyday life so that storied food permeates their experience of the world in a daily fashion, the experiment becomes something more. It is a way to account for one's own ecological debt without slipping into the reductionism of the economic turn. It opens the door to multiple and often contradictory subjectivities and recognizes that humans are not the only subjects with desires, will, and the ability to act. Perhaps most important, the experiment creates the potential for shifting economic discourses in some very specific and productive ways. By encouraging us to live and write the experience of coming into the foodshed, storied food helps to narrativize the profound anxiety and tensions of what Parkins and Craig call the "global everyday,"[139] and thus begin the difficult process of negotiating the scale and scope of the environmental crisis. The foodshed memoir is an attempt to shift one's relationship to nature from an anthropocentric to an ecocentric orientation, using narrative as a technology of self that emphasizes the inseparability of writing the foodshed and inhabiting it and opens the possibility of an alternative future.

3

The Foodshed Memoir:
The Enchantment of Place

"Ruminate": to chew on cud, to regurgitate, to bring to the surface, to consider deeply, to eat. This one word embodies many of the goals of this final chapter, as I consider the foodshed memoir a practice of inhabiting the world, and narrativizing an ecological subjectivity that is conscious of the negotiations, confluences, engagements, translations, and contradictions of food as an object and as a subject of knowledge. I spent the previous chapter ruminating on various narratives of food, categorizing them in order to understand what they do, and what kind of actions or worlds they imagine. While chapter 2 was about imagination, writing, and narratives, this one is about the production of place and the politics that informs and emerges out of those food stories as an embodied and material practice of inhabiting everyday life. This chapter is an attempt to consider the ways in which my own life has become embedded in a narrative arc as I have tried to come into the foodshed of Southern Ontario.

Anthony Giddens posits that in modernity "place becomes phantasmagoric."[1] The global food system, with its vertically integrated pathways of seasonless, jet-setting produce, is but one site of the process of obliterating place. Local food thus becomes a means of embodying place, making it solid once again. This chapter traces my experience of the ghost of place as I struggle to come into the foodshed and account for the ecological debts I have incurred, and also reflect on technologies of self as tools of ecological consciousness[2] and on the work of academic labour as it manifests in this specific place and time. The previous chapters have examined ways in which counter-discourses to economic arguments for solving the environmental crisis become displaced by the very attempt to make nature speak in economic terms. The development of ecological modernization, and specifically of the industrial organic model, exemplifies what happens to an idea when it becomes embroiled in the larger project of green capitalism. I propose that challenging green capitalism as a normalizing force requires forms of enchantment that rely on non-instrumental, non-economic approaches to food. That is, the challenge requires arguments, modes of being, metaphors, and social practices that do not reduce alternative food practices to individual health issues or to arguments for reforming a flawed market mechanism.

Ultimately, alternative food systems cannot avoid the economic turn. The price to pay is too great in the sense of not being heard by the powers that be. However, by understanding the history and consequences of the language of the economy, by fully grasping the price, savvy members of the sustainable food movement are able to use the language to their purposes. This is why the struggle must always exceed the economic, even while using it. It must always be about the excess, about those things that cannot be counted. And this is why utopian, romantic spaces and practices must be sustained in spite of their nostalgic and regressive elements, for looking back in order to look forward is a key element of the enchantment of sustainable food. This dual look is also, however, one of the primary notions that the supermarket pastoral draws on in order to greenwash capitalism, illustrating how powerful pastoral narratives can be. Whether they are a regressive reaction to modernity, an escape to an imagined landscape of harmony, or a legitimate critique of alienation and labour, they represent a powerful structure of feeling that has manifested in a vibrant movement.

Inhabiting the space of enchantment is a means of producing place and thereby challenging the reductionism of economic language. As Laura DeLind argues, we must de-rationalize the arguments surrounding place within local food, focusing instead on the *affective bonds to specific landscapes and ecologies*: "Local is now represented in terms of miles, city blocks, county or state boundaries, and occasionally a natural feature (e.g., mountains, rivers, watersheds). Because such units can be externally measured, mapped, managed, and/or reproduced, they also can be correlated with dollars spent, with calories burned, with milligrams of vitamin A consumed, or with CO_2 emissions released, sold, or exchanged. The outside remains outside."[3] For DeLind, "local and place are not the same. They are not interchangeable and local is not enough. While certainly an aspect of place, local, as both a popular and analytical concept, remains too superficial, too quantifiable, for nurturing or expressing this deeper commitment."[4] In order to generate commitment, the production of place requires that we cultivate language, metaphors, and stories that respect the co-creation of meaning and materiality that occurs within bodies in specific places. As I have said before, we are faced with a crisis of imagination.

The foodshed memoir, in which the author transforms her or his life, is the predominant form of storied food. In this sub-genre, the writing of place and food is always connected with the transformation of self and with a practice that emerges from the act of narrativizing. The projects of writing and inhabiting thus become deeply entwined, and this chapter explores that process, guided by the following questions: how is food becoming a site of struggle for alternative value practices to capitalism? How might storied food aid in the formation of an ecological self capable of participating in less destructive arrangements of production? Can the politics of the pantry escape or push at the boundaries of economic language? Can storied food offer different models of co-production that challenge the social antagonism of capitalism? If so, what emerges? How do the private and public relate? And what role does consumption have in environmentalism?

The most vigorous critiques of Slow Food and the locavore movement come from a basic distrust of the consumer-citizen hybrid model.[5] Chad Lavin, for instance, argues that the model does nothing but recapitulate neoliberal modes of subjectivity by reducing citizenship to consumption. Much of Lavin's critique, to which I return later, rests on a rejection of life politics in favour of a Marxist revolutionary paradigm. Lavin dismisses the kind of intervention offered by Michael Pollan on the grounds that it "offers a food politics that resonates with the lived experience of neoliberalism, in which political agency is all but unthinkable except in the terms of consumerism and in which sovereignty is an embattled concept increasingly difficult to apply to the actions of citizens or states."[6] While Lavin is correct in drawing attention to the limitations of consumer-based politics, I believe that storied food can help expand the notion of politics by developing the concept of *biosocial production*, a dialogic process of producing place through a self-conscious cultivation of situated, embodied knowledge. Thus, while Lavin's criticism that "Pollan's characterization of responsible consumerism as political action is yet another symptom of a consumer society, in which identity formation and social control are largely a function of consumer choices rather than position in a labour hierarchy or workplace management"[7] is important in considering how capitalism incorporates critique into itself, this chapter argues for the significance of life politics in addressing the environmental crisis.

Giddens defines life politics as "happening where the individual and the global meet and influence each other."[8] Because, as Zygmunt Bauman has noted, "lifestyles boil down almost entirely to styles of consumption,"[9] life politics has been discounted by many as privatizing social concern by emphasizing individual choice.[10] While alternative food choices do engage in a form of consumer activism, the environmental crisis demands a different kind of response partly because it is a radically different kind of crisis, one that traditional political forms struggle with.[11] The transboundary nature of pollution, the difficulty nation-states have addressing problems that go beyond borders,[12] the uncertainty of risk, and the challenge of devising a political grammar capable of framing the complexity of the problems and solutions all mean we have to rethink traditional emancipatory politics. This is not to say that emancipatory politics do not matter, but that we must take life politics seriously as a potentially powerful response to the unique configuration of the environmental crisis in late capitalism.

The citizen-consumer model (cautiously) supported by Pollan, Josée Johnston, Gert Spaargaren and Arthur Mol, and Kate Soper, recognizes the changing role of the nation-state in dealing with environmental reform. Increasingly, modern environmentalism hinges on the level of life politics and self-identity. Spaargaren and Mol make a convincing argument that "lifestyle politics are important for sustainable consumption policies primarily because they deal with individual affairs without disconnecting the private and the personal from the public and the global."[13] And yet, as I have shown in earlier chapters, sustainable consumption is a fraught practice that often participates in the very systems it seeks to challenge. Alternative food movements are caught between the poles of capitalism and nature, and between those of agency and incorporation; that being the case, it is important to critically investigate the potential of concepts like life politics, micropolitics, and enchantment in providing alternative modes of agency capable of resisting the discursive, material, and territorial enclosures of capitalism.

Building on the work of Félix Guattari, Jane Bennett argues for the indivisible nature of person, environment, and culture, which will not only require "new 'laws, decrees and bureaucratic programmes' but 'new micropolitical and microsocial practices, new solidarities, new gentleness, together with new aesthetic and new analytic practices regarding the formation of the unconscious."[14] It is precisely in the focus on the role of techniques and forms of expert knowledge in moving beyond politics into science-based policy, that the environmental crisis has become a domain of analysts and bureaucrats, and thus inaccessible to the great majority of people. The techno-utopian paradigm, with its flow charts and dreams of meals in a pill exemplifies this tendency. This is why, within the flows of late capitalist naturecultures, micro- and life politics matter; this is where grassroots alternatives can emerge and begin to challenge the totalizing aspirations of capitalism. The resistance may be temporary and fleeting, but it participates in a process that works to produce common spaces and a common future.

The foodshed memoir participates in this process of self-unfolding. Joseph Tanke, in considering the use of technologies of self in relation to vegetarianism, describes the value of a Foucauldian approach to the situatedness of the self. "Through his genealogy of ethics, Foucault came to understand the self as a network of practices that are tied up with power relations and truth obligations.

The self, for Foucault, is not an ahistorical, worldless subject with an ethics then added on to it. The self exists only by way of a series of practices, in a world where there are relations of power/ politics."[15] Ethics can, according to this approach, be understood as a project that involves a gut-level training of the body in habits of wonder, affect, and love capable of providing the "energy needed to challenge injustice."[16] Following Schiller, Bennett argues that "only a cultivated disposition can bridge the gap between 'acceptance' of truth and the 'adoption' of it."[17] Finding ways of convincing people that being an environmentalist does not only involve deprivation or ascetic frugality is important in shifting the terms of sustainability away from greenwashed, capitalist versions. This is precisely the goal of alternative hedonism and of Juliet Schor's book *Plenitude,* which seeks to redefine progress, happiness, and economic growth in a way that does not demand constant growth and which can cultivate an environmental disposition. Since capitalism trades in desire, the micro and the macro converge on the canvas of the body. To become an ecological self means investing in activities, practices, narratives, and modes of being that recognize and put into practice what it means to be a member of a species with incredible destructive power.

Building upon the idea of technologies of self, Sylvia Bowerbank examines the nature journal as "deployed to construct and narrativize green subjectivity." She looks at nature writing as a means of producing forms of subjectivity that push beyond the "prison-self of separate ego."[18] For Bowerbank, storytelling is "a cultural technology of connectivity and groundedness; stories are told in the flesh, on the ground, by a body in a specific place."[19] By creating "narrative grounded in geography,"[20] we can begin to consider nature "not just as the stage upon which the human story is acted out, but as an actor in the drama."[21] The autobiographical nature of storied food, and the approach I am taking by considering my own journey and life experiment, is an attempt to work through these habits and daily comportments in order to consider the ways in which green capitalism and its attendant codes and obligations, its systems of power/knowledge, are engaging the environmental crisis. Storied food, as a technology of self, as a life(style) politics, offers a nuanced and complex understanding of how various actors and agents are caught up and produce lifeworlds with specific consequences.

The demands of environmentalists and ecocritics for a politics and an ecological subjectivity capable of producing a sustainable way for humans to live on this planet must be answered with more than just policy and technology. The 100-mile diet, for example, can be seen as a technology of self that helps internalize a trust in the foodshed through a daily practice that brings an awareness of the abstract and material costs of one's diet. The act of narrativization, whether through a blog or a book, or even in the establishment of a story of self, is thus part of the self-transformation that is the first step to producing an (ecological) subject position capable of biosocial production. The foodshed memoir functions as an account of this process and invites readers to consider their own everyday lives and practices as embedded in various structures of knowledge, power, and everyday practice.[22] By shifting the tenor from moral codes to embodied knowledge and affect, the foodshed memoir can act as a means of negotiating alternative value practices to capitalism, and as such, is crucial to challenging purely economic notions of sustainability and pleasure. The very process reveals the importance of stories in framing the environmental crisis.

While critics such as Lavin are quick to reject the citizen-consumer as no more than an embodiment of neoliberalism masquerading as sustainability, I believe that certain aspects of this shift are necessary in order to challenge the economic turn. This is one reason I felt it necessary to write myself into the story. I knew from the beginning that I must live the way I read, that I must undertake a transformation of my everyday life to reflect those values and experiences I was reading about. Somehow the topic demands it – you cannot read about fresh-baked sourdough, or the fecundity of a garden in the summer, or the pedagogical impact of school gardens without, in some measure, transforming your own life. I was already a foodie,[23] so I was excited by the prospect of new recipes, techniques, skills, and approaches. Although I hate to use the term, it was a natural step.

In early 2007 I committed myself to a year of eating locally. As one of the most popular manifestations of storied food, the 100-mile diet emerged from the blogosphere and was made popular by

Alisa Smith and J.B. MacKinnon. Aside from reducing the distances food travelled, the experiment mixes narrative with (self)-pedagogy, forcing an intimate awareness of one's own environs by the obligation to consider the story of every piece of food you eat. More than anything, this undertaking forces one to abandon the realm of storyless packaged food almost entirely, to rely on whole foods that must be cooked from scratch. It largely removes the experimenter from an industrial foodshed that exchanges convenience for quality, and requires asking questions of food, treating it like "an active inducer-producer of salient, public effects, rather than a passive resource at the disposal of consumers."[24] For those not accustomed to this, it is a radical transformation of the everyday, involving new skills and a kind of sustained awareness that is both revealing and challenging to maintain. I knew right away that I could not adequately understand the appeal, potential, or limitation of food politics without committing myself to a similar process.

Food is always about negotiation, about the overlapping lifeworlds of slowness and speed, of humans and plants and animals, of bacteria and fermentation, and the intersection of the global within the space of the home. This is my foodshed memoir, one that I am trying to write with a broader question about life politics that considers, self-reflexively, how narrative and practice emerge out of storied food. This is a story of critique and enchantment, which tries to walk the line between academic text and poetic celebration of food in order to consider how alternative food practices relate to the greening of capitalism and to the many value struggles involving environmental and social justice. This is my attempt to write and live through some of the considerations of narrative and pedagogy as they relate to the global everyday. This is my attempt to consider some of the ways in which food signifies, to ruminate about my own journey, and to connect it to a broader politics of the pantry.

BEGINNINGS: HEIRLOOM SEEDS
AND FLUORESCENT LIGHTS

It is a grey and dreary day in Hamilton. The winter has been warm and dry, but today it is raining ever so gently. It might be a bad year for the garden: they're calling for a hot, dry summer and we already had a snow drought, so – unlike the last two years, which were cool and damp – this year may involve a struggle for water. Although, that might be a blessing, since last year's weather transformed my garden into a slug buffet. Gardening is always a joyful negotiation with things outside your control and an effort-bargain regarding the labour and time you are willing to expend dealing with problems that arise. The slugs have a right to part of my harvest, just as much as Thoreau's woodchucks had a right to his beans,[25] but that doesn't stop me from setting out beer traps and oatmeal flakes. The beer lures them with its yeasty aroma and they drown in drunken ecstasy in the saucer, while the oatmeal is slightly more violent. The slugs eat the grain and it begins to expand in their stomachs until they explode. I feel bad about the slugs, but worse about the holes in my tomatoes and the wilted bed of arugula languishing in the damp. All gardeners know their control is a mere illusion, a house of cards dependent on more factors than they can enumerate. To plant a garden is to enter into a negotiation with the world, to transform yourself, to manifest your desire in a material-semiotic[26] form, and to cultivate a world that is resilient enough to satisfy your own needs, and those of the slugs and birds and squirrels. You need to be magnanimous: providing shelter for insects and birds, encouraging beneficial relationships, and building upon the desires of other creatures. The garden doesn't reward solipsism, no matter how much it may seem that you are in control.

Growing your own food changes your relationship to the world. While the effect on the environment might be small, from a pedagogical standpoint it helps "to internalize a trust in one's own food-shed."[27] It is a daily reminder that we survive because of the bounty of the natural world, and not solely thanks to the conveniences and technological innovation of civilization. Planting a garden helps re-establish the material-semiotic chain between nature and culture: "Labors like this help a person appreciate why good food costs what it does. It ought to cost more."[28] The garden is a space where one can supersede alienated forms of labour. It is a place of active transformation, creativity, and co-production, where agency emerges in moments of translation and the slippage between flesh and vegetable. You don't need to be an expert, or rely on technocrats; you see the product of your labour directly, while at the same time realizing the extent to which labour is always an act of co-creation with nature, something that cannot be fully accounted for or controlled, and which must be cultivated on the edges.

I use the term co-production with a number of different valences. First, I draw on Carlo Petrini's understanding that "food consumption cannot be divorced from issues of food production and distribution."[29] The concept of eco-gastronomy (which unites environmental concerns with food), the Ark of Taste (protecting traditional plants, animals and forms of production), as well as Terra Madre (connecting artisanal producers with consumers), all work on the assumption that food is co-produced by farmer and consumer, and by the pact they make with the land, plants, animals, and the whole host of ecological "services" provided by nature. Storied food is largely about sustaining this knowledge and encouraging people to become embodied in their food. I also use the term in the sense employed by Massimo De Angelis, as a way of understanding the social nature of production, without reifying capitalism as a totality, and therefore leaving no room for resistance. De Angelis argues that "the process of social constitution of a reality beyond capitalism can only be the creation, the production of other dimensions of living, of other modes of doing and relating, valuing and judging, and co-producing livelihoods."[30] The focus on co-production emphasizes that resistance and incorporation are always communal acts, and that much of the struggle against capitalism involves seeking ways of sustaining mutual aid and dependence in the face of social antagonism and competition. Where capitalism encourages affective relations of domination in a field of struggle, the garden embodies a deeper species-being: we intervene thoughtfully into nature to coax our existence by providing ideal conditions for certain plants and animals.

De Angelis's analysis of co-production can be extended into what I call biosocial production, a fundamentally open process that tries to bridge the nature-culture divide by self-consciously making connections between nature, economic and political systems, and ethical concerns in a way that fosters human and non-human diversity and moves beyond the economic reductionism of capitalism. The term "co-production" is multivalent and its openness is to some extent necessary in order to accommodate the kind of flexibility required for a revolutionary politics of the everyday. As shown earlier, the "hegemonic redefinition of discourse"[31] is one of the primary ways that green capitalism functions to incorporate alternatives into the logic of growth and profit. I intend to show many different approaches to the term and the practice, and to leave it open enough to accommodate the very diversity it seeks to embrace and produce.

Within storied food, co-production is best revealed in practice. Since I am an academic, the experiences of cooking and gardening are among the few things I do that manifest in direct and immediate ways. Seeing the loaf rise, watching the sprouts poke their verdant first leaves through the moist loam, making a meal with vegetables still warm from the sun – these are satisfying acts for so many reasons. They help connect me to the most basic act of labour as a transformation of nature and culture, an entanglement of self and world before they become caught up in the commodity nexus. Even though my small patch of green earth can by no means support me, the feeling of self-sufficiency, and of learning to decode terroir[32] as a practical semiotics of the land, helps me see the world in a different way. I get pleasure from small moments of pastoral harmony even if I know they are an illusion.

Stories are not enough, however. They can be easily commodified, transformed into the comfortable image of an Aunt Jemima, or applied to labels that assure purity and health. They must also be embodied in everyday life and provide continuity and a sense of history, connecting us to memories, habits, tastes, and experience in a way that the patronizing approach of the commodity biography tends to ignore. It isn't just a matter of giving people the facts – environmentalism has pursued the path of consciousness-raising for decades to little effect. Sure, the message has hit home with some, but as much as apocalyptic statistics are important, it is equally crucial to embody the ideas they represent in everyday experiences and forms of knowledge that can transform the *affective field of domination* characteristic of capitalism into one where hope is felt in the gut, and where alternatives root themselves in more convivial relations of co-production.

Beside my computer, blocking the window of my third floor home office, is a plastic shelving unit with three levels. Each level is a haphazard mixture of fluorescent and halogen lights, some for sheer illumination, and others to cast off heat. This is how the growing season starts for me; actually, it starts earlier, as I thumb through the seed catalogues and luxuriate over heirloom varieties with their narrative pedigrees and colourful names: Amish tongue lettuce, scarlet emperor, orca dry beans, and fairytale eggplants. Heirloom seeds are their own genre of storied food – they have a history, and more important, a future. They tempt us to join a long line of co-production, of farmers and gardeners observing and saving, passing along and trading plants with myriad flavours, styles, and ripening times. All heirloom varieties are open-pollinated, meaning they will stay true to their type and evolve with the landscape. They are living stories, transformed by local microclimates and expressing terroir. Hybrid seeds, those great boons to the holy triad of industrial agriculture – yield, uniformity, and efficiency – produce offspring that do not share the vigour or productivity of their parents. Hybrid seeds need to be bought every year, since trying to save them will yield a different plant all together. This strategy has been great for seed sellers, but has nearly decimated centuries of seed saving as a practice of amateur genetic co-evolution of landscape, plant, and humans.

The industrial simplification of the food chain has had profound effects on the availability of different cultivars, with the result that anyone wanting an alternative has to go outside the typical pathways of corporate agriculture, either by finding a farmers' market with progressive farmers, or by growing it themselves. Many seed catalogues and groups are emerging that are trying to preserve our common agricultural heritage. Since seeds need to be grown every few years in order to be maintained, it is vital that people actually plant the seeds. Groups like Seeds of Diversity in Canada offer a forum for members to exchange heritage, open-pollinated cultivars and thus provide the opportunity to transform the space of the backyard into a site of political, ecological, and social transformation. Buying, sowing, and saving open-pollinated seeds means the gardener can engage in an act of co-production outside the enforced enclosure of genetic diversity that consolidation in the seed industry has produced. It also fosters the process of producing place, literally engaging in a transformative act that brings plant, human, and landscape into a closer relationship. Saving heritage seeds is a recovery of the past in order to regain power over the future. Like utopian pastoralism, it marshals nostalgia as a pining for the past in order to create the conditions of possibility for the future. It isn't so much about a return as a new beginning.

I usually start the eggplants and herbs first, as they need the longest time to mature and cannot stand any frost. Like tomatoes, these tropical plants need a bit of coddling to prosper, but with some care and patience they do well in this climate. My seedling nursery is also where I do my work, where I write and think. It seems like a good combination, and the full-spectrum lights help cut through some of the haze of cloudy days like today, and the little electric heater makes my normally unheated office a bit more comfortable. But it is also a hybrid space, a kind of cyborg that translates between nature and culture. The light from the window is insufficient to produce robust plants, at least not the kinds I desire. I live too far north for tomatoes, so I need to give them some help. They will be spindly and have a harder time surviving the harsh world outside, so I have to make sure they are ready. I try to simulate ideal conditions as best I can. Germination requires moisture and heat. Seeds react to spring when the soil warms to about 21 degrees Celsius. If they jump the gun, the precious reserves of energy saved so carefully in those tiny seeds will be lost to a sudden frost. Consummate opportunists, seeds are also by necessity conservative. They wait until the conditions are just right, so I make sure the temperature is 22°C, the soil is moist, and that they have sixteen hours of light to stimulate their roots to form a resilient ball that will get them through the shock of transplant. It's tough for a seedling accustomed to a controlled environment to make the move into a world filled with wind, bugs, harsh sunlight, cold nights, and cats intent on using my raised beds as a litter box.

It is late March, and only the basil has popped up. It is a blend, and I already see the purple leaves of the Queen Siam variety (from Thailand), but everything else is a bit slower. Once they all come up, I will put a fan on the whole lot, simulating a wind, and encouraging the plants to build up stronger stems. The whole system is fairly automated: everything is on a timer and, although I water them myself every few days, I have toyed with automating the system so that when I am away, the plants don't need a babysitter. It would be rather simple to rig up a drip irrigation system tied into a small moisture sensor and a reservoir of water. I could even connect it to the internet and be able to control the whole system from anywhere in the world, preserving my mobility and shifting the effort-bargain toward a more leisurely pace. For now my watering can and eyes will do, and I don't mind being tied to the fresh green of these first leaves.

Beside the seedlings is my desk where I have written much of this book. It is covered with electronics, computers, screens, books, and other tools that I use. Like the plants, many of which are not native to Ontario, this room is filled with some of the contradictions, possibilities, and intersections of the global and local that emerge and confound the politics of the pantry. I ordered my seeds off the internet from a company in Vancouver at the recommendation of some farmer friends. Besides having a great variety of heirloom plants, their seeds have high germination rates. The first year I planted with some local seeds, I was very disappointed by how few of them actually sprouted, so based on germination prospects alone, I ordered from West Coast Seeds, even though I felt some cognitive dissonance beginning the process of coming into my foodshed with the services of Canada Post. Somehow, the fact that tomatoes and eggplants and basil are not indigenous to this region made me feel absolved, as if I was consciously tapping into an even longer global trade of plants and knowledge. In *Coming Home to Eat*, Gary Paul Nabhan plants some summer squash in an old satellite dish, making a literal connection between mobility, information, and the work of producing place. "I remembered that old adage for peacemakers: 'swords into plowshares.' Perhaps I could offer an amendment for today's *place makers*: satellite dishes into squash planters. We could let the local seeds grow where we had once placed our hope for 'keeping in touch with the outside world'"[33] (emphasis added).

The idea of producing place is very important for alternative food movements, and in this chapter I explore this process from a number of different perspectives. It is precisely in fetishizing the local that food politics can descend into shallow forms of consumer activism and "edible patriotism"[34] that ignore the postcolonial legacy of landscape transformation[35] and the geopolitics of food production. However, as a practice, the production of place can be a mindful and self-conscious activity, a slow practice that can help provide a *temporary space-time commons* that eludes the technocratic forms and structures of ecological modernization. It is exactly in this tension that food can become a site of negotiation between nature and culture, and where alternative value practices to capitalist modes of production can emerge and evolve, challenging even the most persistent and hegemonic discourses of green consumerism.

It can be hard to see how something like planting heirloom seeds can be an act of resistance. How can capitalism be challenged by eating nice bread or buying expensive olive oil? As an ideal, a concentration on local food has come under some criticism from various camps, especially by James McWilliams in his book *Just Food,* where he argues that local eating is nothing but a "symbolic gesture."[36] Taking aim at food miles, he reduces locavores to solipsistic consumers who try to feel better by engaging in a "small act in the larger drama of saving the planet."[37] This assessment is valid to the extent that taking food as a locus for political action and mobilization is often associated with the privatization of responsibility. Lavin makes a convincing argument about locavores: "Reducing politics to consumerism and political economy to ethics, current approaches to responsible foods tend to reflect the actual foreclosure of political opportunity. By locating political action to the actual and metaphorical space of the market, these trends reflect a reduction of political discourse to the terms of global capitalism to the extent that it is only in the rhetoric of free consumption that freedom can be imagined. These trends thus veer toward postpolitical fantasies that differ in content – but not in form – from the neoliberal promise of a harmonious society governed only by voluntary contracts and consumer sovereignty."[38]

On one level McWilliams and Lavin are right. The emphasis on consumption and the market is troubling when it comes to sustaining discourses of green consumerism and providing an alibi for capitalism to continue unsustainable patterns of infinite growth in the name of ecology. In organics, the villains were big business and toxins, whereas for locavores, it is distance and oil. In both cases, there are a number of invisibilities that must be acknowledged and accounted for. Alternative food trades on a significant amount of cultural and monetary capital, drawing on the desires of a largely educated and affluent group that can afford the price premiums usually commanded by organic and local products, and who have the leisure and education to participate in the often time-intensive activities associated with alternative food. This is a very real limitation of the movement, but it does not represent an impasse so much as the necessity to be aware of how food interfaces with larger issues of class, gender, sexuality, and race.

Complex environmental issues are challenging what is considered political, especially as it relates to non-human actors. Storied food as a narrative and material practice of inhabiting and shaping everyday life has the room to tell various narratives, and the demand for connection, for unalienated experiences, can at least begin to account for the privilege associated with good food. The alternative food movement's longevity will depend largely on how successful it is in making connections to issues of environmental justice, gender, economic development, and sustainability, and thus becoming more inclusive over time. Many leftists are attracted to alternative food for exactly this reason.[39] For example, Bennett applauds Slow Food for being a distinctive assemblage that "celebrates, in one fell swoop, ecological sustainability, cultural specificity, nutritional economy, aesthetic pleasure, and the skill needed to make meals from scratch."[40] Eating, like all social practices, is layered with various relations of power and distinction.[41] It is precisely in its polyvalence, in the connection to such a diversity of issues, that food can offer a dual perspective that looks back at traditions while also offering a vision of the future.

McWilliams reduces the value of local eating to an obsession with food miles, a red herring that makes for a convenient argument about the efficacy of the movement, since only a small proportion of the energy required to provide food is used in transportation. He argues that "the prevailing argument for stressing food miles is driven less by concrete evidence of improved sustainability than by a vague quest to condemn globalization. In this respect, buying local is a political act with ideological implications. The ulterior motive of political empowerment ... identity politics and anticorporate angst."[42] I agree that local eating is politically motivated, but disagree that it is largely a feel-good act with little efficacy. For many in the movement, food miles are the least convincing and valuable aspect of the idea and practice. In my own experiences, and on the basis of discussions with others in the movement, thinking about food miles is useful for its effects and affects, not in and of itself; thinking about food miles causes one to fundamentally shift aspects of one's everyday in ways that produce forms of situated knowledge. For myself, limiting my food selection to a geographic area had very little to do with distance measured in miles. It was a way to become involved, to gain a somatic knowledge of my own foodshed. Had I not decided to eat closer to home, I would not have met the various farmers, gardeners, seed savers, and other people passionate about food and politics who have shaped my foodshed. I would not have clambered through the woods, eyes fixed on the forest floor looking for ramps, fiddleheads, and morels. It was in the limitation imposed by the local, that a new world opened up to me, that a new kind of freedom was born.

The mobile, disembodied knowledge prized by capitalism and at the heart of technocratic solutions such as vertical gardens is fundamentally different from embodied knowledge. With so many farmers stuck in the "get-big-or-get-out" mentality of industrial agriculture, we are losing the knowledge that they embodied. There is simply no one way to define sustainable agricultural, for every area has different geography, weather, and micro-climate. These assemblages matter profoundly, and the violence of global food arises largely from the one-size-fits-all approach. Biosocial production is thus primarily concerned with accessing this "sticky," embodied form of knowledge and creating "communities of practice"[43] that can help new farmers create the small and medium-sized farms we need and have lost, which rely on and sustain these forms of embodied knowledge. While reducing food miles may indeed only recapture a small portion of the energy used in agriculture,[44] the emphasis on locality has other effects and affects.

Slow Food projects like the Ark of Taste, whose goal is to preserve traditional modes of production and older varieties of plants and animals, as well as the cultures that emerge from and are shaped by these life-forms and worlds, have little room in an industrial model of high-volume efficiency. As Carlo Petrini explains, the Ark is "trying to resurrect older models of production and revitalize local economies, [by] pointing to a new way for world agriculture."[45] Reducing distance is one of many ways this revitalization can be accomplished.

In addition, by focusing on local production, it becomes much easier to influence how that production plays out, especially when it comes to the kinds of agency available to those of us embedded in neoliberal modes of production. In particular, local food involves cultivating different forms of trust and face-to-face networks, rather than those mediated primarily by cash. Giddens identifies trust as a key component of modern systems, given that we live in a risk society: "the risks of ecological catastrophe form an inevitable part of our horizon of day-to-day life."[46] As a result, according to Giddens's argument, we need people like Al Gore to help establish trust in the wise leadership of dispassionate scientists with our best interests in mind. We must have some trust because nobody can be an expert in all the features of modern life. We make an "effort bargain" with the institutions of modernity in order to allow us to navigate the terrain of modern life without an excess of anxiety.[47]

The provision of food is one of the most profound elements of this effort-bargain, convenience being the hallmark of modern food systems and the justification for everything from monoculture cropping to toxic additives and exploitative labour practices. Thus "a person may go to great lengths to avoid eating foods that contain additives, but if that individual does not grow everything he or she eats, trust must necessarily be invested in the purveyors of 'natural foods' to provide superior products."[48] For the most part, this trust is acquired through a confidence in labelling organizations, organic certifiers, and brands, justifying the interpretation that locavores can easily replicate the contours and logic of the current system. And yet, despite all the advances in food safety, one in four Americans is affected by some food-borne pathogen each year, with 325,000 requiring hospitalization and 3,000–9,000 dying.[49] The high-speed, high-volume, global food system is very convenient for microbes to mutate and travel through, and can turn a local outbreak into a global phenomenon very quickly. Paul Roberts points out that, ironically, "for all the concern about terrorists poisoning the food system, it now seems more likely that our food system will attack itself."[50] The nature of modern agriculture, with its reliance on monoculture and obsession with yield, has created perfect conditions for disease and insects, and has caused a dependence on some extremely toxic chemicals to mitigate the effects generated by the system itself.

A litany of food scares, ranging from BSE, e-coli, and the contamination of waterways, have engendered a widespread distrust in food systems and constitute one of the motivating forces behind the local food movement. Trust is key to understanding the desire for storied food, and as a result of attention to embodied forms of knowledge and direct relationships between consumer and producers, a community of practice can form out of the specific conditions of your foodshed. A distrust in the expert systems of various organic organizations, lobbying groups, industries, and the general trend toward greenwashing forces people to look elsewhere for assurance. For locavores, trust is achieved through the direct acquisition of experience, whether by growing food on your own, or meeting the farmer directly. It is one way of stepping away from federal bureaucracies and certification organizations, whose methods of accreditation often favour large producers and remain largely mystifying. A distrust in organic certification is partly responsible for the popularity of local food.[51] Ecoliteracy programs like the edible schoolyard supported by Alice Waters and Slow Food USA, attempt to reskill and establish a deep trust in the everyday by empowering children with the ability to identify plants and understand what is involved in good food.[52] These programs go a long way toward providing the basis for establishing diverse systems of co-production.

For many in the local food movement, security is based on trust, and food security requires skills and local/individual control. Like many others, Barbara Kingsolver points out that "certified organic does not necessarily mean sustainably grown, worker-friendly, fuel-efficient, cruelty-free, or any other virtue a consumer may wish for."[53] Many growers are now choosing to eschew organic certification and its lengthy and costly bureaucracy in favour of direct relationships with consumers. For example, I was talking to a farmer in my area about her CSA (community-supported agriculture) farm and she told me with pride about an experience she had. Because her farm is close to a highway, many of her customers are commuters who pick up a weekly share on their way home from work. She was out one day in the fields spraying some of the plants with a mixture of vegetable oil and soap to control an outbreak of bugs. Although the spray is harmless, one of her customers who was driving by stopped to ask what she was doing. The farmer was able to reassure the customer that no chemicals were used and the woman left feeling confident that she was supporting a means of production she was content to live with. The relationship of trust, mediated by direct contact or confrontation, is an integral aspect of the CSA experience, and is crucial in pushing beyond the disembodied knowledge of certification bodies. Thus, while the woman is still a "consumer" in the sense that she paid for the share and did not produce the vegetables herself, she takes on a much more active role. She recognizes herself as a co-producer, an active agent who has a say in the production method. The relationship of exchange that emerges from this kind of interaction cannot be reduced to neoliberal forms of subjectivity; nor should it be seen solely as a form of consumer activism.

Most of the genres of storied food that I discussed earlier treat the local as a kind of bioregional primer; coming into the foodshed can be said to be a literary act as much as a physical one. Storied food involves learning about one's environment and forging sustainable links with farmers, labourers, and communities. The local becomes a political space and – in a much greater capacity than organics was ever able to – it defetishizes capitalist relations precisely by establishing a sphere of agency in which the co-producer can emerge and affect and be affected by his or her environment, as well as being self-consciously aware of the role he or she plays in sustaining or destroying certain lifeworlds. Whereas organics was easily incorporated into the marketplace, with its emphasis on the commodity biography, economies of scale, purity, and regulation/labelling, the locavore is impelled to act in a different way, and produces a different kind of model. This does not mean locavores are immune to the lure of green capitalism, but that the locavore movement can cultivate certain buffers to guard against it.

For Lavin, politics are foreclosed by locavorism, which he writes off as a "populist do-it-yourself ethos and belief in American entrepreneurialism that has always evoked a suspicion of institutional politics."[54] Certainly, the history of ecological modernization as a tactic of accommodation by capitalism speaks to the truth of Lavin's critique. However, from the perspective of enchantment and life politics, the kind of consumption that locavores participate in can become a catalyst for something much more radical: the disarticulation of the divide between consumption and production central to the reproduction of capitalism. Capitalism is much too big to topple head on, and from the perspective of inspiring ecopolitical action among diverse groups, fear is not sufficient. By emphasizing the construction of alternatives to capitalism, to the economic rationalization of ecological modernization, lifestyle politics can and is becoming a kind of testing ground for discourses and practices that counter green capitalism. It is also a place where a new kind of commons can emerge, as in the case of the customer and the CSA farmer. Not only does the CSA model encourage a sense of co-production but it places the land at the centre of the relationship. Both consumer and producer take part in a shared stewardship.

For alternative food, the connection between consumer and producer is also mediated partly by pleasure. Unlike voluntary simplicity, which tends to favour the rural over the urban and values ascetic frugality, slow living encourages an "investment in the pleasures of everyday life," pleasures that represent a "conscious negotiation of life in the present, rather than a nostalgic retreat to an imagined community or pastoral golden age."[55] Wendy Parkins and Geoffrey Craig argue that micropolitics and the arts of the self are political sites of great importance in the global economy. Slowness can become "a deliberate subversion and form a basis from which alternative practices of work, leisure, family and relationships may be generated."[56] Moreover, slow living is "not an escape from global culture into an ossified past but rather it is part of contemporary arguments about how we are to live now and in the future. The idea of slow living represents a contemporary interpretation of the past of places and communities and a mobilization of their traditions, principles and values in order to critique the present and provide alternatives for the future."[57] It is precisely in this recovery of the past as a way toward the future that interests me, for it can help stimulate a radical utopian imaginary integral to the politics of the pantry.

Slow Food promises to put pleasure back in the quotidian as a central part of imagining a less destructive way of life. Its critique of globalized, standardized food eaten mindlessly and in a hurry, stems from a valuation of the effects on our lives and on the pleasures of the shared table. For Slow Food, pleasure is much more than just the personal pursuit of what feels good – it is a nexus for considering ways in which we are interpolated and situated as global subjects within the nodes of capitalist agriculture and an economic system obsessed with rationalized efficiency. The pleasure principle of Slow Food is thus both promise and critique, taking up the capitalist colonization of time directly. By cultivating slow experiences, it is possible to become enchanted by the small pleasures of life, for it is often in moments of enjoying time together that we become aware of how interconnected we truly are. Pleasure in slow food has the ability to break the mundane only when it is experienced in connection with great diversity, as with the pleasure of eating seasonally, and thus with social and environmental effect.

While it is important to maintain the goal of challenging the capitalist impulse for growth at the forefront, framing the ecological problem as a possibility for creating a new world has the very positive effect of inspiring a politics of hope. Without a utopian impulse to temper apocalyptic messages, the transformative power of affect cannot break out of the neoliberal solipsism of privatized responsibility. The citizen falls away and is replaced by the consumer in an uneven articulation of desire and choice, without the responsibility or possibility of temporary release. Acknowledging the apocalyptic implications of climate change is important, but so are community gardens, moments of enchantment, and the shared table. Holding these elements in a productive tension is in a sense what biosocial production aims for, and the forms of embodied knowledge produced by local food can change the equation of the economic turn by shifting the balance between price and value. Local food is more expensive because it has to be!

The current food system is largely unsustainable because of the externalities: water pollution, habitat loss, toxic pesticides, and cheap labour, all of which constitute an unpaid debt. The cheapness of global food is based on an illusion, and until people realize these costs and are willing to act on them – until global food is forced to pay its debts – the economic argument will win. Local food will remain elitist and limited in its scope. It is precisely for this reason that I have been moving back and forth between the macro and the micro and why I connect alternative food with the larger project of greening the economy. Currently, economics are based solely on price, but as the sad fate of organics and green capitalism suggests, we desperately need a way of recognizing a moral and environmental dimension to the economy, so that price is no longer the sole measure of everything. The tyranny of the economic is a structural violence that is already being paid by nature and the poor, and will be paid by future generations. As De Angelis points out, "Everyone's externalization of costs, is someone else's internalization."[58]

At its best, the locavore movement is an attempt to cultivate attention to one's environment in a way that is mindful of the everyday and has "positive potential beyond the individual subject to mobilize new forms of political investment and revivify everyday life."[59] As such, local eating as a practice questions the nature of agency within a system capable of incorporating almost anything into itself – a system concerned with policing borders, but also making them nonexistent. Because of this ability to incorporate,

agency is by necessity fractured and impure. The Left has historically eschewed pleasure as somehow suspect, a bourgeois affectation that can provide no basis for true politics.[60] Bennett follows
Foucault in conceptualizing freedom as consisting of "tentative
explorations of the outer edges of the current regime of subjectivity."[61] This is a good way to think of storied food: as circumscribed
within a larger project of the greening of capitalism upon which it
pushes at the boundaries, at the edges. Storied food doesn't break
out with an apocalyptic rupture or utopian leap; it tentatively
expands the space for alternatives to the story of commodification
and alienation. As such, it is vital to understand the movement as
provisional and incomplete, always in a state of becoming.

There are many issues, especially time and class, that limit the
transformative potential of food politics. Despite attempts to reach
out to the developing world in the form of Terra Madre and the
Ark of Taste, the food movements I have examined are particularly
white and bourgeois. My own experiment often required leisure
time, a car, and money, since local food is often more expensive.
During the year-long experiment, I was a graduate student who
worked mainly from home, so I had the time flexibility to cook
from scratch, tend a garden, and spend afternoons rambling
through the woods looking for edibles. This was indeed a luxury
and must be acknowledged as such. However, to dismiss the movement on this basis is to miss some important contributions that
food politics is making to imagining alternatives to capitalism.
Storied food can provide a space for cultivating forms of enchantment and skills that, on a material, spiritual, and social level, can
help foster ecological subjectivity. It helps internalize biosocial production as a practice of self, and also as a way of challenging
econometric appeals to valuing nature. But, precisely because of
the polyvalence of storied food, it is easy to grant too much revolutionary potential to the everyday, or to qualify the whole project
as mere neoliberalism and ineffectual consumer activism. I am
unsatisfied with this stark opposition.

Biosocial production emerges out of these contradictions and
provisionalities. Nabhan exemplifies the required negotiations by
rediscovering desert plants that thrive in low water conditions and

making connections between landscape and identity that are based on a simultaneous consciousness of the global, postcolonial history, and the economy. He begins his journey with a trip to Lebanon, where he reconnects with some of his family's own food traditions and brings back some seeds. And while his local diet would never sustain the current population of Arizona,[62] his underlying desire is foundationally important to creating a sustainable system because it redirects humans from the goal of transforming the desert to transforming themselves, which I think is the basis of the locavore challenge and the goal of biosocial production. The desire to reduce one's own ecological debt, to find a way to tread lightly on the planet, must be understood as a process of translation and transformation, whereby one enters into an uneasy and open negotiation with various actors. This needs to be the goal of the politics of the pantry – to shift our basic approach to nature in terms of material relations, and also in the stories we tell.

We can understand the 100-mile diet as diagnostic of the global problem of sustainability as reinforced by current modes of production, and we must therefore frame it as a form of resistance, a practice of producing place that sustains alternative modes of production. This is the greatest value of storied food and locavorism: they can provide a model, a lived experience of nature that reminds us that we are of the earth. What can emerge is a politics of the pantry that values the everyday act of eating – something so simple and taken for granted in the wealthy West, and yet so foundational to the world's economies, our environmental footprint, and geopolitical relations. Local eating will not solve our food problems: it is not a panacea or silver bullet. But it is a way in, a way of revealing the social mystery of modernity, of the way our lives are invisibly bound together, obscured by global flows of capital, political machinations, and an ecological debt we must somehow account for.

Back to the garden. The seedlings I sit next to as I write this have histories and trajectories that have taken them around the world, and it would be a mistake to ignore their stories. The local should not eclipse the global or lead to what chef Peter Gordon calls "culinary xenophobia."[63] Even foods we equate wholly with certain traditions and cultures – like tomatoes and basil with Italianness – were originally brought from South America and India respectively. For me, being a locavore is about more than geography; it is about sustaining forms of embodied, situated knowledge that can challenge the values associated with capitalism. Following an heirloom tomato that made its way from South America hundreds of years ago, to Italy where it became a part of various local cuisines, through circuits of international commerce that equated particular foods with Italianness, to North America via Eastern Europe where generations of farmers have bred and selected tomatoes for traits they value, and finally to the seed catalogue I am looking at, connects the local and global in an enchanting complexity. The local and global are always imbricated and, it is through gardening and eating locally that their interrelationships are revealed and can be celebrated. Their circuits become manifest in the processes of co-production that tie me into the lifeworlds of plant, soil, animal, and human history. Eating local has ironically made me more aware of mobility, and the ties that bind me to distant others.

For example, a friend of mine returned from Italy with a gift: a small bag of tomato seeds from an old man his mother knew. This man, now close to his end, had cultivated a unique variety of tomato that was extremely delicious. Known only to him and his family, the tomato was an expression of his labour and love, of the dedication of one man to this unique line of co-evolution. Unfortunately, his children were not interested in gardening, so he worried that this variety would die with him. Knowing my passion for gardening, this friend brought over a few seeds for me. They made it across the ocean to my kitchen table, and with excitement I anticipated the joy of continuing the line, saving seeds, and allowing the plant to evolve under my own care in my own land. But, thanks to my carelessness, this line may die. I thought I had put the gift away with my box of seeds, but as I start my seedlings this spring, they are nowhere to be found. Gardening is always precarious, susceptible to the vagaries of chance – in this case, my inability to put things in a safe place. This is perhaps one of the most disturbing aspects of radical localism, that in the name of preserving diversity, it creates false utopian enclaves of illusory isolation that are vulnerable to disruption, and that rely on an imagined and dangerous autonomy that is impossible and undesirable in today's world.[64]

It is important to recognize the global, even as we celebrate the contributions of local flavour, as this is the only way to transform the energy and enchantment of storied food into a broader democratic project. On the tailcoats, ships, furs and feathers of countless people, animals, and birds throughout human history, plants have migrated with us, adapting, transforming, and colonizing, sometimes with devastating consequences, but often with great contributions to the pleasures of life. My little trays of seeds represent a vast historic migration and process of co-evolution which the very local and private act of gardening reveals. This complex interplay between mobility, place, landscape, and labour can only form the basis of a broader ecopolitics if we acknowledge the impossibility of the local in the purest sense, and instead, recognize how the local fosters attachments with human and non-human nature on a broader scale.

At its most basic level, gardening is about producing place. A gardener chooses what to plant and to nourish particular lifeworlds. One of Pollan's most interesting arguments in *The Botany of Desire* reverses the subject and object relationship within agriculture, challenging the notion that the garden is a sovereign human space dominated by our choices and desire. Resonating with Donna Haraway's concept of cyborgs and companion species, Pollan reverses the common thought on domestication and argues that plants have agency as well. Like bumblebees, we have been enlisted by plants, enticed by their fruit, seeds, and sweetness to spread their genetic material for them. It could be said that we are human pollinators, just like bees. This simple reversal, while it seems trite at first glance – a mere philosophical whim – has the effect of overturning the most basic anthropocentric conceit that humans tend to indulge in: the notion that we are in control, that we are the subject and nature the object. While it is certainly true that we make choices, and that the lines of botanists, breeders, farmers, seed savers, gardeners, and the generations of decisions they have made have shaped a large part of the world we live in, the plants are also shaping us.

The seed packets I hold are part of this reversal. The packaging looks "natural," made of recycled paper. It appeals to my organic aesthetic, cultivated by years of so-called ethical and sustainable consumption. Even the electricity powering my seedling nursery is sourced from wind and solar. I long ago heeded the call of green consumption, despite serious reservations about whether buying can be sustainable at all. Obviously some part of me doesn't agree, because I am a very good green consumer. I buy organic food and clothing, seek out natural products, and use a cloth diaper service. But I also produce: these seeds connect me to something much more intricate, more ambiguous and material. They are the stuff of fantasy and stories, transplanted across the world – human history is written in the journey of seeds. Every spring I open the little green and tan packages with glee and thumb through the paper bags of seeds as I plan out my garden.

A lot can be done in a garden in the winter. With the help of some simple cold frames made of wood and plastic, I was able to extend the growing season well into December. Even with snow on the ground, my kale, leeks, carrots, beets, and salad greens thrived. With nothing but some sun and a little greenhouse effect, my family was able to eat from my own labours well into the winter. Unfortunately, that was also the year that we were dumped on by over a metre of snow in one night. I hadn't wanted to commit too much money into covering my 6x12 raised bed, so I had opted for an inexpensive and light frame. The snow crushed it, and many of the plants below were buried before I had a chance to harvest them.

This winter, I left most of the garden work to the mind: it's the time to plot out your garden. I have a very deliberate method that tries to maximize my small backyard by planting intensive groupings in families that have similar nutritional needs and which benefit each other by their proximity. Tomatoes and basil grow well next to eggplants and peppers. All these plants like lots of sun and water. Interspersed within, some borage, one of my favourite plants in the garden. It grows almost as big as the tomatoes and branches off into thick hollow stems that curve and explode with an iridescent violence into azure bumble bee shaped flowers that droop in a purple halo of fuzz. They attract bees, which also enjoy the hundreds of tomato flowers awaiting their quivering hum. Without the bees the flowers would drop off in sexual frustration, dying a virgin death and yielding no delicious fruit for me.

Almost all the plants we eat need pollinators; without them, civilization would literally collapse. So who is to say which of us is subject or object? Am I the subject because I chose to place borage in my garden in order to attract bees? Or does the bee, to whose services I am existentially and materially bound, retain the mantle of agency? Perhaps it is the borage, for seducing the bee with its fragrance and nectar, and for appealing to my aesthetic tastes and utilitarianism? Or the plant catalogue, for appealing to my desire for storied food? I suspect none of us are agents, and that the word is insufficient for explaining the need, desire, and action we are entangled within. The subject-object distinction is meaningless in terms of co-evolutionary relationships. Our awareness of this bargain doesn't change a thing. The bee selects for symmetry and sweetness, and we for intoxication, sweetness, control, and beauty, the four desires that Pollan identifies as central to agriculture.[65] The plants that play on an animal's desires with the most success are the ones that spread their genes most effectively, trading on an animal's ability to move around.

Domesticated animals and plants are a cultural text of our desires, a natural history inscribed on land, language, and bodies. Bennett refers to our relationship with them as "agentic assemblages."[66] She suggests that "eating ... reveals not only the interdependence of humans and edible matter, but also a capacity to effect social change inherent in human and nonhuman bodies alike."[67] We are all caught up in this gastronomic axis, and in some ways I feel as if the plants choose me from the catalogue. I am seduced by the descriptions, by the promise of the smoky flesh of Black Krim tomatoes, or the mottled streaks of purple and white of dragon tongue bush beans. They entice me with their flavour and colours in the same way the bee is intoxicated by the nectar or the shape of a flower. Like an enamoured lover, I want the best for my plants, and so I try to give them what they need. While industrial agriculture favours monocultures, my garden is intentionally wild. In the height of summer, the vegetables are overgrown, crawling upward on poles and trellises, interspersed with herbs and flowers that attract and repel certain insects, and positioned to maximize solar exposure or shade as necessary. I love my garden, and I would like to think it loves me, although I am sure this is a conceit. We have entered a very productive relationship: my little urban space produces hundreds of pounds of vegetables every year, and given the fairly mild climate (for Canada!) in my area, I could easily extend the season almost year-round with a cloche greenhouse or some sturdier cold frames.

The idea of domestication needs to shift to reflect biosocial production as the dialogic process of producing place through a self-conscious cultivation of embodied knowledge. Companion planting is one example. North American Aboriginal groups have long practised this technique, the "three sisters" being the most famous grouping. I have tried this for a few years now, and can attest to the success of the technique, which I employ throughout my garden, and which is instrumental to making organic agriculture more productive than monoculture cropping.[68] One could survive eating the three sisters, which involves a combination of corn, squash, and beans. You start by making a little hill, in the centre of which you plant some corn. Once the corn is two inches high, you plant some pole beans at the base of the stalk. At the same time, you plant some rambling squash or pumpkin plants in between the hills of corn. As the corn grows, it provides a perfect platform for the beans, which need something to climb. The beans, in return, provide a much-needed boost of nitrogen, the result of another co-evolution between the roots of legumes and nitrogen-fixing bacteria. The squash or pumpkin vines wander throughout the empty spaces and choke out the weeds, minimizing my work and yielding an incredible amount of food in a small space with minimal human labour. Haraway describes companion species in terms of the "co-habitation, co-evolution, and embodied cross-species sociality" which constitute the material-semiotic terrain of natureculture.[69] The process of biosocial production, and companion planting in particular, is about translating this knowledge into our lives in ways that help foster modes of being less devastating to nature and other humans. The embodied knowledge and the skills building of utopian pastoralism have the potential of making these kinds of connections felt.

SAUERKRAUT AND SOURDOUGH:
CULTIVATING THE EVERYDAY WILD

"Bread": staff of life, daily ritual, civilization itself. Few foods are as polysemic as bread. For some, it represents home; the smell of fresh-baked bread can transport you into another world – even for those who did not grow up with home bakers, it is powerfully symbolic of the hearth. For generations of women, bread tied them to the kitchen, forcing them to wake up early and bake loaf after loaf to feed their families.[70] Cheap white bread available at the supermarket liberated those women from domestic drudgery. And then, for the 1960s counterculture, white bread came in turn to symbolize what was wrong with the food system, and dense, hearty brown breads, often home-baked, were as much an act of resistance as the housewife buying Wonder Bread had been challenging patriarchal modes of production and consumption.[71] For Richard Manning, on the other hand, bread is part of the fall of civilization from a healthier, more leisurely, and more humane and ecological hunter-and-gatherer way of life. He argues that agriculture has led to a dulling of the senses,[72] the conquest of human desire over natural evolution,[73] sedentary life styles,[74] the spread of disease,[75] and social systems based on hierarchy and patriarchy.[76] More than most foods, bread signifies; and is it useful to think with.

From a culinary standpoint, bread is at once the simplest and most complicated product you can make. Fundamentally, it is just flour, water, and yeast. And yet, baking bread is an activity that can bring fear to cooks: it separates tinkerers from the hardcore, partly because of its polysemic aura. If you have never baked bread, the task seems monumental, hardly worth the effort since bread is so cheap and plentiful in the grocery store. My first serious foray into bread was actually inspired by a class I took in the first year of my PhD. We were discussing Slow Food and I decided to make a soft farmers' cheese and fresh bread for the class as part of my presentation. At first, I began with the predictability of commercial yeast, which for the novice baker is very comforting. It rises when it should and you can pretty much follow a recipe. Although it was delicious, I wanted to try something even more local: sourdough is one of the few foods a cook can experiment with at home that really expresses terroir. San Francisco sourdough is famous because the yeast is unique to that area, not because it was baked there. Every area will yield its own unique flavours and textures, immediately discernible from another. Sourdough takes patience and attention: it demands a different kind of mindfulness and consideration, and a willingness to relinquish control and allow wildness into your life.

My sourdough bread is a three-day process, and in many ways embodies some of the contradictions and possibilities of the politics of the pantry as a social and political movement. Sourdough is the ultimate slow food; at its most basic, you capture wild yeast from the air and nurture a sponge of live culture in a mixture of flour and water. With some time and patience, this is all you need to make the most wonderful bread you have ever eaten. It is so incredibly simple and satisfying – but also frustrating and finicky. Like anything wild, it resists accommodating to clock time. More than many other foods, sourdough is an agentic assemblage, a hybrid being with the power to enchant. It achieves its flavour from a mixture of yeast and lactobacteria, a symbiotic relationship that yields some delicious results. Unfortunately, the bacteria and yeast are out of sync: they exist in slightly different temporalities, and that being so, balancing the rise you get from the yeast with the sourness of the bacteria is a tricky process. For this reason, modern yeast, of the variety you find in packages and jars at your local supermarket, is genetically engineered to be extremely fast and reliable. It eschews the delicate sourness and complexity of lactobacteria in favour of speed, reliability, and loft. The lactobacteria naturally present in bread have no chance to catch up. But it is convenient, and I have been tempted to add some commercial yeast to a loaf of bread that stubbornly refused to fill with the precious exhalations of the teeming billions of microbes for which I have tried to provide a good home. Without these microscopic breaths, the bread comes out like a brick – hardly palatable, dry, and frustratingly dense.

Making good sourdough takes a particular mindset; you must learn to coexist, to imagine the world from the most minute perspective and be generous and accommodating of the microbe's temporality. You must comprehend what the yeast and bacteria want, and if you can provide those conditions, culinary perfection awaits. I have a batch of sourdough that is eight years old, and like a fine wine, it is better today than when I started it. It sits in my refrigerator and provides the basis for breads, pizza, baguettes, waffles, pancakes, and even an experiment with booza, an ancient fermented, beer-like beverage the Egyptians used to drink that is made from sprouted wheat groats, half-baked-sourdough, and water – an acquired taste to be sure, but magical as an example of how two ingredients in different ratios can yield so many different forms. I have tended this batch with care, and it has surprised me with its resilience, coming back from near death on a number of occasions when life has made me negligent of the colony in my fridge.

And wait you must: the fine points usually boil down to time and timing. I start my bread in the evening, proofing a sponge of refrigerated sourdough mixture by adding fresh water and flour, and gently inciting the microbial world from its somnolence by leaving the mixture out for twelve hours. By the morning, the sponge is bubbly and smells wonderful, with a complex, mildly alcoholic smell that is redolent of over-ripe fruit. I take part of this, return it to the clay jar I keep my starter in, and mix in some more fresh flour and water. This goes into the fridge and back into microbial torpidity, awaiting a new feeding or a fresh batch of bread. If tended this way, sourdough cultures will keep for decades and even centuries, becoming tastier and rising with more vigour as they age. Lately, I have been frustrated by the dough because it took so long to rise and was hard to time. Unlike commercial yeast, which generally takes a few hours to rise and re-rise, sourdough is much more particular and susceptible to the vagaries of humidity and temperature. Since I live in a draughty old house where we keep the temperature rather low, it is always a battle to get the right conditions to balance the flavour with the rise, for sourdough is pure terroir, an extension of the local landscape and weather. Every place will yield a different culture, a different flavour, and every time you bake it, the bread is unique. I have baked hundreds of loaves, and each time is always different. It is precisely for this reason that sourdough is artisanal and why even breads advertised as sourdough are in fact rarely leavened by wild bacteria and yeasts alone. Sourdough takes skill and patience and a willingness to engage with the bread on its own terms. Industrial methods always prefer domesticated over wild forms, as they are more predictable and easier to control, having been disciplined to clock time. But like my garden, the wildness gives it vigour and flavour.

After the sponge is ready, I begin the first of three rises. Flour and water are basically all you need, but I like to include flax meal, different kinds of flour, oatmeal, nuts, honey, milk, and dried fruit to enhance the bread. Next, the flour, to which I add water, milk, honey, oil, and salt and then knead until silky smooth. It is a mistake to use precise measurements at this point, as once again, the amount of flour needed will depend on the humidity of the air and the moisture content of the original sponge. It's best to simply feel for a particular texture. It requires that you become viscerally involved with the dough, pulling and stretching, caressing until it becomes an extension of your arm. This is embodied, sticky knowledge at its most delicious. It can be heavy work, and sweat from your brow often mixes with the dough. This is not a process for people who like the comfort of a recipe; you need to be flexible to accommodate the life of the bread, to account for the lifeworld you must nurture. Sourdough is an act of responsibility: you must care for the yeast, tend to it, and feed it like an animal or plant. It is an act of love, of symbiosis.

After ten to fifteen minutes of kneading, the bread goes into a greased bowl and is covered with a damp cloth and popped into the refrigerator, where it will spend the next twenty-four hours proofing, slowing the yeast and allowing the lactobacteria, which are more tolerant of cold temperatures, to impart their tang. The next day, the dough comes out and I add some warm water or milk and some more flour and the nut mixture. This mixture must rise once again, perhaps twelve hours or more, before I punch it down and cuddle it into a loaf pan or shape it onto a baguette tray, after which it still needs another six hours to rise. As you can imagine, timing is tricky, and unless you work from home or are around on a weekend, it can be quite difficult to get it right. Although you can leave it unattended, because of the variability, you must be cautious not to allow the bread to rise too much. If you do, disaster may strike in the form of limp bread. If the carbon dioxide produced by the yeast exceeds the capacity of the gluten to hold together the bread, like a soufflé taken out of the oven too soon, the loaf will collapse into a sad, shapeless, and dense shadow of what could have been. In a cool house, this means watching carefully and, potentially, a very early morning rise or late night bake. Older-style stoves used to have a pilot light that would warm the stove just enough for proofing bread, but I have nothing of the sort.

The solution for me involved a bit of DIY hacking, and I built a grown-up version of an easy-bake oven to control the temperature and humidity for optimal conditions. After the overnight proofing, the bread has more than enough sourness, and it is best to let the yeast take over. The yeast prefers the temperature to be a constant 30 degrees. At this temperature, you can halve the rising time and achieve a levity that rivals commercial yeast. So I lined a large plastic Rubbermaid container with insulating foam, hung a small 35-watt halogen lamp with a dimmer control inside the box, and rigged up a thermometer to register the temperature inside. With this set up, I use the dimmer to adjust the temperature so it sits at exactly 30°C for around four to six hours, after which the bread bursts out of the bowl with a celebratory sigh. One more punch down, a new home in some loaf pans, and back into the box for two to three hours, and the loaf is both sour and lofty. Now I can control the conditions more carefully, providing a better environment for the bread, while also balancing the need for slowness with the real time pressures I must negotiate in the rest of my life. Negotiation with the microbial world takes some patience and flexibility, but it is well worth it. With this set-up, even if I have to work and be away from the house, I can still time the bread properly. I am lucky that I work largely from home and can allow other temporalities into my life.

164 The Politics of the Pantry

Capitalism is largely about time discipline, and allowing other temporalities into your life can be a luxury. Carl Honoré's *In Praise of Slow* looks at how various slow movements are challenging the colonization of time, and how work-sharing arrangements, Slow Food, down-shifting, and other slow practices are shifting the emphasis from labour as a means of upward mobility (higher pay), to questions of time (less work). Honoré advocates the concept of "time autonomy" as a way of resisting the colonization of the fast life.[77] For Juliet Schor, time is the first principle of plenitude and the first step toward an economy of true wealth.[78] She argues that we need more time to change our relationship to consumption, so that rather than buying things, people can spend more time developing their skills. We need to readjust priorities in order to acknowledge that the economy can not continue to grow at the rate it has historically, and that respecting ecological limits will take some profound shifts on the level of culture and economy. This perspective is echoed by Soper: "the affluent lifestyle is generating its own specific forms of disaffection, either because of its negative by-products or because it stands in the way of other enjoyments. Consumerism is today for many people both compromised by the pollution, congestion, stress, noise, ill health, loss of community and personal forms of contact it entails, and viewed as pre-emptive of a distinctive range of pleasures."[79] We must change the way the economy values things like beauty, resilience, and time if we want to move away from the business-as-usual approach. Schor talks about time wealth as a crucial site of struggle, as a reduction in overall paid work hours could help solve unemployment and liberate people to become involved in community, focus on self-provisioning, and create a DIY culture reminiscent of that celebrated by utopian pastoralism and the urban homestead.

Certainly the concept of time autonomy is rooted in bourgeois alienation and expectations and in the desire to have control over one's life; and the specific class position from which it emerges needs to be acknowledged and accounted for. However, an underlying concern about time is crucial, since it is precisely in becoming open to other temporalities in one's life – those associated with family, nature, wildness, and leisure – that alternative value practices such as storied food can challenge the discourses of efficiency and profit that pervade green capitalism.[80] Smith and MacKinnon reflect on the difficulties of the 100-mile diet in relation to time: "We do not live in a world that stops every other activity to bring in the harvest. Putting away food for winter was like adding a part-time job to our full-time lives."[81] Accordingly, when the need for preserving is not paramount, it becomes more convenient to place canning, gardening, and other activities in the category of leisure, allowing them more easily to be reincorporated into green consumption. This is precisely one of the ways in which food politics can be co-opted, relegated to the realm of commodified leisure. But this is also where the seeds of an alternative value practice begin to emerge – where co-production offers up a different sort of relationship between time, value, consumption, and production. Regulating time is perhaps one of the most powerful ways that capitalism disciplines alternatives and brings them back into the fold. The development of organic convenience foods and frozen organic dinners is a utopian bridge between capitalism and nature, offering products that reconcile convenience and morality in an imagined harmony.

The question of time – who has enough, who doesn't – must be understood as central to the politics of the pantry. The concept of time wealth is important because it draws attention to one of the primary ways in which capitalism disciplines works, and illustrates precisely why food can become a fulcrum for considering the greening of the economy, the role of labour, and definitions of wealth, value, and the good life. Moreover, while slowness may take time and be available mainly to the economically advantaged, it is also true that "locally grown food can play an important role in improving the food security of those living on the margins."[82] Time may be one thing that the underemployed have in abundance, and for generations the economically disadvantaged have dealt with precarious labour markets by learning to cook, garden, and preserve food. As we build more resilient and secure food systems, the question of time is less an impasse than a speed bump. Talking about time wealth can also begin to shift value in a redistributive fashion.

William Morris's *News from Nowhere* (1890) illustrates a ro-
manticized time of unalienated labour when artistic production
was seen as a utopian reconciliation of work and life. In a sense,
Kingsolver's experiment is celebrating precisely this kind of life of
self-artistry, and while it is made possible largely through access to
land and money, the resistance that it provides – provisional though
it may be – is nonetheless useful in challenging the economic reductionism and discursive enclosures of green capitalism. Redeeming
housework from the associations of drudgery, celebrating the tilling of the soil with the fecundity of life, transforming work into art,
and celebrating the simple pleasures – these are all ways of bringing
forms of unalienated leisure and work into the centre of life.
Alternative food thus provides friction against global food by
embodying practices and habits that teach the *pleasures of sustainability*, rather than the horrors of potential environmental collapse.
It has the power to make alternative value practices real, in the
sense that they sustain and maintain a sense of the possible. This
shift is crucial at a moment when consumerism is proving to be
unsustainable economically, ecologically, and personally because of
the financial crisis. An alternative hedonism can open the door to a
widespread politics whose values can reorient bodies, affects, and
habits toward practices that are deeply satisfying and sustainable.

All these elements are at the heart of many of the food narratives
I have explored, and are integral to the utopian vision of storied
food as an alternative to capitalist value practices. While provisional and tentative in the resistance they provide – and stemming
from forms of bourgeois alienation that critics such as Lavin find
suspect – gardening, canning, and baking bread represent a more
honest approach to negotiating the entanglements of capitalist
naturecultures than the commodified retreat into wilderness.[83]
Unlike the desire for wilderness, with its concomitant fantasy of
escape and purity, the necessity for labour and time forces the recognition that *the struggle for alternatives is rooted in the process of
producing value*. Any escape must therefore be provisional, for it is
precisely in the liminality of storied food, in the incompleteness of
its escape from consumerism and bourgeois practices, that the discursive enclosure of sustainability can be challenged. In its failure

to escape, alternative food reveals that value is always about negotiation and struggle. It is important, therefore, to temper the revolutionary zeal of storied food with the reality of capitalism. No movement will simply take down the system and replace it with something new. However, by emphasizing time as a locus for alternative value practices, slowness can challenge one of the most powerful sites of capitalist disciplinary mechanisms.

In addition to its work on the level of the utopian imaginary, there are very real economic benefits to supporting a more vibrant local food system. As the economic crisis worsens and employment becomes more flexible and unstable, the local food economy can provide a buffer for the unemployed who have nothing but time. SPIN (Small Plot Intensive Farming) agriculture, farmers' markets, craft fairs, and maker-spaces can provide self-employment opportunities to individuals while increasing individual and community food security. The renaissance of agriculture in Greece is a beautiful example of this. With massive unemployment and cuts to government programs, people are fleeing the city and seeking meaningful and productive employment in agriculture. The irony of ex-bankers and out-of-work financiers learning to make cheese and tend goats attests to the idea that agriculture still remains the base of the economy and a key source of value and pleasure. In a future characterized by increasingly uncertain labour arrangements and climate change, learning to grow your own food may be the smartest thing you can do. With a model such as SPIN, which promises to make agriculture accessible to anyone since it only requires small spaces, focuses on high-value crops, can easily be practised within the city in abandoned lots and community gardens – and doesn't require a lot of capital – the future looks bright for an agricultural renaissance.

The temporality of the microbial world witnessed in sourdough baking is an alternative timescape that provides insight into the politics of the pantry and its connections to economy and ecology. Sandor Katz, in his celebration of bacteria and food, describes fermentation as a process of "developing a symbiotic rhythm with ... tiny fermenting organisms, nurturing them so that they will nourish us."[84] As an extension of the microbial flora within our guts, fermented foods remind us of the unseen world we rely on, a world that modern food sanitation laws and hygiene have set to destroy in a misguided application of industrial standards to small-scale production. Petrini rejects the "disastrous agricultural policies that don't respect natural biorhythms, the threat of environmental degradation, and hygiene laws drafted for large industries that are absurd when applied to small artisan producers."[85] Whether through laws that prohibit the purchase of raw milk and cheese or home-cured meats, or make it illegal for people to process animals on their own farms, "small-scale production methods have effectively been outlawed by hygiene regulations that are designed for mass production."[86] Small producers often find it impossible to comply with such strictures, even though their techniques rarely result in bacterial outbreak – and, even if they do, the scale of toxicity is contained. Whereas a small beef producer might risk contaminating a couple of hundred pounds of beef and make a few people sick, a single burger processed in a modern slaughterhouse may have meat from a thousand animals in it[87] and in such conditions, one sick cow can infect tens of thousands of pounds of meat.

Following the logic that bureaucracy provides the only way to ensure safety, governments consider massive facilities to be safer than a small farm butchering its own chickens or cows. In Ontario, Michael Schmidt, a farmer who provided raw milk for members of his farm community through a cow-share arrangement, was embroiled in a three-year legal battle with the government over the safety of his product, which when tested had lower levels of bacteria than pasteurized milk. Katz refers to "the raw milk underground [as] one of the most widespread civil disobedience movements in the United States today,"[88] a response to a bacteria-phobic regulatory regime in the United States and Canada that disallows local control over food security. In this case, hygiene laws add to the deskilling characteristic of modernity, shifting responsibility for safety into the factory and licensed kitchen. Cooking from scratch, baking, fermenting, and preserving are all skills that need to be demystified and relearned for a vibrant food culture to emerge.

Katz makes a connection between health, biodiversity, and microbes: "your body is an ecosystem that can function most effectively when populated by diverse species of microorganisms."[89]

Once again, we meet the importance of perception. The ecological crisis is largely a crisis of culture, and we need to shift the basic understanding of how we relate to the world, especially in terms of the value assigned to nature within economic systems. Even seeing dandelions as food rather than weeds is important as it shifts from antagonism (killing with Roundup) to a much more gracious worldview accommodating of difference. This is especially true of fermented foods, which require one to abandon the modern obsession with hygiene. For Katz, the act of fermenting foods in your home makes you more "interconnected with the life forces of the world around you. Your environment becomes you, as you invite the microbial populations you share the Earth with to enter your diet and your intestinal ecology."[90]

Along the same lines, Neil Evernden uses ecology to undermine the sense of the self being bound by skin, and moves into an expanded mode of "fields of self."[91] Drawing on observations about organisms such as lichen that are composed of cooperative algal and fungal elements, he asks the question: where does one organism begin and another end? Are the bacterial flora that help people digest "human," even though they are "separate" organisms without which we could not survive? Are mitochondria, which "replicate separately and independently of the cells, and are made up of RNA that is quite unlike the RNA of the cells," a separate organism, symbiotic, or are they simply an aspect of the collective human being?[92] Ultimately, any multi-cellular organism exemplifies such blurring of categories. The notion of literal interconnectedness changes the quality of border zones from vulnerable areas in need of patrol and careful surveillance, to always-incomplete processes of biosocial production in which mutual interpenetration, co-operation, and survival require the active participation of all parties involved. Biosocial production is always concerned with making borders more permeable and self-reflexive.

Live foods, raw milk, unpasteurized cheese: all these foods are highly regulated by a system that is geared toward large processors. But we need their microbes: they improve digestion of food, immune functions, and nutrition. The lactase in raw milk breaks down lactose, making it more digestible.[93] The war on bacteria has led to a rise in rates of asthma and allergies[94] as the immune systems of children raised in increasingly sterile environments fail to learn what constitutes a threat. As Katz reminds us, "health and homeostasis requires that humans coexist with microorganisms," to which the human body is host in excess of 100 trillion.[95] But I am not here to argue about the health effects of unprocessed food. What is most worrying is the effect that this hyper-vigilance has on small producers like Schmidt, who cannot sell raw milk to willing customers because of government regulations favouring large-scale producers whose very methods generate pathogens. As much as we may want to point to developments such as farmers' markets as shining examples of the new green economy, an appeal to individual entrepreneurialism isn't sufficient, as changes to agricultural policy, subsidies, and sanitation laws will also have to be made if a vibrant local food system is to emerge.

Changes on the level of culture and value will help this process along and perhaps provide a buffer against some of the more alluring promises of green capitalism. With the raw milk underground and other forms of civil disobedience showing a genuine desire for small-scale production, people must demand that government regulations respect the unique conditions of production that local producers face. Mutual co-operation and coexistence, the goal of biosocial production, manifests in even the smallest places. The lessons we learn from making sauerkraut, fermenting a pot of kimchi, or tending carefully to a crock of sourdough starter for years and decades extend into the production of sustainable communities. Learning how to be accepting of wildness is a start, a way of resisting the logic of green capitalism. Biosocial production moves in this direction, shifting the basic compact so that humans relearn to adapt to nature, learning from the smallest examples of co-operation, applying them to designing our cities and economic systems, and internalizing a generosity of spirit.

The small act of baking bread, brewing homemade wine or beer, or making a crock of sauerkraut with friends helps generate alternative value practices and creates communities that can resist the commodification and alienation of techno-utopianism and ecological modernization, both of which lead toward large bureaucratic

modes of addressing the environmental crisis, and tend to accentu-
ate the social antagonism of capitalist modes of production. This is
not to say that we don't need global treaties and global thinking.
Both are necessary. But keeping in mind the ways that the organic
movement was largely co-opted and contained by capitalism, Slow
Foodies and locavores need to be aware of the ways in which they
are embedded within a larger project of the greening of capitalism.
The demand for storied food is best satisfied within a much smaller,
direct and human-scale economic engagement that eschews technocratic solutions, bureaucratic regulations, and marketing campaigns in favour of face-to-face food communities. Storied food
can help transform a consumer into a food citizen.

MEAT: THE GENEROSITY OF (EATING) LIFE

I have a friend who has travelled along a culinary path similar to
mine. Over the last few years, we have challenged each other,
shared countless meals, and tried to find outlandish new recipes
and techniques to hone our skills and celebrate the joys of the
kitchen as a space of transformation. One such project was a goose.
We called a local butcher a couple of weeks in advance and began
to plan. We knew we wanted to use every part, truly engaging with
the bird in its entirety. I was inspired by an episode of *River Cottage*
that featured a recipe for a goose neck sausage that used the skin of
the neck, the organs, and the neck meat in order to make a large
coil of sausage. Although I always use every part of the animal I
get, to have the bird the way we wanted it we had to request it.
Even the butcher rarely gets the bird with the neck on, since most
people don't know what to do with it and are slightly repulsed by
the reminder of the goose's fleshly materiality. I wanted to celebrate
the entirety of the bird by highlighting its animality and not hiding
from it.

Taking responsibility always begins with knowledge, and the
boneless, skinless, almost deathless package of meat from the supermarket just would not do. Using whole animals or whole parts is an
economical and delicious way to eat meat and can largely offset the
cost of buying organic, free-range animals. Many of the texts in the

commodity biography are very critical of the loss of knowledge and skills related to animals precisely because the meat that comes to us – drained of blood, deboned, seasoned, or worse yet, mechanically reclaimed – performs a kind of erasure that allows us to forget we are eating something that was once alive. This deliberate forgetting is instrumental in transforming the animal into something Other, unworthy of our sympathy and respect. I buy most of my meat directly from farmers, and I prefer whole cuts. Bones in particular have pretty much disappeared from the grocery shelf. By learning a few basic skills, even someone on a tight budget can get the same value from a whole organic chicken as from a cheaper a boneless, skinless chicken breast in the grocery store.

Unfortunately for us, it wasn't goose season. In order to get a goose with a neck, we would need to special order from the farm, so we settled for a frozen bird with its neck already cut off. The organs would go into the gravy, but we still wanted to make a sausage, so instead of a piece of skin, the butcher gave us a long piece of hog intestine. Most sausage today is made either with a processed collagen casing, cellulose, or even plastic. Traditionally, sausage was made when the animal was butchered in the fall and every part was utilized. After the fat and mucous are scraped from the intestines, they can be stuffed with a mixture of meat, herbs, honey, spices, and organs. Our casing was already prepared by the butcher, so all we had to do was stuff it. This was the fun part, and since we didn't really have the proper equipment, we had to improvise. The intestine is very strange: it looks like an oily white rope. It is surprisingly strong and resilient, and yet delicate. We tore a hole in it a couple of times and had to push the whole sausage down further to avoid the tear. The trick was getting the meat inside without the proper device. I found an unused piece of plastic tubing from a shelving unit in my basement, cut it to size, and filed down the edges. It was surprisingly efficient for the task, but it demanded a slow and methodical push and pull from us.

Making the sausage was a very visceral experience, literally of the viscera – the tumescent intestine slowly swelling in our oily hands, the sexual sound of the meat slurping down the tube, the tenderness of our hands as we tried not to rip the precious casing.

I felt as if we were transported back, that we were doing something basic, ritualistic. We had our hands in something real, something deep inside the animal. It took us much longer than we anticipated – over an hour, but in the end we had a beautiful, continuous coil over a metre long, and five, individual sausages twisted and tied in a fashion echoing the original organ. We were actually surprised by how much sausage we got, especially since the cost of the meat was so low. For under ten dollars, we had approximately twenty sausages and the labour was truly a pleasure. Neither my friend nor I had much idea what we were doing, but with some patience, a search on the internet, and some common sense, we were able to figure out the process.

Jamie Oliver's *Ministry of Food* and Hugh Fearnley-Whittingstall's *River Cottage* series both put a high premium on teaching basic skills so that the audience can make ethical decisions without spending a fortune. Cooking skills are the only means of breaking the seductive cycle of food convenience, and learning to cook from scratch is part of the process of coming into the foodshed. The kind of disembodied knowledge gained by the commodity biography needs to be supplemented by the embodied knowledge and pleasure of utopian pastoralism. The two combined can resist the seductive path of green capitalism. The utopian pastoral is concerned primarily with reviving skills as a way of encouraging people to face their food directly, while at the same time enabling them to cook delicious and often inexpensive meals. Having been a longtime vegetarian, I understand the mental block people have with handling raw meat. There is something unsettling about the sound it makes, the sheen of the flesh, the bones and skin, even its weight. All of it is too real, too hard to hide from. I remember the first fish I gutted. After crushing its skull with a rock, I had to slit the belly and literally tear out the organs. The fish was still twitching a bit, but it is best to clean it quickly. Working with whole animals reminds you of the compact we make with nature. For there to be life, there must be death. It is also one of the only ways to know the story of the animal. I buy my meat from a couple of farmers, and I usually get a half or quarter pig or elk and keep it in the freezer for the year. It is truly economical and most of the money gets to the farmers directly, supporting them so that they can treat their animals and their land with respect.

Last year, I ordered a half Tamworth pig from a local farmer. The Tam is an heirloom variety that has nearly gone extinct because it likes to be outside and takes twice as long to grow to half the size of commodity pigs. Ironically, the only way to ensure the survival of this breed is to eat it. When I called the farmer, he asked me if I wanted the half in its entirety, literally cut down the middle and delivered to me in all its glory. For a moment I thought about it seriously, but then I realized the logistics of over a hundred pounds of pig in my kitchen and my wife threatening divorce as I boiled the head and bumbled through a butchery job I really did not understand in a space unsuited to the task. Instead, I got it cut up and vacuum-packed, but I did take as much as I could see using, including the fat (for rendering into lard), the cheeks and jowl, and the ears. Being cognizant of this interplay, of the push and pull, of the negotiation, is central to biosocial production as a practice of inhabiting place responsibly and sustainably.

In the course of my research on Slow Food and local food movements, I spent a season working on an organic farm that runs a CSA program. One of my hardest decisions was whether I would maintain my vegetarianism. Before I started the 100-mile diet I had been an ardent vegetarian for almost a decade. I was sure that this was the morally and environmentally superior position, but as I started getting more involved in food production, I realized that vegetarianism often relies on highly processed meat substitutes, long-distance transportation, and an agricultural-industrial complex that I was in principle against. Moreover, many of the problems of modern industrial agriculture stem from the separation of animals and crops, for animals are an integral part of the farm ecosystem. Without animals, farmers must buy artificial fertilizers from far away, or convert grasslands, which are indigestible to humans, into crops that probably should not grow there. Farms with both plants and animals tend to be much more diverse than those with just one or the other. From a personal standpoint, I was concerned that as winter set in and I was relying on my preserves for vegetables, with only a few humble roots providing a fresh source, that I would begin to waste away. I was unable to get locally sourced tofu or beans and thus my protein choices were severely limited. Ultimately I chose to include local and ethically raised animals in my diet.

Without getting into a protracted discussion of vegetarianism and meat eating, I would like to consider a specific encounter I had with some chickens I was looking after, because the encounter helps elucidate an important concept related to biosocial production. As I see it, biosocial production is a de-commodified biography of food that self-consciously participates in producing a place that respects the diverse needs and desires of both human and non-human actors. Biosocial production recognizes that co-production of food is made possible by both the farmer and the consumer, and by the pact that they make with the land, plants, animals, and the whole host of ecological "services" provided by nature. Rather than dividing up the process, biosocial production seeks to reconnect people with the means of production, and in the case of food, reconnect the rural and the urban. This is precisely the goal of Community Supported Agriculture and organizations such as "farm-folk city-folk," which try to make consumers realize they need to take responsibility for the lifeworlds they help produce. Sustaining this awareness is crucial to creating a sustainable economic system that can relate to nature beyond the cash nexus and the reductionism of profit and growth. Without this fundamental shift in the relationship between production and consumption, storied food becomes nothing more than another adjunct to the greening of capitalism. By agitating on the borderlines where capitalism's measures and values abut onto those of other systems, imagined communities, and modes of being, food initiatives can become a site of hybridity and an alternative value practice.

Like most people, I get my eggs from the sterile, brightly lit aisles of the local supermarket. Since I became a vegetarian, I have always tried to buy and eat only free-range or organic eggs. I had read about the sad life of the modern chicken and reacted with the anger and indignation that sustains many environmentalists. The industrial chicken is a horrible example of what capitalism is capable of with minimal regulation and when guided solely by the profit motive. Having decided not to be a vegan, I felt better knowing that the eggs I was eating came from free-range chickens. I imagined that these chickens, although probably not nestled in the bowers of the pastoral landscape of an idyllic pre-industrial farm, at least had room to wander, roost, and do other chicken-like things. The particular chickens I was taking care of were allowed to roam freely around the whole farm, roosting as they saw fit, and engaging in the activities that make a chicken a chicken. Not only did their lives seem to be relatively happy, but their eggs were of a different category all together, with brilliant orange yolks, firm whites, and a taste that echoed the quality of their lives.

Perhaps the greatest lesson I have learned while working on the farm relates to the subtle violence that nonetheless prevails even in the most beneficial symbiosis. While these chickens were "free" in a sense, it also remained the case that eating eggs involves using another animal for your benefit. Chickens are nurturing creatures, expending one-eighth of their body mass on the production of eggs every day. They roost and instinctively hide their eggs to protect them from the animals who covet this nutritious and dense source of food. They are the archetypal good parent of the animal kingdom. Having been tasked with feeding the chickens and collecting the eggs, I lifted the back flap of the chicken-coop and looked in on the mothers. There weren't many eggs; most of them were under one chicken who was doing the work of tending a few eggs at once. I tentatively reached in and was pecked at by the hen. I had been told it was important to get the eggs out from under her as soon as possible, for if the eggs are warmed, they begin to develop bloody spots, which most of us don't enjoy in our morning omelette. So as I reached in, I blocked her pecking with the egg carton – an irony not lost on me that morning. To the hen's dismay, I was successful in providing for my lunch. What struck me the most, however, was the plaintive clucking that followed me as I walked away. I could hear her indignation as she lamented her lost children, and for the first time I was truly aware of the cost of eating an egg. This was a face-to-beak encounter that left a mark on me because I was responsible, in a direct way, for that specific chicken's suffering. In the most basic sense, it was an unmediated and unalienated experience.

However, I also felt responsible, in that I had chosen to support a farmer who respects his chickens and allows them to live as chickens, in what I can honestly say within the limits of human imagination, is a good life. I was part of the biosocial production of a lifeworld that respected the being of that chicken. In the wild, these chickens would be hunted by foxes, coyotes, weasels, and all sorts of other animals that want both eggs and hens. At the farm, they are relatively safe and live to see many of their chicks hatch before they join the fate of all creatures in the human gastronomic axis and make their way to the soup pot. I always knew of the abstract costs of my diet, but that day, I saw a more complete picture. I had to be comfortable with myself and the system I was part of and, rather than handing over a few dollars and hiding behind the false civility of commerce, I reached in behind an actual chicken and stole an egg from a mother. Instead of being a passive consumer who purchases eggs, I had an encounter that commodification precludes from occurring, or at least makes it difficult to experience. I felt I was part of a mundane enchantment that revealed the true costs of eating, and in the process connected me to a much more complete economic, political, social, and ethical system. As Michael Carolan points out, "if one's embodied knowledge of chickens is based significantly on encounters with Chicken McNuggets why should anyone expect them to feel ethically connected to this fried mass of bleached meat? We shouldn't."[96]

Whereas the experience of buying organic, free-range eggs is mediated by the cash nexus, the face-to-beak encounter of taking an egg from its mother forced me into a realization of co-habitation, a shared fleshly presence that helps defend against the instrumentalization of being that is characteristic of so much of our agricultural system. The chicken and I become enmeshed in an ethico-political dynamic that protects against the symbolic and real violence of commodification that occurs within the factory farming system. While by no means clean or morally clear, my encounter was productive in the sense that it produced a reciprocal being, a biosocial network of need and desire that suffuses chicken, human, and landscape in a way that forces reflection, adaptation, and negotiation, which are lacking in the somnolent and alienated act of supermarket store shopping. By hearing an individual hen's expressive appeal, rather than the inarticulate squawking of a mass of birds, or the dead silence of the egg carton, I acknowledged that she was asking me something, that she was an articulate being with her own world, desires, and needs. She demanded from me the right of hospitality and inclusion in a community with a right to a good life. She called on my generosity, and in turn, provided her eggs. The next time I took eggs, she was more welcoming.

Interactions of this kind are only possible when vibrant local economies thrive, where people can meet those who produce their food, and where they share a stake in that production. The CSA model is particularly emblematic of biosocial production because it requires that consumption and production be reconciled. When you purchase a share at the beginning of the season, you make a pact with the farmer. Your share of the produce depends on the weather, temperature, precipitation, availability of labour, and so on. Being a locavore is so much more than distance. Shortening the miles your food travels makes it possible – necessary even – to know the story in a material way. Most CSAs are by definition open to the public, inviting their members to participate in harvesting, farm tours, dinner nights, and school tours. The CSA I am currently a member of hosts regular events, focusing especially on school-age children. Since most people in North America do not live on farms or have little access to farm animals, giving children the opportunity to witness the actual lives of their food is an important step in establishing a cultural ecology that fosters respect. From a pedagogical standpoint, the CSA can help bridge the gap between town and country, and at the same time foster a sense of co-production. Joel Kovel goes as far as to say that "a community garden is an excellent model for a pathway towards an ecological society,"[97] acknowledging the powerful role of embodied knowledge in transforming the affective field of domination characteristic of capitalism into a system based on mutual aid and co-operation.

One of the most interesting sections of the *Omnivore's Dilemma* is the portrait of Joel Salatin. He owns and operates Polyface Farms, a beautiful example of biosocial production. Salatin describes his farm as "management-intensive grazing."[98] He rotates his cows along the pasture so they do not overgraze. After they have eaten and fertilized a section of the pasture, he waits three days to give the grubs in the cow paddies time to become plump, and then sends in the chickens to feed on them, in the process sanitizing the field. Salatin mimics the natural relationship between herbivores and birds. His kind of farming requires a deep, embodied understanding of the local landscape – a bioregional knowledge that cannot be reduced to feed charts and applied to every landscape. In nature, predators keep herbivores mobbed and moving, and thus they never overtax the grass. Salatin accomplishes this natural motion by means of movable electric fences and a chicken tractor that allows him to pull the chicken coops after the cows. His system results in healthier grass, as the cow's rumen takes over the nutrient recycling role of the grass during the dry months. He works within the economy of nature, modelling his farm after natural processes that improve rather than degrade the soil and the land.

Biosocial production releases some degree of control or hierarchy, and recognizes that humans cannot and should not seek to control nature completely. It moves from notions of conquest to notions of co-operation and co-production – from a model of green capitalism and techno-utopian fantasies of control, to something like my sourdough proofing box where negotiations are made in good faith. In recognizing the dynamic nature of the partnership between nature, culture, and the economy, alternative value practices can push at the boundaries of green capitalism as a redefinition of hegemonic discourse. This revaluation begins with recognizing that nature is an agent, which for Salatin means taking on the role of an "orchestra conductor," making sure everybody is in the right place at the right time.[99] While he nonetheless remains in control and functions within a capitalist system, his animals retain dignity and can live their lives well, and the landscape thrives. Moreover, where an Intensive Livestock Operation has a waste problem, Salatin is able to transform cow patties into happy chickens and healthy and delicious eggs. There is no waste anywhere, and his reliance on fossil fuels is minimal. His farm functions as an integrated system with complex loops that mimic those found in nature. This must be the goal of biosocial production: to encourage, nurture, and replicate the kinds of co-productive relationships found in healthy ecosystems, by integrating human culture into them. By building upon co-evolutionary relationships, like the reciprocal need-fulfillment of grass, herbivores, and birds, Salatin orchestrates beneficial cycles that improve rather than degrade the quality of the land.

A Gardener's Utopia

In his book *Liquid Times*, Zygmunt Bauman considers the social, political, ethical, and institutional effects of the passage from "solid" to "liquid" modernity,[1] a transition that involves relentless movement as the dynamo of capitalism, with its power of creative destruction, is unleashed on a population universally undergoing uncertainty and fear. Globalization is experienced in ways that depend on class. For the well off, it provides opportunities, but for those of us limited by the local, it is often characterized by insecurity. Bauman reflects on the effects of uncertainty and constant flux on our communities, governments, and individuals, as the foundations of society and nature crumble under the gathering weight of the growth and profit imperative, and suffer the "collapse of long-term thinking, planning and acting."[2] He argues that this new global system is geared toward generating human and natural waste as quickly as possible and that, as a result, an endemic uncertainty accompanies what he calls a collapse into the present, the end of history, and perhaps also an end of the utopian imaginary.

In his final chapter, Bauman considers the question of utopia in the age of uncertainty. He defines utopia as "an image of another universe … a universe originated entirely by human wisdom and devotion" and impelled by a feeling that something is wrong and a confidence that we can fix it.[3] The very concept of a utopia requires a sense of the possibility of progress, a trust in movement toward a better world, and the fundamental capacity and desire of humans to first imagine and then put into practice the relations that would make that world possible. Bauman breaks utopian thinking into three modalities: the gamekeeper, the gardener, and the hunter, metaphors that roughly map onto the pre-modern, modern, and postmodern. Gamekeepers believe that "things are at their best when they are not tinkered with."[4] They maintain the balance of nature by keeping people out, since order is preordained and the keeper's job is to maintain divine harmony. Gardeners, on the other hand, make plans, distinguish plants from weeds, cultivate, and generally understand order to emanate from the mind: "It is the gardeners who tend to be the most keen and expert (one is tempted to say, professional) utopia-makers. It is at the gardeners' image of ideal harmony, first laid out in blueprint in their heads, that 'the gardens always land,' a prototype for the way in which humanity, to recall Oscar Wilde's postulate, would tend to land in the country called utopia."[5] In a conclusion similar to that of Fredric Jameson, Bauman identifies the death of the utopian vision with a postmodern "weakening of the sense of history and of the imagination of historical difference"[6] that occurs when the past, present, and future are collapsed into the singularity of the individual body. The demise of utopia occurs because "the posture of the gardener is nowadays giving way to that of the hunter."[7] Unlike the gardener who is impelled by a mental image of perfection, the hunter is alone and mobile, and worries less about depleting stocks than about filling his bag with the spoils of the hunt. The hunter is the epitome of the neoliberal individual, free from social constraints and surviving by his wits and will in a brutal world where the strongest survive and the weak are left behind.

If this sounds like something from Ayn Rand or the Republican National Convention, it is because we find ourselves today in a hunter's utopia; which is to say, in a collapse into the present, where progress is no longer an "urge to rush ahead, but ... a desperate effort to stay in the race."[8] Escape is the only available substitute for utopia today; we seek refuge in our gated communities and suvs, the very opposite of what the utopian drive would accomplish if understood as collective wish-fulfillment fantasy. All that remains is a positional game of maintaining what we have, a desperate attempt to stay in the ranks of the hunters rather than the hunted. We can understand the alternative food movement as a garden oasis in a hunter's paradise, caught between the end and the beginning of history. Ambitions to build community, to root individuality in land, as well as to develop an ecological self, rely on a gardener's approach to utopia, which has the potential to break through the individualization so endemic to neoliberal models of citizenship and agency.

I want to thicken this idea of the garden utopia by suggesting that a garden is in itself not enough. Gardening can involve domination and fantasies of complete control, as in the case of the techno-utopian promise of the vertical garden, for that is a garden cleansed of diversity and sustained by the expulsion of nature in favour of scientific purity. It is utopian in the same sense as the gated community: order is maintained by eviction notice. In the purity of an Enlightenment faith in reason, the gleaming tower glows green and bathes the city in a cleansing light. It may seem to move toward a future, but dreams of techno-utopia actually represent a failure of imagination, an inability to think differently or to venture beyond the entrenched ideology of growth and development. Such a garden is in fact an anti-utopia, in the sense that it becomes trapped in an end-of-history limbo where the logic and trajectory of the pre-existing system are mapped onto faith in technological advancements capable of ushering in a cornucopia of abundance. It offers the promise of continuing business as usual, since we can always engineer a better future. But what we desperately need is a hybrid between the gamekeeper and the gardener, which would allow biosocial production and permaculture, in a conscious effort to design gardens as living ecosystems, to create an exuberance and excess that feeds everyone, not just those lucky enough to be contained by the walls.

Jameson maintains that utopian and revolutionary thought is shaped by a number of oppositions, especially between town and country, and the timeworn antithesis of asceticism and pleasure. The Franciscan vision of simplicity and poverty that is recommended by the apocalyptic mode, and the fantasy of escape that sustains the utopian space of gated communities both emerge from and are equally bound by ideology. Each in its own way represents an ideological position that cannot be divorced from its class content. Yet, rather than fixate on utopian fantasies as hopeless articulations of a specific class position, Jameson argues that "the value of each term ... lies not in its own substantive content but as an ideological critique of its opposite number. The truth of the vision of nature lies in the way in which it discloses the complacency of the urban celebration; but the opposite is also true, and the vision of the city exposes everything nostalgic and impoverished in the embrace of nature."[9] According to Jameson, these two opposites must not be allowed to cancel each other out, but rather, add up to something more.

This potential dialectic is precisely what attracts me to the ideologically laden, class-inflected, romantic turn of pastoralism. The romantic position can be embraced for its power to enchant and celebrate pleasure while at the same providing a dialectic opposition, an ideological critique that reveals something fundamental about its opposite, and thus also about itself. Utopian pastoralism, especially the kind that celebrates the urban homestead, embraces exactly this kind of dialectic, whereby town and country unite in a productive middlescape, and where the pleasures and pitfalls of each reveal a new path toward a more satisfying and sustainable vision of urban development. Perhaps this is nothing more than the garden city that became suburbia; but I would like to think that what is emerging is a new hybrid, a natureculture fusion of urban and rural that can help address some of the most pressing problems associated with climate change, peak oil, and agriculture by treating the solution as inter-related. One of the reasons for separating storied food into a series of sub-genres is that the separation enables us to isolate competing ideologies which, although working together, can tend toward contradiction and negation. We need to pay particular attention to pleasure, asceticism, hedonism, and the relationship between town and country. For while alternative food has emerged from a specific class position, it can reveal something about its dialectic opposite (apocalyptic asceticism) while at the same time becoming more aware of something about itself – namely the limits of consumption as an organizing logic for society.

Perhaps it will help to return to the basics of the utopian impulse, which Jameson identifies which as wish fulfillment and construction. Enchantment comes in the vision of an alternative and in the politics of hope that emerges from the mundane, micro-utopian politics of the pantry. Ironically, this vision manifests most potently in the apocalyptic mode which, by rejecting evolution from within in favour of revolution, refuses to succumb to the end of history. As I have mentioned earlier, the apocalyptic clean sweep, as a pedagogical move, is actually utopian in character, wiping the slate clean in the hope of building something better upon the ruins of the old. Despite the possibility of a clean slate, the apocalyptic mode tends to leave people stuck, waiting for some great change to undo the wrongs of the past. The clean sweep relies on a classically Marxist view of history as a linear process in which revolution progresses through a series of stages until a new system emerges out of the rubble of capitalism. This is a view that tends to reinforce the paralysis of actors as they face off against a system too big to fail. De Angelis proposes a different view of revolution, one that involves value struggles and must ultimately emerge, or at least solidify, on the level of the everyday. Contrary to conventional economic wisdom, according to which the market is rational and value-free, the market is a system governed by an ethics that encourages us to behave in antisocial and ecologically destructive ways. The market value system codifies our actions within a set of norms; and thus, to resist it, we must step outside the system to see it for what it is. We can step out in a variety of abstract ways, and also, and perhaps more significantly, in concrete, embodied ways. On the front line of green capitalism we see how value struggles push against capitalist modes of production, and thus make way for the possibility of an economic system based on sharing, mutual aid, and the flourishing of ecosystems.

In order to push beyond the system, we must retain a sense of the existence of the outside, of a field of relations that are not reduced to manifestations of, or even oppositions to capitalism, but are understood as autonomous social forms. Once again, we must learn to think as gardeners and not as hunters. The ultimate value of this way of thinking is to provide a lived experience on the level of the concrete and everyday – as well as on the level of the abstract and global – of the processes of struggle, containment, and resistance. "History does not begin after the revolution, but it begins any time there are social forces whose practices rearticulate phase, cyclical and linear time autonomously from capital, whatever their scale of action."[10] In a sense, an experimental locavore year, and even smaller actions like the one-pot pledge, do precisely this. They allow different temporalities into our lives in a way that can plant revolutionary seeds of possibility by opening the future to our greatest dreams. The moments of sensed freedom might be fragmentary and fleeting, but they can be profound in their effects. In my case, the year led me to try and find ways to recover the relations and modes of production it revealed. Such moments can give us a panoramic view that allows us to "see more clearly how things are related, so that on our return into the midst of the scenery, we can measure ourselves and others, our relations of co-production, and the values that give meaning to our actions more thoughtfully."[11] They give us a sense of the world we want to fight for, not just the world we fight against.

Green capitalism is a way of normalizing the idea that there is no alternative. It is a way of enchanting people with the idea that growth, greed, and green can be reconciled in a techno-utopia of abundance liberated by competition and rational planning. For the politics of the pantry, this must be the front line of the struggle. By reinforcing the metaphoric and lived practice of the shared table, of values that surpass the logic of capitalism, values that cannot be counted, we can be part of the beginning of history. By resisting the logic of the economic turn, even while making use of it to our benefit, we can help push at the boundaries of capitalism and expand the space for gardens in a world of hunters.

While the wish-fulfillment fantasy of a clean sweep or a techno-utopian world of abundance may provide a form of pleasure, the everyday character of the politics of the pantry also enables and encourages the pleasure of construction, of building bridges. This pleasure is central to Jamie Oliver's *Ministry of Food*, and to campaigns that work toward edible school gardens, or taste education.

The pleasures of cooking, gardening, and preserving are all examples of the gardener's utopia. Plans take form. Seeds are planted. Worlds are shaped. In the spirit of non-alienated labour, where the product emerges from our own hands and by our own creativity, we are able to break free from the dreamy quality of a utopia as wish-fulfillment fantasy by rooting pleasure in the everyday. In both cases, as wish fulfillment and as construction, the utopian imagination helps to reveal limitations as well as possibilities. To the extent that we embrace this duality, a truly dynamic movement can respond to the historically given conditions of capitalism, while at the same time pushing beyond those limits. It is in the combination of concrete prescriptions and programs, in building new structures and institutions for promoting local food, that the pleasure of construction roots individuals in the world. But it is also beyond the political, in the wild visions of a world that is not defined by capitalism, a world where it is possible to live simply, beautifully, and without harming the planet, that the politics of the pantry gains a vital store of energy. It is precisely in this dialectic movement between apocalypse and utopia that something more emerges, something which can break through oppressive structures while also building new ones.

More than anything, this is what our world needs as an antidote to the politicians and businesspeople whose overriding message is that the processes we already have in place are the best we can do – that we simply have to stay the course and things will continue to get better. You need a map to get somewhere, but perhaps more important, you need a compass, a sense of direction, or a distant goal. Let us then become gamekeepers and gardeners who understand that control is an illusion, and build intentionally wild gardens in which plants have as much agency as humans, and where co-evolution and not domestication is a metaphor for utopia. We need gardeners who recognize the agency of nature and gardens that embrace the incredible power unleashed by humans as geological agents of the anthropocene.

Before we move on, let us consider how the hunter has come to dominate, and how the politics of the pantry can participate in making space for a garden in a world of hunters. The "success" and subsequent industrialization of organic food has shown that the economic turn leaves alternative food in a pickle. We speak a necessary language when we talk about investment in local economies, agrotourism, voting with one's dollar, and sustainable development. And yet, that language comes with the weight of history, or more accurately, with the hollowness of a future dispossessed of alternatives. The economic turn is a radical simplification of human motives to the language of profit, advantage, and a market that naturalizes the hunter's utopia. Naturalizing economic language is a key way in which neoliberalism maintains power, exercising a metaphoric tyranny that has been enthusiastically embraced by the local food movement in an attempt to effect "real world" changes. Much in the same way that sustainable development has sought a win-win scenario that reconciles growth, capitalism, and the environment through the discourse of ecological modernization, local food advocates themselves frequently draw on the undeniable benefits that supporting local food systems can provide to communities and regions. And why not? When seeking support from a local council or district, or trying to convince a school board to buy locally produced food, one needs to speak the language that will make you heard. This is perhaps the most insidious aspect of the economic turn: that it slowly and imperceptibly begins to change the terms of the debate from values such as conviviality, community, and nature, toward exchange, profit, balance, and development.

When I decided to commit to a year of local eating I wondered what it would accomplish. Why bother replicating an experiment found in books? Is it not enough to simply read and think deeply? Surely the isolated nature of the change, the fact that it is an "experiment," reduces its utility. Chad Lavin and James McWilliams both see the undertaking of a year of eating politically as fundamentally flawed, either replicating the hunter's utopia in the form of escape and neoliberal modes of subjectivity, or coming as a hollow political gesture that fails to grasp the scale of the problem. There are major time, money, and structural constraints that make the relationship to food I achieved during that year hard to attain for many people. Indeed, now that I am no longer a student, have children, and am balancing work and life in a precarious academic labour market, my efforts at slow living have sped up in many ways. To a certain extent, my experiment was a utopian enclave, a temporary escape into a pastoral fantasy. I am certainly more mediated by consumerism now than I was during the *annus mirabilis*. The year was a kind of perfect enchantment; it brought me a sense of wonder by making me pay attention to things I otherwise never would have noticed. It was a luxury, an island, and therefore unreal. And I think I love it more because of that artificiality. I have also discovered a lot in the act of "returning" to the "real" world, in that I had to learn to not mourn the passage of that time by crystallizing it into something it was not. In many ways, the hybrid diet I have now is more real, more muddled, and therefore more of a lived politics than a utopian enclave. While I would like to always cook and live the way I did that year, I simply cannot, at least not on the life path I am on now. I don't have the time.

And yet, perhaps it is precisely this isolation, the artificial purity of the experiment that gives it power. The locavore *annus mirabilis* accomplishes a number of interconnected tasks. First, the sensuous, embodied knowledge offers an alternative value practice that can help reorient people toward a form of sustainability that is more localized and truly aware of limits. The techno-utopian knowledge of the environmental crisis predicated on disembodied, portable scientific knowledge is insufficient in and of itself for dealing with the problems we are facing today. Many have argued that the techno-utopian approach, which involves breaking the world up into distinct pieces arranged along a series of hierarchical binary relations between nature/culture, man/woman, reason/emotion and so on is exactly what has caused us to become agents of the anthropocene. The knowledge gained through participating in alternative food schemes helps to build relations of interdependence, and perhaps most fundamentally, sustains a belief that a different world is possible. Unlike organics, local food necessitates face-to-face encounters that encourage non-economic relations of trust, solidarity, and pleasure. While it is certainly vulnerable to the economic turn, the experience of embodied knowledge can help resist some of the more typical and powerful circuits of incorporation deployed by the force field of capitalism as it cannibalizes value into capital flows.

I may not preserve food as much as I did, or bake all my own bread, but the skills I have learned have helped me foster a more vibrant local food system and allowed me to maintain a much lower ecological footprint on a number of levels. From a practical standpoint, learning to cook from scratch can reduce food costs and waste. Using whole animals and learning how to use every part, for example, is not only practical and inexpensive, but it begins to transform environmental critiques based on Franciscan poverty, frugality, and sacrifice, into celebrations of unique flavours, the transformation of nature into culture, and an alternative hedonism essential to any future environmental politics. As many have pointed out, affluent countries must drastically cut back their consumption and reduce their ecological footprint, while poorer countries are given an opportunity to grow.[12] A politics of scarcity can rapidly lead to hoarding, and as the great rice panic of 2008 showed, even the belief that there is not enough has the ability to send people into the me-first mentality of the hunter. A single decision in the government of India to give away 60 million tonnes of wheat and rice to the poor, and the subsequent banning of rice exports by the government, initiated a chain reaction and global panic that led to skyrocketing rice prices and hoarding by countries and individuals around the world, even when there was more than enough rice to feed everyone.

Elspeth Probyn identifies "the predicament of how to practice restraint in a culture of more"[13] as a key problem for contemporary environmental politics. I would argue that, especially from the perspective of the affluent in the West, who will have to be convinced to radically reduce consumption, this is a crucial impasse, and not just a collapse of politics into the space of the market. To reduce Slow Food to a dinner club for left-wing yuppies is to naturalize the end-of-history position. Thus, while it may seem strange to focus on politics of the pantry within the context of slow and local food, doing so actually reveals a dynamic that is felt across the spectrum of class. In fact, it may be even more crucial to deal with this issue from within the worldview of the West, since many of the values normalized by capitalism emerge from a Western class position and become a model for development, both in terms of aspirational consumerism and also in terms of structural forces like the IMF, World Bank, and policy frameworks.

However incomplete or problematic it may be, the first world comes across as a land of plenty, and thus becomes a model for development that, simply and irrefutably, cannot be universalized. As my students found out in their exercise of measuring their ecological footprints, even their modest lifestyle, if universalized, would require three to five planets to sustain at current levels of population. It is therefore crucial to come up with alternative models of plenitude and pleasure that do not follow the consumerist path. Ironically, the very front line of green consumption provides crucial insight into the way capitalism works to colonize all lifeworlds and subsume all value into itself, and also into the peculiar set of dissatisfactions and problems generated by that process. The idea that limits need not lead to deprivation, that development is still possible, and that we can flourish on a finite planet, is a lesson that needs to be internalized, felt, and digested. It is an idea that must take hold before alternative values can provide a different system. The unique combination of enchantment and embodiment in local food is a powerful way to bring into being a gardener's utopia.

Jane Bennett describes enchantment as "a feeling of being connected in an affirmative way to existence; it is to be under the momentary impression that the natural and cultural world *offer gifts* and, in doing so, remind us that it is good to be alive. This sense of fullness ... encourages the finite human animal, in turn, to give away some of its own time and effort on behalf of other creatures."[14] In Bennett's view, "an enchantment tale disrupts the apocalyptic tenor of the news and the despair or cynicism it breeds ... For such attentiveness can help transform shock at tragedy into a political will to reform painful social structures."[15] When it comes to environmental problems, whose scope and scale and implications seem so huge and unwieldy that they genuinely paralyze people, enchantment is a vital store of energy for generating change. The clean sweep of the apocalyptic narrative, the techno-utopian tale of the scientist-hero releasing a cornucopian abundance, the ecological modernizer reuniting economics with ecology – all fail to capture a vital moral energy capable of knitting together a resilient and sustainable system that also acknowledges non-human agency.

Storied food can easily slip into a disenchantment tale, especially within nostalgic pastoral narratives that fetishize the harmony and innocence of a prelapsarian world and turn a blind eye to the complexities of modern life. Likewise, the commodity biography participates in a narrative of disenchantment, suggesting that knowledge is power and offering emancipation only through enlightened shopping experiences. A story can easily become a brand and be folded back into the very social mystery it seeks to reveal, and for that reason, the kind of disembodied knowledge provided by organic labelling, the counting of food miles, and the general economic turn will not do the job. The alternative food movement needs instead to fix its sights on alienation, responsibility, and control and ask: what do stories of food reveal about agency, collectivity, power, and nature? Do they help challenge some of the fundamental categories that naturalize exploitation? Can they provide an alternative vision to the hunter's utopia? Can they foster utopian agency and wonder capable of challenging the end-of-history rhetoric of capitalism or the impasse of apocalyptic thinking?

My answer is yes, precisely because of the interface between the actual and the representation, between production and consumption, and nature and culture that emerges dialectically from these narratives. But in order to be successful, the politics of the pantry has to focus less on the problems of distorted representation, on revealing the commodity's biography, and more on the biosocial relations made possible or impossible by competing narratives. This is precisely what biosocial production involves – a reflexive awareness of narrative as power and, as such, a localization of the ability to write one's own story in a way that reveals the multiple connections between natural and cultural agents. Biosocial production must be magnanimous, accommodating of difference in its most radical sense. Many of the distinctions between apocalyptic, ecological modernism, and techno-utopian alternatives rest on the ability to write one's life story, to participate in the production of place, rather than simply experiencing the after-effects as victims of modernization. The feeling that we must constantly run just to stay in one place – that the future is a threat and not a promise – induces fantasies of escape and rugged individualism that can only hasten our demise. Especially in terms of technocratic management, the question of scale and locus of power is the true struggle that food politics is engaged in. For example, Vandana Shiva's concern about seeds is fundamentally related to the capitalist enclosure of common resources, as corporations scramble to privatize and profit from traditional, embodied forms of knowledge. Likewise, the critique of agribusiness boils down largely to concerns about the alienation of control from the level of the individual and community. Storied food opens up a space of possibility, where relations of social power can be revealed and contested, and where new commons are created.

The politics of the pantry must also take care not to replicate the fundamental disenchantment narrative of modernity. The pastoral is an interesting site of ambiguity in this regard because, on the one hand, by pining for an imagined harmony with nature, it reinforces the notion that modernity is disenchanting. The utopian pastoral, on the other hand, embraces the moments of enchantment associated with unalienated labour within actual landscapes as fragments of clarity, windows into new ethical and political arrangements, and affective ties to other members of the community. By promoting co-production, the utopian pastoral encourages garden cities that can overcome age-old dichotomies between town and country, pleasure and asceticism. Without a dialectic construction of this sort, we are left with the impasse of the apocalyptic clean sweep or the scientist-manager and his bureaucracy. Without such a bridge, the system becomes cannibalistic, consuming itself in the name of profit. This is why the pastoral dimension is so important: it helps us escape the path of a cultural critique that creates a dichotomy of victims and heroes. Bennett reminds us that "an ethical politics requires more than rational demystification."[16] We need to crave change, to hunger for it. After wandering around as solitary hunters for so long, our bodies must become tuned to the gardener's utopia.

Elements of storied food that emphasize pedagogy and the everyday, such as community gardens, kitchens, and even shows like *Jamie at Home*, are immensely helpful because they reintroduce pleasure into politics and help internalize an embodied form of ethics that resonates on the level of the gut. While it is essential to maintain a sense of the huge scale of the crisis and the changes necessary, it is equally important to maintain hope for the possibilities inherent in that crisis, for the chance to remake the world. Within the alternative food movement, a sense of play, of somatic reverence, and ethical energetics emerges in the pastoral. Even though the pastoral has its conservative and regressive elements, utopian pastoralism can enliven and enchant – make a better world seem possible and indeed necessary. Without this possibility, without a sense of hope, the apocalyptic mode will limit the power of storied food, and fail to inspire change precisely because it can only recognize rupture as the means towards a new world.

Enchantment is crucial to the transition from the end of history to the beginning, from understanding food movements as ineffectual forms of consumer activism to focusing on the positive affirmations and dispositions suggested by lived stories. In a sense, my final chapter has tried to weave theory and life into an affirmation of possibility. It's not that I don't see any place for critique; as the rest of this book has shown, without critique and awareness, storied food will very easily become the next organic food or cloth shopping bag, an artifact of its own incorporation. Only in a spirit of critique, awareness, regulation, and pleasure can the politics of the pantry emerge as a challenge to green capitalism. Only in this spirit can we resist the economic orthodoxy that requires all limits to be exceeded, all boundaries to be cast aside in deference to the economy. Somehow, we must begin to see limitation to freedom as the very foundation of freedom; to understand that regulations and governmental intervention are not stifling, but can be enabling.

The spirit of pleasure, celebration, and enchantment central to the politics of the pantry can offer a new beginning, a new set of value practices that contain the seeds of a better world, in which the currents of the economy no longer run in opposite directions to the currents of ecology. This world must be nurtured and tended to, engaged with like a garden, not as a site of domination and manifestation of colonizing human will but as a site of co-production, of biosocial production, with enough generosity and wildness to accommodate a world of true difference – a world in which there are enough beans for the woodchuck, and where slugs dine on lettuce and then drown in beer. I have an affinity for Georges Bataille's concept of "wild exuberance,"[17] which shifts the tenor from an economics of scarcity to one of fecundity and wildness that can accommodate cross-species encounters, desires, and enchantments, and produce a world capable of sustaining human life without destroying countless others. As apocalypsarians continue to recommend the path of austerity and the world is gripped by the iron logic of debt, it has never been more crucial to keep the future fundamentally open on the level of the imagination and also on the level of everyday life.

For myself, the slow shift from apocalypse and enforced austerity that drove me to try the 100-mile diet, to a delight in the conviviality and abundance liberated by exercising new-found skills is a source of empowerment and pleasure. What began as a supermarket artificially emptied by my experiment was soon replaced with a new world of possibility. But this transformation on the individual level must also extend into a new economic system. In other words, while sustainability must emerge from a code (enforced by regulations and laws), it also requires a transformation of self that can internalize, perform, and at times resist these codes, to impel bodies to make productive choices. Because food is something most of us experience multiple times a day, it can provide a platform for this process. And while many of the texts, particularly those concerned with life narratives, recollect the hardships of such experiments, the overall tenor is one of enchantment, conviviality, and pleasure.

The activation of an ethical system capable of responding to ecological problems requires more than guilt and heavy-handed regulation. It wasn't my mother's anxiety about McDonald's that scared me away from fast food; it was, rather, the pleasure of her perogies that tuned my body to good food. Despite the fact that I do not bake all my own bread or pickle as much, the skills I learned are still part of my body of knowledge. They inform me in the choices I make at the market, and perhaps most important, in how I will teach my daughters to understand food. I will always have a garden, even if it takes too much time, because of the pleasure I already receive from watching my three-year-old play in the bean bower. In the summer, many of her calories come from grazing in the garden. With her open mind and insatiable lust for knowledge, her understanding of food is already rooted in the soil, and I can see that she already craves the story behind her food.

When I came into my first winter as a locavore, I was anxious about what I was going to eat. This is Canada of course, and even in Southern Ontario, winter is long and greenery disappears well before it seems possible to survive through the cold and dark. I compensated for this with local dinners shared with friends, putting out dish after dish – arrays of homemade pickles, cheeses, fresh bread and sausage, as if saying to myself and my guests: this is not a barren land. We can survive here, even in the winter, and it can be delicious and prolific. What it takes is labour and planning and love. To eat a local diet in the winter, you must begin in the summer: freezing, drying, pickling, canning, and jamming. Nature provides her largesse in bouts: an extravagance of seasons that can overwhelm even the most prepared. Some of my fondest memories of my locavore year involve the days I needed to complete big projects. Making 250 perogies, canning 25 jars of tomato sauce, making 30 jars of salsa, or preparing a 100-litre crock of sauerkraut. Although each of these projects was exhausting and took a lot of time and effort, with the help of some friends, the task was transformed into a communal event. We took the opportunity to share in the bounty, transforming the kitchen into a space of enchanted materialism that connected us to a legacy of survival and celebration, an activity as old as the human species. Most of us have lost the joys of preparing for winter, of squirreling away and sharing, and finding ways to transform decay into delicacy. Some of our most delicious foods – cured meats, cheeses, miso, pickles, beer and wine – emerged out of this necessity to juggle the seasons, to accommodate nature's bounty when it arrives, and to plan for her coming miserliness. Eating in season helps internalize this valuable lesson; the line between famine and feast is often razor-thin, and on this line, culture emerges by preserving nature.

Bennett points out that one of the ways enchantment works is by "slowing down or speeding up the usual tempo of something."[18] This temporal shift is precisely the pleasure I receive from looking at my wall of pickles, jams, salsas, and preserves. It represents labour frozen, plans enacted, seasons respected, and time compressed and expanded. I look at the thirty jars of salsa, and I think about my friend and the afternoon we spent chopping and dicing, sipping wine, and enduring the heat from the water bath we used to sanitize the mason jars. Or the night my wife and I set up a camp stove on the porch to make pickled asparagus in order to avoid heating the house up during an early heat wave in May. I am enchanted, transfixed by the sight of a loaded pantry – I admit, sometimes I steal away into my basement and just look at the jars, their myriad colours, the small flecks of pepper and coriander, the almost artificial glow of turmeric, the sheen of the metal catching the light. They transfix me with the miracle of preservation and the transformation of flavours that salt, sugar, and vinegar can accomplish.

One of the biggest and most obvious changes that occurs when eating locally is the force of seasonality. The end of summer is always a flurry of activity in my kitchen as I think about the upcoming winter. Giant crock pots and mason jars are permanent fixtures as I madly try to keep up with the summer harvest. One year I put away nearly two hundred jars of preserves – I am still eating from that embodied labour two and a half years later. The labour is hot and long at times, but not only do you have a store of food produced locally, at minimal cost and with a small environmental footprint, but the satisfaction is truly intoxicating. It gives you a sense of the fecundity of nature, of the lascivious bounty of flowering plants and the possibility of a solar economy. Each jar reveals its story, standing bare before my eyes in its connection to land and labour.

Preserving your own food and preparing for the winter is one way of becoming a gardener rather than a hunter. It doesn't matter if you don't accomplish self-sufficiency, and perhaps it is better if you don't, for the very desire can lead us toward the hunter's fantasy of individualism. We must learn to internalize the ethical comportment of wild exuberance and participate in biosocial production on the micro level before it can become the basis for a new economic system. Without this sense of possibility, there is no hope of resisting the instant pleasures offered by the techno-utopian reconciliation of capitalism and nature. The politics of the pantry can be an everyday site where guilt mixes with joy to offer an alternative to the momentum and trajectory of greenwashing and shallow forms of sustainability, the effect of which is to enclose more of nature and culture. The politics of the pantry can open up the utopian possibilities of the everyday, a material politics of enchantment that reunites the public and the private. Environmentalism is largely a discourse of futurity and design, in the sense that it is preoccupied simultaneously with the possible end of life and the shape of the future.

While capitalism does encompass many aspects of our lives, it is a mistake to reify it into an all-encompassing totality. It is a word that suggests an all-encompassing force, a totalizing system or logic that has no outside. But there is an outside, a field of relations that is defined not only by commodities and money but also by conviviality, commons, and gifts. The huge scale of the idea of capitalism tends to close the cracks and openings necessary for the emergence of new commons. The resistance to capitalism is often framed as a fight for a particular system, whereas what we should be fighting for is the ability to write a collective story and for the chance to reopen the commons. We must strive to become the authors of our stories, rather than spectators. Ironically, the very failure of alternative food to change the system ensures that it remains, at least provisionally, on the outside. By emphasizing the moments and values that exceed the logic of capitalism, we can challenge the idea of limitless growth with an equally powerful notion of abundance within limits, of a garden utopia. Food is a key site of this process, precisely because of the polyvalent ways in which it signifies, engages, supports, and challenges the reduction of all value to the economic. Because, and not in spite of its liminality, we must engage the politics of the pantry as central to establishing a better future. After all, we must eat.

We are at a very interesting point in human history, where a global system is coming up against its own limits and must transform in order to survive its internal contradictions. What system emerges depends on numerous factors, but to sink into despair and announce every push outside the logic of capital as bound to fail is to admit defeat before the fight has even begun. Even the very act of struggling against various enclosures and commodifications helps to expand the number of ethical and environmental accommodations capitalism must make. The politics of the pantry, the conviviality of the shared table, the abundance of the farmers' market, the smell of home baked-bread – all of this is part of the shifting landscape of economy and ecology in the twenty-first century. The shapes it will take are still a mystery, but the struggle must continue. The future must be contested.

Notes

INTRODUCTION

1 Petrini, *Slow Food*.
2 Hawken, *The Ecology of Commerce*, 8.
3 Rees, "The Eco-Footprint of Agriculture," 89.
4 Pfeiffer, *Eating Fossil Fuels*, 21.
5 Rees, "The Eco-Footprint of Agriculture," 90.
6 Vidal, "Time is Running Out."
7 Brown, "The Environmental Revolution."
8 Carolan, *Embodied Food Politics*, 6.
9 Ibid., 13.
10 Probyn, *Carnal Appetites*, 7
11 See: Spaargen and Mol, "Greening Global Consumption," 350–9; Hobson, "Competing Discourses of Sustainable Consumption," 95–120; Soper, "Rethinking the Good Life," 111–16; Johnston, "The Citizen-Consumer Hybrid," 229–70; and Nordhouse and Shellenberger, *Break Through*.
12 Johnston, "The Citizen-Consumer Hybrid," 229–70.
13 McKibben, *Deep Economy*, 105.
14 Lavin, "The Year of Eating Politically," 1.
15 Jameson, *Archaeologies of the Future*, 199.
16 McKibben, "Global Warming's Terrifying New Math," n.p.
17 Chakrabarty, "The Climate of History," 209.
18 Bennett, *The Enchantment of Modern Life*, 3.
19 Jameson, "The Politics of Utopia," 36.

20 Ibid., 38.
21 Bennett, *The Enchantment of Modern Life*, 4.

CHAPTER ONE

1 For example, the Soil Association in Britain has proposed denying
   organic status for anything that has been shipped via airplane, in effect
   decimating the organic cash crop industry of Northern Africa that
   formed in response to consumer demand for organic produce outside
   British seasons. Averill, "African Trade Fears," n.p.
2 See: McKibben, *Deep Economy*; Kingsolver, *Animal, Vegetable, Miracle*.
3 Næss and Høyer, "The Emperor's Green Clothes," 74.
4 Hajer, *The Politics of Environmental Discourse*, 9.
5 Carl Sagan commented on an equally suggestive image taken by Voyager
   1 on February 14, 1990. As the craft left the solar system, engineers
   turned it around to take a photo of the earth, which from a distance of
   6.4 billion kilometres looks like a pale blue dot. Reflecting on that image,
   Carl Sagan states: "It has been said that astronomy is a humbling and
   character-building experience. There is perhaps no better demonstration
   of the folly of human conceits than this distant image of our tiny world.
   To me, it underscores our responsibility to deal more kindly with one
   another, and to preserve and cherish the pale blue dot, the only home
   we've ever known." Sagan, *Pale Blue Dot*, 6.
6 Stern, *Stern Review*, 1.
7 Ibid., 2.
8 Stewart, "Nicholas Stern: 'I got it wrong on climate change – it's far,
   far worse.'"
9 For example, Bjørn Lomborg accepts that global warming exists but
   disputes that we need to address it by limiting the emission of carbon.
   Instead, he argues that "if we invest smartly, we will essentially have no
   people flooded by 2085, simply because we are richer and can afford
   greater protection." Using cost-benefit analysis, one can argue that in
   order to avoid the effects of climate change, such as flooding, it is
   cheaper to simply build bigger dikes. This is one danger of economic
   arguments: it can rationalize almost anything because of the difficulty
   of calculating risk and valuing nature. Lomborg, *Cool It*, 68.
10 Stern, *Stern Review*, 12.

11 Beck, "Climate for Change," 255.

12 Hajer, *The Politics of Environmental Discourse*, 65.

13 Solow, "Responses to the Stern Review," 2.

14 See: Hourcade et al., "Beyond the Stern Review," 2479–84; Dasgupta, "Comments," n.p.; Mendelsohn, "A Critique of the Stern Report," 42–6; Nordhaus, "A Review of the Stern Review," n.p.; Tol and Yohe, "A Review of the Stern Review," 233–50.

15 Giddens, *The Politics of Climate Change*, 201.

16 Spash, "The Economics of Climate Change," 712.

17 Foucault et al., *Security, Territory, Population*, 3.

18 See: Darier, "Foucault and the Environment," 1–33; Murdoch and Clark, "'Sustainable Knowledge,'" 115–32; Mills, *Discourse*, 26–38.

19 "Earth on Course for Eco 'Crunch.'"

20 Richard Black, "Nature loss 'dwarfs bank crisis,'" 10 October 2008. See also http://www.teebweb.org

21 See Di Chiro, "Nature as Community," 69–90; Woodhouse, "The Politics of Ecology," 53–84.

22 See White, "'Are You an Environmentalist?'" 171–85.

23 Anthony Van Jones was appointed the White House green jobs czar in 2009, signalling a significant shift of the American political landscape in accepting the notion that capitalism and nature can coexist within a framework of growth.

24 Similarly, Shellenberger and Nordhaus's controversial essay "The Death of Environmentalism" lambastes the environmental movement for its narrow self-interest, lack of vision, failure to inspire alternatives, and fetishization of an external environment. They argue for a grand vision framed around a win-win scenario among labour, capital, government, and individuals. See Nordhaus and Shellenberger, *Break Through*.

25 Jones and Conrad, *The Green-Collar Economy*, vii.

26 Ibid., 4.

27 See: Hawken et al., *Natural Capitalism*; Daly and Farley, *Ecological Economics*, 6; Stern, *Stern Review*.

28 Giddens, *The Politics of Climate Change*, 10.

29 Ibid., 11.

30 Soper, "Alternative Hedonism," 576.

31 Beck, "Climate for Change," 263. Bennett discusses ecopolitics in terms of facilitating "affective attachments to the world" capable of providing

the kinds of moral energetics necessary for a deeper environmental and social justice ethics. Susan McManus makes a similar argument for cultivating wonder and affect as a means of opening spaces of alterity and critique that can bridge the utopian gap. See: Bennett, *The Enchantment of Modern Life*, 3; McManus, "Theorizing Utopian Agency," 1–42.

32 Brown, "The Environmental Revolution," n.p.

33 See Fukuyama, *The End of History and the Last Man*.

34 James O'Connor refers to this as the second contradiction of capitalism. O'Connor, *Natural Causes*.

35 Popularized by Austrian economist Joseph Schumpeter, the term "creative destruction" refers to the process of capitalist accumulation whereby radical innovation leads to the destruction of old infrastructure, monopolies, or markets, making way for new growth. Marx and Engels refer to this as the process by which capitalism reinvents itself by "constantly revolutionising the instruments of production." The effect is generally destabilizing, requiring that the old make way for the new, and often resulting in labour redundancy. See: Schumpeter, *Capitalism, Socialism, and Democracy*; Engels and Marx, *The Communist Manifesto*, 64.

36 This approach is often referred to as "weak sustainability." See: Auty and Brown, *Approaches to Sustainable Development*; Hobson, "Competing Discourses," 96.

37 Nordhaus and Shellenberger make a similar claim in *Break Through*. See also: Hawken et al., *Natural Capitalism*; Brown, "The Environmental Revolution," 1.

38 Jones and Conrad, *The Green-Collar Economy*, 6.

39 See: Næss and Høyer, "The Emperor's Green Clothes," 80; Giddens, *The Politics of Climate Change*, 71–90.

40 Bennett, *The Enchantment of Modern Life*, 9.

41 De Angelis, *The Beginning of History*, 222.

42 Ibid., 143.

43 Ibid., 176.

44 Latour, *Politics of Nature*.

45 Haraway, *The Companion Species Manifesto*.

46 See: Deleuze and Guattari, *A Thousand Plateaus*; Bennett, *Vibrant Matter*.

47 Castells, *The Rise of the Network Society*.

48 Hajer, *The Politics of Environmental Discourse*, 64–5.

49 Manes, "Nature and Silence," 15.

50 Hubert Zapf discusses the importance of the concept of cultural ecology, which "considers the sphere of human culture not as separate from but as interdependent with and transfused by ecological processes and natural energy cycles. At the same time, it recognizes the relative independence and self-reflexive dynamics of cultural processes." Zapf, "Literary Ecology and the Ethics of Texts," 851.

51 Buell, *The Environmental Imagination*, 2.

52 De Angelis, *The Beginning of History*, 43.

53 Hajer, *The Politics of Environmental Discourse*, 24.

54 Ibid., 25.

55 Ibid.

56 Ibid.

57 Ibid.

58 Ibid., 26.

59 Ibid., 32.

60 Åkerman, "What Does 'Natural Capital' Do?" 37.

61 In 1972 Herman Daly proposed the idea of the steady-state economy: "he argued that the physical flows of production and consumption must be minimized, not maximized. The central concept must be the stock of wealth, not the flow of income and consumption. Furthermore the stock must not grow. The important issue brought to the fore by the steady-state concept was distribution, not production." Næss and Høyer, "The Emperor's Green Clothes," 77.

62 Natural Capitalism and Environmental economics share a similar historic path and I treat them as the same. The idea of natural capital is used in environmental economics to discuss primitive accumulation and the worth of ecological services. Hawken uses the term to describe a broader shift in the capitalism that is occurring as stocks of natural capital become worth more than stocks of human or industrial capital. Hawken et al., *Natural Capitalism*, 5.

63 See: Åkerman, "What Does 'Natural Capital' Do?" 38–41; Næss and Høyer, "The Emperor's Green Clothes," 74–95; Spash, "The Economics of Climate Change," 706–13.

64 Åkerman, "What Does 'Natural Capital' Do?" 39.

65 Næss and Høyer, "The Emperor's Green Clothes," 76.

66 Åkerman, "What Does 'Natural Capital' Do?" 48.

67 Ibid., 44.

68 Daly and Farley, *Ecological Economics*, xviii.

69 Ibid., 5.

70 Ibid., 6.

71 Ibid.

72 Ibid., 55.

73 Næss and Høyer, "The Emperor's Green Clothes," 78.

74 Hawken et al., *Natural Capitalism*, xiii.

75 Ibid., 2.

76 Ibid., 261.

77 Guthman, *Agrarian Dreams*, 3.

78 Pollan, *The Omnivore's Dilemma*, 158.

79 Ibid., 137.

80 Ibid., 138.

81 Obach, "Theoretical Interpretations," 234.

82 Guthman, *Agrarian Dreams*, 119.

83 Pollan, *The Omnivore's Dilemma*, 158.

84 DeLind, "Of Bodies, Place, and Culture," 123.

85 Guthman argues that "certifying agencies became institutions of
    surveillance." Local food must be careful not to give the same emphasis
    to labels and consumer clarity, as in the case with organic, labels replace
    the more direct relationships of co-production in favour of distinct
    consumer-producer paradigms typical of industrial agriculture.
    Guthman, *Agrarian Dreams*, 111.

86 Laura DeLind emphasizes two major arguments in local food, which
    have a similarity to organics. "The first of these arguments is economic
    and political in nature. From this standpoint, local food tends to be
    viewed as a development (or redevelopment) tool, a means to support
    small to mid-sized farmers and a sustainable agriculture … The second
    argument is far more individually focused. From this standpoint, local
    food represents a vehicle for personal improvement. Here, local food is
    understood to be fresher, riper, more nutritious, and thus a healthier
    product than its long distance counterpart." DeLind, "Of Bodies, Place,
    and Culture," 123.

87 Ibid., 126.

88 See: Lavin, "Pollanated Politics"; Johnston, "The Citizen-Consumer
    Hybrid," 256.

89 See: Cuddleford, "When Organics Go Mainstream," 14–19; DeLind, "Transforming Organic Agriculture Into Industrial Organic Products," 198–208; Guthman, *Agrarian Dreams*.

90 Obach, "Theoretical Interpretations," 235.

91 See Di Chiro, "Nature as Community," 69–90.

92 Giddens, *The Politics of Climate Change*, 55.

93 Gillis, "British Panel Clears Scientists."

94 Anthony Giddens discusses this in terms of disconnecting climate change from a green agenda and environmental politics. Giddens, *The Politics of Climate Change*, 49.

95 Luke, "Rethinking Technoscience in Risk Society," 240.

96 Ibid., 239.

97 Giddens, *Modernity and Self-Identity*, 124.

98 Beck, "Climate for Change," 261. Emphasis in original.

99 Guggenheim et al., *An Inconvenient Truth*.

100 Harvard biologist E.O Wilson coined this term, referring to human's innate desire or need to connect to other life forms. Wilson, *Biophilia*.

101 Guggenheim et al., *An Inconvenient Truth*.

102 Ibid.

103 Ibid.

104 Foucault et al., *Security, Territory, Population*, 70.

105 Guggenheim et al., *An Inconvenient Truth*.

106 Ibid.

107 Ibid.

108 Ibid.

109 Giddens, *Modernity and Self-Identity*, 114.

110 Luke, "Generating Green Governmentality," 10.

111 Margolis, "Growing Food in the Desert."

112 Despommier, *Vertical Farm*, n.p.

113 Ibid.

114 Ibid.

115 Wilson, *The Culture of Nature*, 167.

116 Belasco, *Meals to Come*, 37.

117 Chlorella is an algae that can be grown in warm sunny water and can convert upwards of 20 percent of the light available, orders of magnitude more than the typical plant. When dried, it contains 50 percent protein and has a complete assortment of amino acids, fats, and vitamins. Belasco, *Meals to Come*, 203.

118 It's hard not to notice similarities with current discussions of algae-based biofuels.

119 Belasco, *Meals to Come*, 212.

120 Ibid., 213.

121 Cox and Van Tassel, "'Vertical Farming' Doesn't Stack Up," n.p.

122 Ibid.

123 Ibid.

124 Despommier, *Vertical Farm*, n.p.

125 Shiva, *Biopiracy*.

126 Bauman, *Liquid Times*, 77.

127 Suzuki, *The David Suzuki Reader*, 107. Suzuki's current position is an example of the power of the economic turn. He is now the host of "The Bottom Line," a show on CBC radio that examines the partnership between industry and environmentalism. The first episode features Stern as a kind of hero, a stark contrast to Suzuki's earlier positions against economic arguments. Suzuki, "The Bottom Line."

128 Evernden, *The Natural Alien*, 134.

129 Heise, "The Hitchhiker's Guide to Ecocriticism," 507.

130 Devall and Sessions, *Deep Ecology*, 67.

131 Latour refers to this as the "antimodern" position, which attempts to jump out of progress and back into a purer nature. Latour, *We Have Never Been Modern*, 9.

132 Heise, "The Hitchhiker's Guide to Ecocriticism," 507.

133 Szeman, "System Failure," 816.

134 One could add Kunstler's *World Made by Hand* and *The Long Emergency*, *King Corn*, *The Age of Stupid*, *Against the Grain*, as well as social movements like the Slow Food Presidia, and many more.

135 Buell, *The Environmental Imagination*, 93.

136 Bennett, *The Enchantment of Modern Life*, 3.

137 "Barack Obama created a White House Task Force on Childhood Obesity, which issued a ground-breaking new national obesity strategy in May 2010 that included the bold goal of reducing child obesity rates from 17 percent to 5 percent by 2030 and contained concrete measures and roles for every agency in the federal government." Levi et al., "F as in Fat," 3. See also Neville, "The Obesity Crisis is Growing."

138 Roberts, *The End of Food*, 185.

139 Manning, *Against the Grain*.

140 See: Petrini, *Slow Food*, 87; Shiva, *Monocultures of the Mind*, 65–88.

141 Roberts, *The End of Food*, xiv.

142 Ibid.

143 Ibid., 223.

144 Pawlick, *The End of Food*, 7.

145 Ibid., 79.

146 Pfeiffer, *Eating Fossil Fuels*, 7.

147 Richard Manning argues that we practise catastrophic agriculture, a strategy that involves a yearly resetting of the biological clock after a disaster and the use of colonizing plants and succession communities. "And as grain is the foundation of civilization, so, by extension, is catastrophe." Manning, *Against the Grain*, 29.

148 Pfeiffer, *Eating Fossil Fuels*, 8.

149 Roberts, *The End of Food*, 223.

150 Vaclav Smil argues that the industrial synthesis of ammonia (which requires natural gas) is the most significant invention of the twentieth century. It has allowed the population to rise from 1.6 billion in 1900 to over 6 billion in 2000, making synthetic nitrogen the most important aspect of the human diet. Smil, *Enriching the Earth*, xiv.

151 Bennett, *The Enchantment of Modern Life*, 4.

152 Szeman, "System Failure," 817.

153 See Kovel, *The Enemy of Nature*, 83.

154 Kovel, *The Enemy of Nature*, 39.

155 See: Kovel, *The Enemy of Nature*; Foster, *Marx's Ecology*; Escobar, "Constructing Nature," 46–68. Ecosocialism is a philosophy that looks at the interrelated dimensions of ecology and human liberation from capital. The journal *Capitalism, Nature, Socialism* is representative of this philosophy.

156 Roberts, *The End of Food*, 242.

157 Ibid., 249.

158 Ibid.

159 Pollan, *The Omnivore's Dilemma*, 20.

160 Ibid., 26.

161 Thirty-seven percent of world grain production goes to animal feed. Wheeler and Thompson, "Brand Barons and the Business of Food," 212.

162 In the sense that it represents what is evil about the current system. See: Kenner, "Food, Inc"; Woolf et al., "King Corn"; Pollan, *The*

Omnivore's Dilemma; Kingsolver, *Animal, Vegetable, Miracle*; Smith and MacKinnon, *The 100-Mile Diet*; Manning, *Against the Grain*.

163 Pollan, *The Omnivore's Dilemma*, 45.

164 Ibid., 102.

165 This influential thesis by Horkheimer and Adorno argues that culture has become little more than an arm of industrial production, infected by the same homogeneity and alienation characteristic of commodity production under industrialism. The machine logic of the cultural industry serves bourgeois interests by taking the leisure-production distinction and transforming leisure into consumption and reproduction, thereby extending the domain of capitalist control. Horkheimer and Adorno, *Dialectic of Enlightenment*, 124.

166 Pollan, *The Omnivore's Dilemma*, 106.

167 For Pollan and others, real food simply means food that your grandmother would recognize as such, emphasizing simple, whole ingredients produced with minimal processing and prepared at home with love. See Pollan, *In Defense of Food*.

168 Guthman, *Agrarian Dreams*, 75.

169 Guthman, "Can't Stomach It," 77.

170 Ibid.

171 Ibid., 78.

172 Ibid.

173 Brownell, "Overfeeding the Future," 164.

174 See Pollan, "Farmer in Chief."

175 Sharp, "School Meals in England," 114.

176 See Hollows and Jones, "'At Least He's Doing Something,'" 307–22.

177 Ibid., 308.

178 Parkins and Craig, *Slow Living*, 86.

179 Ibid., 27.

180 Hollows and Jones, "'At Least He's Doing Something,'" 312.

181 Ibid., 319.

182 Ibid., 316.

183 Carolan, *Embodied Food Politics*, 56.

184 Ibid., 16.

185 Ibid.

186 Shiva, *Monocultures of the Mind*, 12.

187 Haraway, "Situated Knowledges," 581.

188 Carolan, *Embodied Food Politics*, 79.

CHAPTER TWO

1 Brownell, "Overfeeding the Future," 168.
2 Badgley et al., "Organic Agriculture and the Global Food Supply," 86.
3 Badgley et al. concluded that "organic methods could produce enough food on a global per capita basis to sustain the current human population, and potentially an even larger population, without increasing the agricultural land base." They found this is particularly true for developing nations that practise low-input subsistence agriculture.
4 Pollan, *The Omnivore's Dilemma*, 19.
5 Ibid.
6 Parkins and Craig, *Slow Living*, 23.
7 Vandana Shiva's work with the Navdanya movement looks at the connection between biodiversity, economic security, and bioprospecting (the patenting of life by pharmaceutical and seed companies). Shiva argues that seed saving is a right that must be defended because it represents a way of life and a means for addressing climate change.
8 See: Roberts, *The End of Food*; Pawlick, *The End of Food*; Belasco, *Meals to Come*; Nestle, *Food Politics*.
9 Belasco, *Meals to Come*, viii.
10 Brown, *Plan B 3.0*, 107.
11 De Angelis, *The Beginning of History*, 64.
12 Rose et al., "Thinking Through the Environment," 3.
13 Bennett, *The Enchantment of Modern Life*, 3
14 De Angelis, *The Beginning of History*, 8.
15 See McIntyre and Rondeau, "Individual Consumer Food Localism," 1–9.
16 Slow Food is a global movement concerned with challenging the dominance of fast food as a social institution and way of life. It emerged from the Arcigola group in 1986 in opposition to the opening of a McDonald's on the Piazza di Spagna in Rome. Since then, the organization has challenged many conventions of social movements, with a core emphasis on slowness, eco-gastronomy, the preservation of traditional foods and techniques, and the promotion of artisanal products from around the world. Parkins and Craig, *Slow Living*, 19. See also: Andrews, *The Slow Food Story*; Parkins and Craig, *Slow Living*, 18–37; Petrini, *Slow Food*; Petrini and Padovani, *Slow Food Revolution*.
17 For example, Lillydale Chicken features an image of a verdant green field on its packaging, and many packages of meat contain empty words like

"All Natural" to invoke a sense of connection to the farm. Fortino's brand "Naturally Raised" meat and Metro's "Traditionally Raised," both trade on pastoral appeal but do nothing to clarify what these terms actually mean or who certifies the natural and traditional conditions.

18 Berry, "The Pleasures of Eating."
19 Pollan, *The Omnivore's Dilemma*, 7–8.
20 Ibid., 409.
21 Other examples include: *Fast-Food Nation*, *Black Gold*, *King Corn*, *Sweetness and Power: The Place of Sugar in Modern Histor*, and *Supersize Me*.
22 Morris, "The Globalisation of 'Italian' Coffee," 3.
23 Kenner, *Food, Inc.*
24 Ibid.
25 Ibid.
26 Marx, *The Machine in the Garden.*
27 Ibid.
28 Heintzman and Solomon, *Feeding the Future*, x.
29 Pollan, *The Omnivore's Dilemma*, 63.
30 Oliver, *Jamie's Fowl Dinners.*
31 There is a perverse way in which the process of extracting MRM can be argued as environmentally friendly, since the whole process is designed to minimize waste. Every part of the chicken is utilized and consumed.
32 De Angelis, *The Beginning of History*, 64.
33 RSPCA, "Farm Animal Welfare Standards."
34 Petrini defines the Ark of Taste as a: "protective receptacle for quality produces that should be saved from the deluge of standardization and world-wide distribution." Parkins and Craig, *Slow Living*, 23.
35 Ibid., 27.
36 Ibid., 25.
37 Guthman, *Agrarian Dreams*, 111.
38 Johnston, "The Citizen-Consumer Hybrid," 235.
39 See: Obach, "Theoretical Interpretations," 229–44; Guthman, *Agrarian Dreams*; LaSalle and Hepperly, "Regenerative Organic Farming"; DeLind, "Transforming Organic Agriculture," 198–208.
40 Oliver, *Jamie's Fowl Dinners.*
41 DeLind, "Transforming Organic Agriculture," 203.
42 Marx, *The Machine in the Garden*, 71.

43 Ibid., 22.

44 Ibid., 112.

45 Cannavò, "American Contradictions and Pastoral Visions," 77.

46 See: Cronon, "The Trouble With Wilderness," 69–90; Morton, *Ecology Without Nature*; Phillips, *The Truth of Ecology*.

47 Marx, *The Machine in the Garden*, 226.

48 Williams, *The Country and the City*, 9.

49 Ibid., 18.

50 Ibid., 22.

51 Ibid.

52 Ibid., 32.

53 Ibid., 35.

54 Ibid., 39.

55 See Phillips, *The Truth of Ecology*, 42–82.

56 Morton, *Ecology Without Nature*, 67.

57 Both Timothy Morton and Slavoj Zizek argue that we need to abandon notions of nature as a domain of organic harmony and purity. Following Morton, Zizek argues that "what we need is ecology without nature: the ultimate obstacle to protecting nature is the very notion of nature we rely on." For Zizek, ecology is the new opium of the masses. Morton, *Ecology Without Nature*, 84; Zizek, "Nature and Its Discontents," 58; ibid., 55.

58 See: Braun, *The Intemperate Rainforest*; Haraway, *Simians, Cyborgs, and Women*; Deleuze and Guattari, *A Thousand Plateaus*; Latour, *We Have Never Been Modern*; Latour, "'It's Development, Stupid!'" 1–13; Bennett, *The Enchantment of Modern Life*; Bennett, *Vibrant Matter*; Beck, "Climate for Change," 254–66; Giddens, *Modernity and Self-Identity*.

59 Buell, *The Environmental Imagination*, 31. For Glen Love, "the redefinition of pastoral ... requires that contact with the green world be acknowledged as something more than a temporary excursion into simplicity which exists primarily for the sake of its eventual renunciation and a return to the 'real' world at the end." Thus Love works towards a definition of pastoralism as "literature which recognizes and dramatizes the integration of human with natural lifecycles." Love, "Revaluing Nature," 234–5; ibid., 235.

60 Buell, *The Environmental Imagination*, 44.

61 Ibid., 52.

62 Ibid., 44.
63 Carolan, *Embodied Food Politics*, 82.
64 Bennett, *Vibrant Matter*, 18.
65 Ibid., 17.
66 Ibid., viii.
67 Ibid., ix.
68 Kingsolver, *Animal, Vegetable, Miracle*, 3.
69 O'Brien, "'No Debt Outstanding,'" 4.
70 Kingsolver, *Animal, Vegetable, Miracle*, 6.
71 Ibid., 5.
72 Ibid., 11.
73 Guthman, *Agrarian Dreams*, 10. Agrarian populism echoes the Jeffersonian yeoman tradition, with its understanding of democracy, family values, the connection between ownership and stewardship, and the negative role of government in ensuring that the small farmer/citizen isn't trampled by corporate interest.
74 Guthman, *Agrarian Dreams*, 11.
75 Buell, *The Environmental Imagination*, 34.
76 Kingsolver, *Animal, Vegetable, Miracle*, 13.
77 McWilliams, *Just Food*, 6.
78 Ibid.
79 Zizek, *Mapping Ideology*, 10.
80 Kingsolver, *Animal, Vegetable, Miracle*, 11.
81 Her book is filled with examples such as this, which use rhetorical hyperbole to reveal the connection between food and oil: "transporting a single calorie of a perishable fresh fruit from California to New York takes about 87 calories worth of fuel. That's as efficient as driving from Philadelphia to Annapolis, and back, in order to walk three miles on a treadmill in a Maryland gym." Ibid., 68.
82 Kingsolver, *Animal, Vegetable, Miracle*, 15.
83 Ibid., 338.
84 See: Katz, *The Revolution*, 33; Nabhan, *Coming Home to Eat*, 252.
85 Kingsolver, *Animal, Vegetable, Miracle*, 150.
86 Guthman, *Agrarian Dreams*, 10.
87 Ibid., 12.
88 Ibid., 11.
89 Katz, *The Revolution*, 95.

90 McIntyre and Rondeau, "Individual Consumer Food Localism," 6.

91 Buell, *The Environmental Imagination*, 4.

92 Bauman, *Liquid Times*, 104.

93 Bowerbank, "Nature Writing as Self-Technology," 174.

94 De Angelis, *The Beginning of History*, 25.

95 Ibid., 36.

96 Ibid., 37.

97 Ibid., 24.

98 Ibid., 23.

99 McManus, "Theorizing Utopian Agency," 3.

100 Jameson, *Archaeologies of the Future*, 38.

101 Belasco notes that vegetarian crusaders have been arguing for over two hundred years that the planet could be fuller and happier if we simply gave up the extravagance of meat. Those opposed to the eat-less paradigm, argue that meat eating creates superior civilizations. For example, arguing for increased consumption of British beef was a key rhetorical strategy that pitted the "superior" British people against the "the rice-eating Hindoo and Chinese, and the potato-eating Irish." Thus, "whether posed in racial, economic, or nutritious terms, these evolutionary tales usually locate utopia in the meat-eating West and dystopia in the grain-based East." Belasco, *Meals to Come*, 9; ibid., 12.

102 Cannavò, "American Contradictions," 86. Emphasis mine.

103 See: Brown, *In Timber* Country; Reed, *Taking Stands*; White, "'Are You an Environmentalist,'" 171–85; Wilson, *The Culture of Nature*.

104 Bauman, *Liquid Times*, 82.

105 Giddens, *Modernity and Self-Identity*, 137.

106 The "techno" in techno-utopian participates in this process of deskilling by placing the solutions of environmental problems in the hands of technocrats and government.

107 Sharp, "School Meals in England," 114.

108 Pollan, *The Omnivore's Dilemma*, 110.

109 See: Honoré, *In Praise of Slow*; Kingsolver, *Animal, Vegetable, Miracle*; Estill, *Small Is Possible*.

110 See: Nabhan, *Coming Home to Eat*.

111 See Pollan, *The Omnivore's Dilemma*; Oliver, *Food Revolution*.

112 See Petrini, *Slow Food*.

113 See Shiva, *Earth Democracy*.

114 See McKibben, *Deep Economy*.

115 Wilson, *The Culture of Nature*, 203.

116 Parkins and Craig, *Slow Living*, 14.

117 Thomas, "Alternative Realities," 690.

118 Soper, "Alternative Hedonism," 571.

119 Jameson, "The Politics of Utopia," 43.

120 Buell, *The Environmental Imagination*, 54.

121 Berry, "The Pleasures of Eating," 4.

122 DeLind, "Of Bodies, Place, and Culture," 126.

123 Parkins and Craig, *Slow Living*, 25.

124 Like Pollan in his emphasis on real food, Fearnley-Whittingstall emphasizes eating unprocessed whole foods as a means of detaching from the worst aspects of industrial food system.

125 Fearnley-Whittingstall, "Escape to River Cottage."

126 Fearnley-Whittingstall, "The River Cottage Treatment."

127 Thomas, "Alternative Realities," 689.

128 Coyne and Knutzen, *The Urban Homestead*, 16.

129 Ibid., 25.

130 Bennett, *Vibrant Matter*, xv.

131 Nabhan, *Coming Home to Eat*, 163.

132 Ibid., 32.

133 Ibid., 33.

134 Smith and MacKinnon, *The 100-Mile Diet*, 3.

135 Ibid., 4.

136 Ibid., 33.

137 Parkins and Craig, *Slow Living*, 11.

138 Giddens, *Modernity and Self-Identity*, 76.

139 Parkins and Craig, *Slow Living*, x.

CHAPTER THREE

1 Giddens, *Modernity and Self-Identity*, 146.

2 Bowerbank, "Nature Writing as Self-Technology," 163–76.

3 DeLind, "Of Bodies, Place, and Culture," 129.

4 Ibid., 134.

5 See: Johnston, "The Citizen-Consumer Hybrid," 229–70; Pollan, *The Omnivore's Dilemma*.

6 Lavin, "Pollanated Politics," n.p.

7 Ibid.

8 Giddens, *Modernity and Self-Identity*, 214.

9 Bauman, *Thinking Sociologically*, 207.

10 The emphasis on how healthy organic food is, rather than on the environmental benefits, would be one example of life politics.

11 See: Giddens, *The Politics of Climate Change*, 55; Beck, "Climate for Change," 254–66; Nordhaus and Shellenberger, *Break Through*.

12 Spaargaren and Mol argue that "the diminishing management capacities of nation–states are not just related to global environmental problems that transcend the national level, e.g., ozone layer depletion, loss of biodiversity and climate change. The regulatory autonomy of states also declines with respect to 'normal' environmental problems as for example the implementation of import restrictions and export bans (of hazardous waste, toxic substances)." Spaargaren and Mol, "Greening Global Consumption," 351.

13 Ibid., 357.

14 Bennett, *Vibrant Matter*, 114.

15 Tanke, "The Care of Self and Environmental Politics," 89.

16 Bennett, *The Enchantment of Modern Life*, 128.

17 Ibid., 139.

18 Bowerbank, "Nature Writing as Self-Technology," 164–5.

19 Bowerbank, "Telling Stories About Places."

20 Cheney, "Postmodern Environmental Ethics," 31.

21 Glotfelty and Fromm, *The Ecocriticism Reader*, xxi. Michael Ziser and Julie Sze argue that "one way to tell the climate story in its historical complexity is through large-scale economic studies and sweeping historical narratives of fossil-fuel use. In the realm of culture, however, a more effective approach can be found in narrative forms that combine individual biography with environmental history in order to provide concrete examples of environmental damage that can become the basis for redress and reform." Ziser and Sze, "Climate Change," 403.

22 Henri Lefebvre points out the duality of the everyday: "I see the humble events of everyday life as having two sides: a little, individual, chance event – and at the same time an infinitely complex social event, richer than the many 'essences' it contains within itself … It remains for us to explain why the infinite complexity of these events is hidden, and to

discover why – and this too is part of their reality – they appear to be so humble." Lefebvre, *Critique of Everyday Life*, 57.

23 Josée Johnston and Shyon Baumann take up the tension between access and distinction in gourmet food by considering two story lines. The first deals with food as democratic and often celebrates local, family-owned eateries. The second looks at food as a source of distinction and cultural capital. Johnston and Baumann, *Foodies*.

24 Bennett, *The Enchantment of Modern Life*, 134.

25 Thoreau and Atkinson, *Walden*, 157.

26 Donna Haraway uses the term "material-semiotic actor" to move away from conceptions of nature that treat it as a resource. The material-semiotic actor can be human or non-human, but it must be an "active, meaning-generating axis of the apparatus of bodily production." This term is crucial for Haraway's attempt to shift agency in a much broader, less objective direction and forms the basis of considerations of cyborgs and companion species. Haraway, *Simians, Cyborgs, and Women*, 200.

27 Kingsolver, *Animal, Vegetable, Miracle*, 343.

28 Ibid., 102.

29 Petrini, *Slow Food*, xii.

30 De Angelis, *The Beginning of History*, 1.

31 Ibid., 143.

32 Terroir is defined as the "combination of natural factors (soil, water, slope, height above the sea level, vegetation, microclimate) and human ones (tradition and practice of cultivation) that gives a unique character to each small agricultural locality and the food grown, raised, made, and cooked there." Trubek, *The Taste of Place*, 238.

33 Nabhan, *Coming Home to Eat*, 41.

34 Kingsolver, *Animal, Vegetable, Miracle*, 338.

35 See: O'Brien, "'No Debt Outstanding;'" Sluyter, *Colonialism and Landscape*.

36 McWilliams, *Just Food*, 11.

37 Ibid., 22.

38 Lavin, "The Year of Eating Politically," 1.

39 Parkins and Craig are attracted to Slow Food for its notion of artful or mindful consumption and eco-gastronomy, with its emphasis on situated pleasure and mindful eating that promotes conviviality, diversity, and an ethical understanding of one's relationship to the lives connected the act

of eating. They compare the focus of traditional gastronomy, which is about the elite cultivation of taste based on an "omniscient connoisseur's knowledge of world cuisine," to that of situated pleasure based on taste education, which they argue is more democratic. Parkins and Craig, *Slow Living*, 86.

40 Bennett, *The Enchantment of Modern Life*, 50.

41 See Rachel Slocum for consideration of how race plays into alternative food movements. Slocum points out that while "shopping local is often shopping white," it is important to consider the progressive aspects of the movement in working through various forms of privilege and producing forms of "embodied ecologies: situated, corporeal ways of connecting across differences through engaged universals. Embodied ecologies would build on a global sense of place, enact ethical relations with nonhuman life, and devise a politics out of the friction of difference. The questions of how and what and whom, like the outcomes, are open." Slocum, "Whiteness," 8; ibid., 4.

42 McWilliams, *Just Food*, 30–1.

43 Carolan, *Embodied Food Politics*, 131.

44 Transportation only accounts for 11 percent of the energetic costs of food. Most comes in the production. McWilliams, *Just Food*, 25–6.

45 Petrini, *Slow Food*, 16.

46 Giddens, *Modernity and Self-Identity*, 4.

47 Ibid., 23.

48 Ibid.

49 Roberts, *The End of Food*, 177.

50 Ibid., 178.

51 DeLind, "Of Bodies, Place, and Culture," 123.

52 See Vallianatos et al., "Farm-to-School," 414–23. Wendy Parkins and Geoffrey Craig argue that "if they can manage to avoid the twin pitfalls of the instrumentalism of traditional nutritional education and the distinction of traditional gastronomy, school gardens can reconnect daily practices of food with larger questions of ethics and pleasure." Parkins and Craig, *Slow Living*, 29.

53 Kingsolver, *Animal, Vegetable, Miracle*, 121.

54 Lavin, "The Year of Eating Politically," 2.

55 Parkins and Craig, *Slow Living*, 3.

56 Ibid., 39.

57 Ibid., 78.

58 De Angelis, *The Beginning of History*, 60.

59 Parkins and Craig, *Slow Living*, 5.

60 See: Petrini and Padovani, *Slow Food Revolution*; Andrews, *The Slow Food Story*.

61 Bennett, *The Enchantment of Modern Life*, 146.

62 One of the irrational, intransigent circumstances with which alternative food politics must reckon is this: humans have settled parts of the world that cannot sustain the kinds of lifestyles and cultures living in them. Both Arizona and California, for example, rely extensively on fossil fuels and fossil aquifers to provide for domestic and agricultural use. Marc Reisner deals with this situation in the *Cadillac Desert*.

63 Gordon, "Our Love Affair With Home-Grown Ingredients."

64 Latour talks about this as the anti-modern position, which attempts to retreat into a pure nature and rejects any intervention into that same nature. For Latour, "the sin is not to wish to have dominion over nature but to believe that this dominion means emancipation and not attachment." He uses the example of Frankenstein and argues that his sin wasn't creating the monster so much as it was abandoning him and thus not taking responsibility. Latour, "'It's Development, Stupid!'" 12.

65 Pollan, *The Botany of Desire*.

66 Bennett, *Vibrant Matter*, 137.

67 Ibid., 134.

68 See LaSalle et al., "Regenerative Organic Farming," 1–13.

69 Haraway, *The Companion Species Manifesto*, 4.

70 In *Animal, Vegetable, Miracle*, Kingsolver talks to a local cheese monger and asks about rennet, revealing that she makes cheese at home. In response, the cheese monger states: "You are a real housewife." To which Kingsolver adds: "It has taken me decades to get here, but I took that as a compliment." The question of gender and domestic labour complicates many of the celebratory discourses of the shared table, which is often shorthand for mother's cooking. Pollan is guilty of talking about Real Food in the same way, glossing over questions of gender, class, and unpaid labour. For example, Pollan argues that nutritionism has displaced "the influence of tradition and habit and common sense – and the transmitter of all those values, mom." This can lead to a devastating

critique of Slow Food in the same vein as nostalgic narratives of nature. ·
It is crucial to acknowledge and work through the cultural and political
dynamics of gender, especially as they relate to domestic labour, though
a detailed consideration of these questions is beyond the scope of my
book. Kingsolver, *Animal, Vegetable, Miracle*, 156; Pollan, *In Defense
of Food*, 81. See also: Parkins and Craig, *Slow Loving*, 8; Slocum,
"Whiteness," 10; Shiva, *Earth Democracy*, 111.

71 Josée Johnston points out that alternative food politics is rooted in
feminist understandings of social reproduction: "Food shopping is not
simply a banal, private concern, but represents a key private/public
nexus, as well as a potential entry-point to political engagement.
This understanding draws from feminist understandings of social
reproduction, which emphasize that food choices are not neutral, private
matters, but rather represent a politicized, gendered, and globalized
terrain where gendered labor and households intersect with states,
capital, and civil society in varying balances." Johnston, "The Citizen-
Consumer Hybrid," 239.

72 Manning, *Against the Grain*, 22.

73 Ibid., 26.

74 Ibid., 29.

75 Ibid., 57.

76 Ibid., 32.

77 Honoré, *In Praise of Slow*, 209.

78 Schor, *Plenitude*.

79 Soper, "Alternative Hedonism," 571.

80 Wendy Parkins and Geoffrey Craig refer to this as "time poverty," which
they challenge by emphasizing the irreducibility of time contra the popular
notion that time is money. Parkins and Craig, *Slow Living*, 47.

81 Smith and MacKinnon, *The 100-Mile Diet*, 161.

82 Carolan, *Embodied Food Politics*, 53.

83 Wendy Parkins and Geoffrey Craig argue that, unlike the folk revivalism
popular in Italy, Slow Food's lament of the loss of tradition does not
ossify the past in a static and facile nostalgia, but engages with a
dynamic global everyday in much more subtle and productive ways. It is
an engagement and not an escape from the world. "In the discourse and
philosophy of Slow Food, authenticity is not a pristine or timeless state

but a quality derived from *terroir*, understood as a distinct cultural and historical identity in which "the resources of the past are activated to build the future." Parkins and Craig, *Slow Living*, 102.

84 Katz, *Wild Fermentation*, 4.
85 Petrini, *Slow Food*, 85.
86 Katz, *The Revolution*, 143.
87 Roberts, *The End of Food*, 180.
88 Katz, *The Revolution Will Not Be Microwaved*, 163.
89 Ibid., 11.
90 Ibid., 12.
91 Evernden, *The Natural Alien*, 33.
92 Evernden, "Beyond Ecology," 95.
93 Katz, *The Revolution Will Not Be Microwaved*, 164.
94 Katz, *Wild Fermentation*, 9.
95 Ibid., 10.
96 Carolan, *Embodied Food Politics*, 108.
97 Kovel, *The Enemy of Nature*, 108.
98 Pollan, *The Omnivore's Dilemma*, 180.
99 Ibid., 212.

CONCLUSION

1 Zygmunt Bauman defines liquid modernity as a state in which social forms, institutions, and patterns of acceptable behaviour can no longer keep shape for long "because they decompose and melt faster than the time it takes to cast them." Bauman, *Liquid Times*, 1.
2 Ibid., 3.
3 Ibid., 97–8.
4 Ibid., 99.
5 Ibid.
6 Jameson, "The Politics of Utopia," 36.
7 Bauman, *Liquid Times*, 100.
8 Ibid., 103.
9 Jameson, "The Politics of Utopia," 50.
10 De Angelis, *The Beginning of History*, 6.
11 Ibid., 23.
12 See Correia, "Degrowth, American Style," 105–18.

13 Probyn, *Carnal Appetites*, 99.
14 Bennett, *The Enchantment of Modern Life*, 156.
15 Ibid., 160.
16 Ibid., 128.
17 Bataille, *The Accursed Share*, 33.
18 Bennett, *The Enchantment of Modern Life*, 127.

Bibliography

Abbey, Edward. *Desert Solitaire: A Season in the Wilderness*. New York: McGraw-Hill, 1968.

Achbar, Mark, and Jennifer Abbott. *The Corporation*. Toronto: Mongrel Media, 2004. DVD.

Adamson, Joni, Mei Mei Evans, and Rachel Stein. *The Environmental Justice Reader: Politics, Poetics, and Pedagogy*. Tucson: University of Arizona Press, 2002.

Adorno, Theodor W. "On Popular Music." In *Cultural Theory and Popular Culture: A Reader*, edited by John Storey, 73–84. New York: Prentice Hall, 2006.

Åkerman, Maria. "What Does 'Natural Capital' Do? The Role of Metaphor in Economic Understanding of the Environment." *Environmental Education Research* 11, no. 1 (2005): 37–52.

Althusser, Louis. *Lenin and Philosophy, and Other Essays*. Translated by Ben Brewster. London: NLB, 1971.

Andrews, Geoff. *The Slow Food Story: Politics and Pleasure*. Montreal: McGill-Queen's University Press, 2008.

Armbruster, Karla, and Kathleen R. Wallace. *Beyond Nature Writing: Expanding the Boundaries of Ecocriticism*. Charlottesville: University Press of Virginia, 2001.

Armstrong, Franny. *The Age of Stupid*. Toronto: Mongrel Media, 2008. DVD.

Arnold, Mathew. "Culture and Anarchy." In *Cultural Theory and Popular Culture: A Reader*, edited by John Storey, 6–11. New York: Prentice Hall, 2006.

Auty, R.M, and Katrina Brown. *Approaches to Sustainable Development.*
New York: Pinter, 1997.

Averill, Victoria. "African Trade Fears Carbon Footprint Backlash."
BBC News, February 22, 2007. http://newsvote.bbc.co.uk/mpapps/
pagetools/print/news.bbc.co.uk/2/hi/business/6383687.stm

Bachram, Heidi. "Climate Fraud and Carbon Colonialism: The New
Trade in Greenhouse Gases." *Capitalism Nature Socialism* 15, no. 4
(2004): 5–20.

Badgley, C., J. Moghtader, E. Quintero, E. Zakem, M.J. Chappell,
K. Aviles-Vazquez, A. Samulon, and I. Perfecto. "Organic Agriculture
and the Global Food Supply." *Renewable Agriculture and Food
Systems* 22, no. 02 (2007): 86–108.

Bataille, Georges. *The Accursed Share.* Translated by Robert Hurley.
3 vols. New York: Zone Books, 1988–91.

Bauman, Zygmunt. *Thinking Sociologically.* Oxford: Blackwell, 1990.
– *Liquid Times: Living in an Age of Uncertainty.* Cambridge: Polity
Press, 2007.

Beck, Ulrich. "Climate for Change, Or How to Create a Green Modernity?"
Theory, Culture & Society 27, no. 2–3 (2010): 254–66.
–, and Mark Ritter. *Risk Society: Towards a New Modernity.* London:
Sage, 1992.

Belasco, Warren James. *Meals to Come: A History of the Future of Food.*
California Studies in Food and Culture 16, edited by Darra Goldstein.
Berkeley: University of California Press, 2006.

Bell, David, and Gill Valentine. *Consuming Geographies: We Are Where
We Eat.* New York: Routledge, 1997.

Bennett, Jane. *The Enchantment of Modern Life: Attachments, Crossings,
and Ethics.* Princeton: Princeton University Press, 2001.
– *Vibrant Matter: A Political Ecology of Things.* Durham: Duke
University Press, 2010.

Berardi, Franco. *The Uprising: On Poetry and Finance.* Los Angeles:
Semiotext(e), 2012.

Berry, Wendell. "The Pleasures of Eating." *Center for Ecoliteracy*, 1990.
http://www.ecoliteracy.org/publications/rsl/wendell-berry.html

Bird, Jon. *Mapping the Futures: Local Cultures, Global Change.*
New York: Routledge, 1993.

Black, Richard. "Nature Loss 'Dwarf Bank Crisis.'" *BBC News*,
   10 October 2008, http://news.bbc.co.uk/go/pr/fr/-/2/hi/science/nature/
   7662565.stm
– "Climate Law 'Could Cost Billions.'" *BBC News*, 25 November 2008,
   http://news. bbc.co.uk/go/pr/fr/-/2/hi/science/nature/7747167.stm
– "Lovelock Urges Ocean Climate Fix." *BBC News*, 26 September 2007,
   http://news.bbc.co.uk/2/hi/science/nature/7014503.stm
Boulding, Kenneth E. "The Economics of the Coming Spaceship Earth."
   In *Environmental Quality in a Growing Economy: Essays From the
   Sixth RFF Forum*, edited by Henry Jarrett, 3–14. Baltimore: Johns
   Hopkins University Press, 1966.
Bourdieu, Pierre. "Distinction & the Aristocracy of Culture." In *Cultural
   Theory and Popular Culture: A Reader*, edited by John Storey, 466–76.
   New York: Prentice Hall, 2006.
Bourdieu, Pierre. *The Field of Cultural Production: Essays on Art and
   Literature*. European Perspectives: A Series in Social Thought and
   Cultural Criticism. Edited by Randal Johnson. New York: Columbia
   University Press, 1993.
Bowerbank, Sylvia. "Nature Writing as Self-Technology." In *Discourses
   of the Environment*, edited by Eric Darier, 163–78. Oxford: Blackwell,
   1999.
– "Telling Stories About Places: Local Knowledge and Narratives Can
   Improve Decisions About the Environment." *Alternatives Journal* 23,
   no. 1 (winter 1997).
Braun, Bruce. *The Intemperate Rainforest: Nature, Culture, and Power
   on Canada's West Coast*. Minneapolis: University of Minnesota Press,
   2002.
Brown, Lester. "The Environmental Revolution." In *Plan B 2.0: Rescuing
   a Planet Under Stress and a Civilization in Trouble. Earth Policy
   Institute*, 2006, http://www.earth-policy.org/books/pb2
– *Plan B 3.0: Mobilizing to Save Civilization*. New York: W.W. Norton,
   2008.
Brownell, Kelly. "Overfeeding the Future." In *Feeding the Future: From
   Fat to Famine: How to Solve the World's Food Crises*, edited by
   Andrew Heintzman and Evan Solomon, 155–90. Toronto: House of
   Anansi Press, 2004.

Brundtland, G. ed. *Our Common Future: World Commission on Environment and Development.* New York: Oxford University Press, 1987.

Buell, Lawrence. *The Environmental Imagination: Thoreau, Nature Writing, and the Formation of American Culture.* Cambridge, Massachusetts: Belknap Press of Harvard University Press, 1995.

Cannavò, Peter F. "American Contradictions and Pastoral Visions." *Organization & Environment* 14, no. 1 (March 2001): 74–92.

Carolan, Michael S. *Embodied Food Politics.* Burlington, Vermont: Ashgate, 2011.

Carson, Rachel. *Silent Spring.* 40th anniversary ed. Boston: Houghton Mifflin, 2002.

Castells, Manuel. *The Rise of the Network Society.* Cambridge, Massachusetts: Blackwell Publishers, 1996.

Chakrabarty, Dipesh. "The Climate of History: Four Theses." *Critical Inquiry* 35 (winter 2009): 197–222.

Cheney, Jim. "Postmodern Environmental Ethics: Ethics as Bioregional Narrative." In *Postmodern Environmental Ethics,* edited by Max Oelschlaeger, 23–42. Albany: State University of New York Press, 1995.

Chenje, Munyaradzi, Michael Keating, and Mirjam Schomaker, eds. *Global Environmental Outlook Four (Geo4): Environment for Development.* United Nations Environment Programme. Malta: Progress Press Ltd., 2007.

Cohen, Michael P. "Blues in the Green: Ecocriticism Under Critique." *Environmental History* 9 (2004): 9–36.

Conners, Nadia and Leila Conners Petersen. *The 11th Hour.* United States: Warner Independent Pictures, 2007. DVD.

Correia, David. "Degrowth, American Style: *No Impact Man* and Bourgeois Primitivism." *Capitalism Nature Socialism* 23, no. 1 (March 2012): 105–18.

Costanza, R., R. d'Agre, and R. de Groot. "The Value of the World's Ecosystem Services and Natural Capital." *Nature* (1997): 253–60.

Cox, Stan, and David Van Tassel. "'Vertical Farming' Doesn't Stack Up." *Synthesis/Regeneration* 52 (spring 2010): n.p.

Coyne, Kelly, and Erik Knutzen. *The Urban Homestead: Your Guide to Self-Sufficient Living in the Heart of the City.* Los Angeles: Process Media, 2008.

Cronon, William. "The Trouble With Wilderness; Or, Getting Back to the Wrong Nature." In *Uncommon Ground: Toward Reinventing Nature*, edited by William Cronon, 69–90. New York: W.W. Norton & Co, 1996.

– *Uncommon Ground: Toward Reinventing Nature*. New York: W.W. Norton & Co, 1996.

Cuddleford, V. "When Organics Go Mainstream." *Alternatives Journal* 29, no. 4 (2003): 14–19.

Daly, Herman E. "On Economics as a Life Science." *Journal of Political Economy* 76 (1968): 392–406.

–, ed. *Toward a Steady-State Economy*. New York: W.H. Freeman & Co. Ltd, 1973.

–, and Joshua C. Farley. *Ecological Economics: Principles and Applications*. Washington: Island Press, 2004.

Darier, Eric. *Discourses of the Environment*. Malden, Massachusetts: Blackwell, 1999.

– "Foucault and the Environment: An Introduction." In *Discourses of the Environment*, edited by Eric Darier, 1–34. Malden: Blackwell, 1999.

Dasgupta, Sir Partha. "Comments on the Stern Review's Economics of Climate Change." Seminar presented at the Foundation for Science and Technology at the Royal Society, London, UK, 11 November 2006. http://econ.tau.ac.il/papers/research /Partha%20Dasgupta%20on%20Stern%20Review.pdf

de Certeau, Michel. "The Practice of Everyday Life." In *Cultural Theory and Popular Culture: A Reader*, edited by John Storey, 516–27. New York: Prentice Hall, 2006.

De Angelis, Massimo. *The Beginning of History: Value Struggles and Global Capital*. London: Pluto, 2007.

De Lissovoy, Noah. "Dialectic of Emergency/Emergency of the Dialectic." *Capitalism Nature Socialism* (2008): 27–40.

Debord, Guy. *The Society of the Spectacle*. Translated by Donald Nicholson-Smith. New York: Zone Books, 1994.

Deleuze, Gilles, and Felix Guattari. *A Thousand Plateaus: Capitalism and Schizophrenia*. Minneapolis: University of Minnesota Press, 1987.

DeLind, Laura. "Transforming Organic Agriculture Into Industrial Organic Products: Reconsidering National Organic Standards." *Human Organization* 59, no. 2 (2000): 198–208.

– "Of Bodies, Place, and Culture: Re-Situating Local Food." *Journal of Agricultural and Environmental Ethics* 19 (2006): 121–46.

Despommier, Dickson. *Vertical Farm: Feeding the World in the 21st Century*. New York: Thomas Dunne Books, 2010.

– "The Vertical Farm: Reducing the Impact of Agriculture on Ecosystem Functions and Services." *The Vertical Farm*, n.d. http://www.verticalfarm.com/more?essay1

Devall, Bill, and George Sessions. *Deep Ecology*. Salt Lake City: G.M. Smith, 1985.

Di Chiro, Giovanna. "Nature as Community: The Convergence of Environment and Social Justice." In *Uncommon Ground: Rethinking the Human Place in Nature*, edited by William Cronon, 298–320. New York: Norton & Company, 1996.

Diamond, Jared M. *Collapse: How Societies Choose to Fail or Succeed*. New York: Viking, 2005.

"Earth on Course for Eco 'Crunch.'" *BBC News*, 29 October 2008. http://news.bbc.co.uk/2/hi/science/nature/7696197.stm

"The Economist: Ecology Edition," *The Economist*, 31 May 2007.

Ehrlich, Paul R. *The Population Bomb*. New York: Ballantine Books, 1968.

Ellis, Jeffrey C. "On the Search for a Root Cause: Essentialist Tendencies in Environmental Discourses." In *Uncommon Ground: Toward Reinventing Nature*, edited by William Cronon, 256–68. New York: W.W. Norton & Co, 1996.

Engels, Friedrich and Karl Marx. *The Communist Manifesto*. Edited by L.M Findlay. Peterborough, Ontario: Broadview Press, 2004.

Ervine, Kate. "The Greying of Green Governance: Power Politics and the Global Environment Facility." *Capitalism Nature Socialism* 18, no. 4 (December 2007): 125–42.

Escobar, A. "Constructing Nature. Elements for a Poststructural Political Ecology." In *Liberation Ecologies: Environment, Development, Social Movements*, edited by Richard Peet and Michael Watts, 46–68. New York: Routledge, 1996.

Estill, Lyle. *Small Is Possible: Life in a Local Economy*. Gabriola Island, British Columbia: New Society Publishers, 2008.

Evernden, Lorne Leslie Neil. *The Natural Alien: Humankind and Environment*. 2nd ed. Toronto: University of Toronto Press, 1993.

– "Beyond Ecology: Self, Place, and the Pathetic Fallacy." In *The Eco-criticism Reader: Landmarks in Literary Ecology*, edited by Cheryll Glotfelty and Harold Fromm, 92–104. Athens, Georgia: University of Georgia Press, 1996.

Fearnley-Whittingstall, Hugh. "Escape to River Cottage." *The River Cottage Collection*. Directed by Garry John Hughes. Silver Spring, Maryland: Acorn Media, 1999. DVD.

– *The River Cottage Treatment*. London, UK: KEO Films, 2006. DVD.

Flannery, Tim F. *The Weather Makers: How We Are Changing the Climate and What It Means for Life on Earth*. Toronto: HarperCollins Canada, 2006.

Foster, John Bellamy. *Marx's Ecology: Materialism and Nature*. New York: Monthly Review Press, 2000.

Foucault, Michel. *Discipline and Punish: The Birth of the Prison*. 2nd Vintage Books ed. New York: Vintage Books, 1995.

Foucault, Michel, Mauro Bertani, Alessandro Fontana, and David Macey. *"Society Must Be Defended:" Lectures at the Collège de France, 1975–76*. London: Allen Lane, 2003.

Foucault, Michel, Michel Senellart, and Graham Burchell. *Security, Territory, Population: Lectures at the Collège de France, 1977–78*. Basingstoke: Palgrave Macmillan, 2007.

Francis, Marc, and Nick Francis. *Black Gold: Wake Up and Smell the Coffee*. Toronto: Mongrel Media, 2007. DVD.

Friedman, Thomas L. "The Post-Binge World." *New York Times*, 12 October 2008. http://www.nytimes.com/2008/10/12/opinion/12friedman.html?_r=0

Fukuyama, Francis. *The End of History and the Last Man*. New York: Avon Books, 1992.

Gelpke, Basil, Ray McCormack, and Reto Caduff. *A Crude Awakening: The Oil Crash*. New York: Docurama Films, 2006. DVD.

Georgescu-Roegen, N. *The Entropy Law and the Economic Process*. Cambridge: Harvard University Press, 1971.

Giddens, Anthony. *Modernity and Self-Identity: Self and Society in the Late Modern Age*. Cambridge, UK: Polity Press, 1991.

– *The Politics of Climate Change*. Malden, Massachusetts: Polity Press, 2009.

Gifford, Terry. "Recent Critiques of Ecocriticism." *New Formations* 64 (spring 2008): 15–24.

Gillis, Justin. "British Panel Clears Scientists." *New York Times*, 7 July 2010. http://www.nytimes.com/2010/07/08/science/earth/08climate.html

Glotfelty, Cheryll, and Harold Fromm. *The Ecocriticism Reader: Landmarks in Literary Ecology*. Athens, Georgia: University of Georgia Press, 1996.

Goodman, Michael. "Towards Visceral Entanglements: Knowing and Growing Geographies of Food." *Environment, Politics and Development Working Paper Series Department of Geography, King's College London* (2008): 1–25.

Gordon, Peter. "Our Love Affair with Home-Grown Ingredients is Killing Innovation in Our Restaurants." *The Independent*, 11 March 2010. http://www.independent.co.uk/life-style/food-and-drink/features/peter-.rown-ingredients-is-killing-innovation-in-our-restaurants-1919364.html

Guggenheim, Davis. *An Inconvenient Truth*. Los Angeles: Paramount, 2006. DVD.

Guha, Ramachandra, and Joan Martinez Alier. *Varieties of Environmentalism: Essays North and South*. New York: Oxford University Press, 1998.

Guthman, Julie. "Fast Food/Organic Food: Reflexive Tastes and the Making of 'Yuppie Chow.'" *Social and Cultural Geography* 4, no. 1 (2003): 45–58.

– *Agrarian Dreams: The Paradox of Organic Farming in California*. California Studies in Critical Human Geography. Berkeley: University of California Press, 2004.

– "Can't Stomach It: How Michael Pollan et al. Made Me Want to Eat Cheetos." *Gastronomica: The Journal of Food and Culture* 7, no. 3 (summer 2007): 75–9.

Hajer, Maarten A. *The Politics of Environmental Discourse: Ecological Modernization and the Policy Process*. Oxford: Clarendon Press, 1995.

Hall, Stuart. "Notes on Deconstructing 'the Popular.'" In *Cultural Theory and Popular Culture: A Reader*, edited by John Storey, 477–86. New York: Prentice Hall, 2006.

Haraway, Donna Jeanne. "Situated Knowledges: The Science Question in Feminism and the Privilege of Partial Perspective." *Feminist Studies*, 14, no. 3 (1988): 575–99.

– *Simians, Cyborgs, and Women: The Reinvention of Nature*. New York: Routledge, 1991.

– "Universal Donors in a Vampire Culture: It's All in the Family: Biological Kinship Categories in the Twentieth-Century United States." In *Uncommon Ground: Rethinking the Human Place in Nature*, edited by William Cronon, 321–66. New York: W.W. Norton & Company, 1996.

– *The Companion Species Manifesto: Dogs, People, and Significant Otherness*. Chicago: Prickly Paradigm Press, 2003.

Hardt, Michael, and Antonio Negri. *Empire*. Cambridge: Harvard University Press, 2000.

– *Multitude: War and Democracy in the Age of Empire*. New York: Penguin Press, 2004.

Harvey, David. *The Condition of Postmodernity: An Enquiry into the Origins of Cultural Change*. Cambridge, Massachusetts: Blackwell, 1990.

– "What's Green and Makes the Environment Go Round?" In *The Cultures of Globalization*, edited by Fredric Jameson and Masao Miyoshi, 327–55. Durham: Duke University Press, 1998.

Hawken, Paul. *The Ecology of Commerce: A Declaration of Sustainability*. New York: HarperBusiness Publishers, 1993.

Hawken, Paul, L. Hunter Lovins, and Amory B. Lovins. *Natural Capitalism: Creating the Next Industrial Revolution*. Boston: Little, Brown and Co., 2000.

Heintzman, Andrew, and Evan Solomon. *Feeding the Future: From Fat to Famine: How to Solve the World's Food Crises*. Toronto: House of Anansi Press, 2004.

Heise, Ursula K. "The Hitchhiker's Gudie to Ecocriticism." *PMLA* 121, no. 2 (2006): 503–16.

– *Sense of Place and Sense of Planet: The Environmental Imagination of the Global*. New York: Oxford University Press, 2008.

Hobson, Kersty. "Competing Discourses of Sustainable Consumption: Does the 'Rationalization of Lifestyles' Make Sense." *Environmental Politics* 11, no. 2 (2002): 95–120.

Hofrichter, Richard. *Reclaiming the Environmental Debate: The Politics of Health in a Toxic Culture*. Cambridge, Massachusetts: MIT Press, 2000.

Hollows, Joanne, and Steve Jones. "'At Least He's Doing Something:' Moral Entrepreneurship and Individual Responsibility in Jamie's Ministry of Food." *European Journal of Cultural Studies* 13, no. 3 (2010): 307–22.

Honoré, Carl. *In Praise of Slow: How a Worldwide Movement Is Challenging the Cult of Speed.* Toronto: Vintage Canada, 2004.

Horkheimer, Max, and Theodor W. Adorno. *Dialectic of Enlightenment.* New York: Herder and Herder, 1972.

Hourcade, Jean-Charles, Philippe Ambrosi, and Patrice Dumas. "Beyond the Stern Review: Lessons From a Risky Venture at the Limits of the Cost-Benefit Analysis." *Ecological Economics* 68 (2009): 2479–84.

Jacobs, Jane. *The Nature of Economies.* Toronto: Vintage Canada, 2001.

Jameson, Fredric. *Postmodernism, Or, the Cultural Logic of Late Capitalism.* Post-Contemporary Interventions, edited by Stanley Fish and Fredric Jameson. Durham: Duke University Press, 1991.

– *The Cultural Turn: Selected Writings on the Postmodern, 1983–1998.* London: Verso, 1998.

– "The Politics of Utopia." *New Left Review* 25, (January–February 2004): 38–54.

– *Archaeologies of the Future: The Desire Called Utopia and Other Science Fictions.* New York: Verso, 2005.

–, and Masao Miyoshi. *The Cultures of Globalization.* Post-Contemporary Interventions, edited by Stanley Fish and Fredric Jameson. Durham: Duke University Press, 1998.

Johnston, Josée. "The Citizen-Consumer Hybrid: Ideological Tensions and the Case of Whole Foods Market." *Theory and Society* 37 (2008): 229–70.

Johnston, Josée, and Shyon Baumann. *Foodies: Democracy and Distinction in the Gourmet Foodscape.* New York: Routledge, 2009.

Jones, Van, and Ariane Conrad. *The Green-Collar Economy: How One Solution Can Fix Our Two Biggest Problems.* San Francisco: HarperOne, 2008.

Jowit, Juliette. "Why Greed Is Good for All." *Guardian Unlimited,* 26 November, 2007. http://business.guardian.co.uk/print/0,331368865-126926,00.html

Katz, Sandor Ellix. *Wild Fermentation: The Flavor, Nutrition, and Craft of Live-Culture Foods.* White River Junction, Vermont: Chelsea Green, 2003.

‒ *The Revolution Will Not Be Microwaved: Inside America's Underground Food Movements*. White River Junction, Vermont: Chelsea Green, 2006.

Kenner, Robert. *Food, Inc.* Toronto: Alliance Films, 2008. DVD.

Kerridge, Richard, and Neil Sammells. *Writing the Environment: Ecocriticism and Literature*. New York: Zed Books, 1998.

Kingsolver, Barbara. *Animal, Vegetable, Miracle: A Year of Food Life*. New York: HarperCollins, 2007.

Klein, Naomi. *The Shock Doctrine: The Rise of Disaster Capitalism*. New York: Metropolitan Books, 2007

Kovel, Joel. *The Enemy of Nature: The End of Capitalism Or the End of the World?* New York: Zed Books, 2002.

Kunstler, James Howard. *The Long Emergency: Surviving the End of the Oil Age, Climate Change, and Other Converging Catastrophes of the Twenty-First Century*. New York: Atlantic Monthly Press, 2005.

‒ *World Made By Hand: A Novel*. New York: Grove Press, 2009.

Lampitt, R.S., E.P. Achterberg, T.R. Anderson, J.A. Hughes, M.D. Iglesias-Rodriguez, B.A. Kelly-Gerreyn, M. Lucas, E.E. Popova, R. Sanders, and J.G. Shepherd. "Ocean Fertilization: A Potential Means of Geoengineering?" *Philosophical Transactions of the Royal Society A: Mathematical, Physical and Engineering Sciences* 366, no. 1882 (2008): 3919.

Larsen, Janet. "Grain Harvest Indicator." *Earth Policy Institute*, 17 January 2013. http://www.earth-policy.org/indicators/C54

LaSalle, Tim J., and Paul Hepperly. "Regenerative Organic Farming: A Solution to Global Warming." *Rodale Institute* (2008): 1–13.

Latour, Bruno. *We Have Never Been Modern*. Cambridge: Harvard University Press, 1993.

‒ *Politics of Nature: How to Bring the Sciences into Democracy*. Cambridge: Harvard University Press, 2004.

‒ "Why Has Critique Run Out of Steam? From Matters of Fact to Matters of Concern." *Critical Inquiry* 30, no. 2 (2004): 225–48.

‒ "'It's Development, Stupid!' Or: How to Modernize Modernization." In *Post-Environmentalism*, edited by Jim Proctor, 1–13. New York: MIT Press, 2008.

Lavin, Chad. "Pollanated Politics, Or, the Neoliberal's Dilemma." *Politics and Culture* 2 (2009): 57–68.

– "The Year of Eating Politically." *Theory and Event* 12, no. 2 (2009): 1–16.

Lean, Geoffrey. "Greenhouse Gasses Will Heat Up Planet 'Forever.'" *Independent UK*, 30 November 2008. http://www.independent.co.uk/ environment/climate-change/greenhouse-gases-will-heat-up-planet-for-ever-1041642.html

Lefebvre, Henri. *Critique of Everyday Life*. New York: Verso, 1991.

Leopold, Aldo, and Charles Walsh Schwartz. *A Sand County Almanac, with Other Essays on Conservation From Round River*. New York: Oxford University Press, 1966.

Levi, Jeffrey, Serena Vinter, Rebecca Laurent, and Laura Segal. "F as in Fat: How Obesity Threatens America's Future." *Trust for America's Health*, June 2010. http://healthyamericans.org/reports/obesity2010/ Obesity2010Report.pdf

Little, Amanda Griscom. "Friends with Benefit Packages: Romance Blossoms Between Big Biz and Enviros Over a Candlelit Dinner." *Grist*, 17 February 2007. http://www.grist.org/ cgi bin/printthis.pl? uri=/news/muck/2007/02/16/WRI/index.html

Lomborg, Bjørn. *Cool It: The Skeptical Environmentalist's Guide to Global Warming*. Toronto: Random House, 2008.

Love, Glen. "Revaluing Nature: Toward an Ecological Criticism." In *The Ecocriticism Reader: Landmarks in Literary Ecology*, edited by Cheryll Glotfelty and Harold Fromm, 225–40. Athens, Georgia: University of Georgia Press, 1996.

Lovelock, J. "A Geophysiologist's Thoughts on Geoengineering." *Philosophical Transactions of the Royal Society A: Mathematical, Physical and Engineering Sciences* 366, no. 1882 (2008): 3883.

Lovelock, James, and Crispin Tickell. *The Revenge of Gaia: Why the Earth Is Fighting Back – and How We Can Still Save Humanity*. London: Penguin, 2007.

Luke, Timothy W. "On Environmentality: Geo-Power and Eco-Knowledge in the Discourses of Contemporary Environmentalism." *Cultural Critique* (1995): 57–81.

– "Generating Green Governmentality: A Cultural Critique of Environmental Studies as a Power/Knowledge Formation." Unpublished manuscript, last modified December 1, 2004. http://www.cddc.vt.edu/tim/ tims/Tim514a.htm

– *Ecocritique: Contesting the Politics of Nature, Economy, and Culture.*
Minneapolis: University of Minnesota Press, 1997.
– "Environmentality as Green Governmentality." In *Discourses of the
Environment*, edited by Eric Darier, 121–51. Oxford: Blackwell, 1999.
– "Rethinking Technoscience in Risk Society: Toxicity as Textuality." In
*Reclaiming the Environmental Debate: The Politics of Health in a
Toxic Culture*, edited by R. Hofrichter, 239–54. Cambridge: MIT
Press, 2000.
Manes, Christopher. *Green Rage: Radical Environmentalism and the
Unmaking of Civilization.* Boston: Little, Brown and Co., 1990.
– "Nature and Silence." In *The Ecocriticism Reader: Landmarks in
Literary Ecology*, edited by Cheryll Glotfelty and Harold Fromm,
15–29. Athens, Georgia: University of Georgia Press, 1996.
Manning, Richard. *Against the Grain: How Agriculture Has Hijacked
Civilization.* New York: North Point Press, 2004.
Margolis, Jonathan. "Growing Food in the Desert: A Solution to
the World's Food Crisis?" *The Observer*, 24 November 2012. http://
www.guardian.co.uk/environment/2012/nov/24/growing-food-in-the-
desert-crisis
Martinez, Alier, Joan. "Environmental Justice." In *The Cultures of
Globalization*, edited by Fredric Jameson and Masao Miyoshi, 312–
26. Durham, North Carolina: Duke University Press, 1998.
Marx, Leo. *The Machine in the Garden; Technology and the Pastoral
Ideal in America.* New York: Oxford University Press, 1964.
Mazel, David. *American Literary Environmentalism.* Athens, Georgia:
University of Georgia Press, 2000.
McIntyre, Lynn, and Krista Rondeau. "Individual Consumer Food
Localism: A Review Anchored in Canadian Farmwomen's Reflec-
tions." *Journal of Rural Studies* 27, no. 2 (2011): 1–9.
McKibben, Bill. *The End of Nature.* 2nd ed. Toronto: Anchor Books,
1999.
– *Deep Economy: The Wealth of Communities and the Durable Future.*
New York: Times Books, 2007.
– "The Most Important Number on Earth." *Mother Jones*, 2008.
http://www.commondreams.org/view/2008/12/16-3
– *Eaarth: Making a Life on a Tough New Planet.* New York: Time
Books, 2010.

– "Global Warming's Terrifying New Math." *The Rolling Stone*, 19 July 2012. http://www.rollingstone.com/politics/news/global-warmings-terrifying-new-math-20120719

McManus, Susan. "Theorizing Utopian Agency: Two Steps Toward Utopian Techniques of the Self." *Theory and Event* 10, no. 3 (2007): 1–42.

McWilliams, James E. *Just Food: Where Locavores Get It Worng and How We Can Truly Eat Responsibly*. New York: Little, Brown and Co., 2009.

Meadows, Donella H. *The Limits to Growth: A Report for the Club of Rome's Project on the Predicament of Mankind*. New York: Universe Books, 1972.

Mendelsohn, R.O. "A Critique of the Stern Report." *Regulation* (winter 2006): 42–6.

Merchant, Carolyn. "Reinventing Eden: Western Culture as a Recovery Narrative." In *Uncommon Ground: Rethinking the Human Place in Nature*, edited by William Cronon, 132–59. New York: W.W. Norton & Company, 1996.

Mikulak, Michael. "The Rhizomatics of Domination: From Darwin to Biotechnology." *Rhizomes* 15 (winter 2007): n.p.

Mills, Sara. *Discourse*. London: Routledge, 1998.

Mintz, Sidney Wilfred. *Sweetness and Power: The Place of Sugar in Modern History*. New York: Penguin Books, 1986.

Monbiot, George. "This Stock Collapse Is Petty When Compared to the Nature Crunch." *The Guardian UK*, 14 October 2008. http://www.guardian.co.uk/commentisfree/2008/oct/14/climatechange-marketturmoil

Morris, Jonathan. "The Globalisation of 'Italian' Coffee: A Commodity Biography." http://www.hist.uib.no/ebha/papers/Morris_ebha_2008.pdf

Morris, William. *News From Nowhere*. Edited by Stephen Arata. Peterborough, Ontario: Broadview Press, 2003.

Morton, Timothy. *Ecology Without Nature: Rethinking Environmental Aesthetics*. Cambridge: Harvard University Press, 2007.

Murdoch, Jonathan, and Judy Clark. "'Sustainable Knowledge.'" *GeoForum* 25, no. 2 (1994): 115–32.

Nabhan, Gary Paul. *Coming Home to Eat: The Pleasures and Politics of Local Foods*. New York: Norton, 2002.

Næss, Petter, and Georg Høyer. "The Emperor's Green Clothes: Growth, Decoupling, and Capitalism." *Capitalism Nature Socialism* 20, no. 3 (September 2009): 74–95.

Nelleman, C., M. MacDevette, T. Manders, B. Eickhout, B. Svihus, A.G. Prins, B.P. Kaltenborn, eds. "The Environmental Food Crisis: The Environment's Role in Averting Future Food Crises." *UN EFC*, February 2009. http://www.grida.no/files/publications/FoodCrisis_lores.pdf

Nestle, Marion. *Food Politics: How the Food Industry Influences Nutrition and Health*. Rev. ed. California Studies in Food and Culture 3, edited by Darra Goldstein. Berkeley: University of California Press, 2007.

Neville, Rigby. "The Obesity Crisis is Growing." *The Guardian UK*, 5 July 2010. http://www.guardian.co.uk/commentisfree/2010/jul/05/growing-obesity-crisis

Nordhaus, Ted, and Michael Shellenberger. *Break Through: From the Death of Environmentalism to the Politics of Possibility*. Boston: Houghton Mifflin, 2007.

Nordhaus, W.D. "A Review of the Stern Review on the Economics of Global Warming." *Journal of Economic Literature*, XLV (September 2007): 682–702. http://nordhaus.econ.yale.edu/stern_050307.pdf

O'Brien, Susie. "'No Debt Outstanding': the Postcolonial Ecology of Local Food." Paper presented at the The New Exotic? Postcolonialism and Globalization Conference, Dunedin, New Zealand, June 24–26, 2009.

O'Connor, James. *Natural Causes: Essays in Ecological Marxism*. New York: Guilford Press, 1998.

Obach, B K. "Theoretical Interpretations of the Growth in Organic Agriculture: Agricultural Modernization Or an Organic Treadmill?" *Society & Natural Resources* 20, no. 3 (2007): 229–44.

Oelschlaeger, Max. *The Idea of Wilderness: From Prehistory to the Age of Ecology*. New Haven: Yale University Press, 1991.

Oliver, Jamie. *Jamie's School Dinners*. London: Fremantle Home Entertainment, 2005. DVD.

– "Jamie's Fowl Dinners." *YouTube*. 10 parts. 22 August 2008. http://
www.youtube.com/watch?v=PCBtkVSk3OU

– "Jamie's Ministry of Food." *Channel* 4 video. 4 episodes. October
2008. http://www.channel4.com/programmes/jamies-ministry-
of-food/4od#2920502

– "Jamie Oliver's Food Revolution." *Channel* 4 video. 6 episodes.
September 2010. http://www.channel4.com/programmes/jamies-
american-food-revolution/4od

Parkins, Wendy, and Geoffrey Craig. *Slow Living*. New York: Berg, 2006.

Pawlick, Thomas. *The End of Food*. Fort Lee, New Jersey: Barricade
Books, 2006.

Petrini, Carlo. *Slow Food: The Case for Taste*. New York: Columbia
University Press, 2003.

Petrini, Carlo, and Gigi Padovani. *Slow Food Revolution: A New
Culture for Eating and Living*. Translated by Francesca Santovetti.
New York: Rizzoli, 2006.

Pfeiffer, Dale Allen. *Eating Fossil Fuels: Oil, Food and the Coming Crisis in
Agriculture*. Gabriola, British Columbia: New Society Publishers, 2006.

Phillips, Dana. *The Truth of Ecology: Nature, Culture, and Literature in
America*. New York: Oxford University Press, 2003.

Pollan, Michael. *The Botany of Desire: A Plant's Eye View of the World*.
New York: Random House, 2001.

– *The Omnivore's Dilemma: A Natural History of Four Meals*. New York:
Penguin Press, 2006.

– *In Defense of Food: An Eater's Manifesto*. New York: Penguin Press,
2008.

– "Farmer in Chief." *New York Times Magazine*, 12 October 2008.
http://michaelpollan.com/articles-archive/farmer-in-chief/

– *Food Rules: An Eater's Manual*. New York: Penguin Books, 2009.

Probyn, Elspeth. *Carnal Appetites: Foodsexidentities*. New York:
Routledge, 2000.

Rees, William. "The Eco-Footprint of Agriculture: A Far-From-
(Thermodynamic)-Equilibrium Interpretation." Paper presented at
Agricultural Biotechnology: Finding Common International Goals,
Guelph, Ontario, 13–15 June 2004. http://wwwdata.forestry.
oregonstate.edu/orb/BiotechClass/2005%20materials/Probsteing/
Eco-footprint,%20Rees.pdf

Richardson, Ben. "Business Embraces Its Ethical Future." *BBC News*, 1 November 2006. http://news.bbc.co.uk/2/hi/business/6102450.stm

Roberts, Paul. *The End of Food*. Boston: Houghton Mifflin, 2008.

RSPCA. "Farm Animal Welfare Standards." *RSPCA*, n.d. http://www.rspca.org.uk/sciencegroup/farmanimals/standards

Sagan, Carl. *Pale Blue Dot: A Vision of the Human Future in Space*. New York: Random House, 1994.

Schlosser, Eric. *Fast Food Nation: The Dark Side of the All-American Meal*. New York: Perennial, 2002. First published by Houghton Mifflin.

Schor, Juliet. *Plenitude: The New Economics of True Wealth*. New York: Penguin Press, 2010.

Schumpeter, Joseph Alois. *Capitalism, Socialism, and Democracy*. 3rd ed. New York: Harper & Row, 1975.

Sharp, G. "School Meals in England and the Contradictions of Capital." *Capitalism Nature Socialism* 18, no. 3 (2007): 103–21.

Shiva, Vandana. *Monocultures of the Mind: Perspectives on Biodiversity and Biotechnology*. London: Zed Books, 1993.

– *Biopiracy: The Plunder of Nature and Knowledge*. Boston: South End Press, 1997.

– *Stolen Harvest: The Hijacking of the Global Food Supply*. Cambridge: South End Press, 2000.

– *Earth Democracy: Justice, Sustainability, and Peace*. Cambridge: South End Press, 2005.

Sinclair, Upton. *The Jungle*. Penguin Classics Deluxe ed. New York: Penguin, 2006. First published by Doubleday, Page & Co.

Slocum, Rachel. "Whiteness, Space and Alternative Food Practice." *GeoForum* 38, no. 3 (May 2007): 520–33.

Sluyter, Andrew. *Colonialism and Landscape: Postcolonial Theory and Applications*. Lanham, Maryland: Rowman & Littlefield Publishers, 2002.

Smil, Vaclav. *Enriching the Earth: Fritz Haber, Carl Bosch, and the Transformation of World Food Production*. Cambridge: MIT Press, 2001.

Smith, Alisa, and J.B. MacKinnon. *The 100-Mile Diet: A Year of Local Eating*. New York: Random House, 2007.

Snyder, Gary. *The Practice of the Wild: Essays*. San Francisco: North Point Press, 1990.

Solow, Robert et al. "Responses to the Stern Review." *The National Archives,* n.d. http://webarchive.nationalarchives.gov.uk/+/http://www.hm-treasury.gov.uk/media/1/2/20061028_Quotes-7.pdf

Soper, Kate. *What Is Nature? Culture, Politics and the Non-Human.* Cambridge: Blackwell, 1995.

– "Rethinking the Good Life: Consumer as Citizen." *Capitalism Nature Socialism* 15, no. 3 (2004): 111–16.

– "Alternative Hedonism, Cultural Theory and the Role of Aesthetic Revisioning." *Cultural Studies* 22, no. 5 (September 2008): 567–87.

Spaargaren, Gert, and Arthur P.J. Mol. "Greening Global Consumption: Redefining Politics and Authority." *Global Environmental Change* 18 (2008): 350–9.

Spash, Clive. "The Economics of Climate Change Impacts à la Stern: Novel and Nuanced or Rhetorically Restricted?" *Ecological Economics* 63 (2007): 706–13.

"Special Issue: The Future of the Environment," *Popular Science,* August 2007.

Spurlock, Morgan. *Supersize Me.* United States: Sony Pictures, 2004. DVD.

Stern, Nicholas. *Stern Review on the Economics of Climate Change.* Cambridge, UK: Cambridge University Press, 2006.

Stewart, Heather and Larry Elliot. "Nicholas Stern: 'I Got It Wrong on Climate Change – It's Far, Far Worse.'" *The Guardian UK,* 26 January 2013. http://www.guardian.co.uk/environment/2013/jan/27/nicholas-stern-climate-change-davos

Suzuki, David T. *The David Suzuki Reader.* Vancouver: Greystone Books, 2003.

– "The Bottom Line." CBC podcast. 10 episodes. 2011. http://www.cbc.ca/player/Radio/

Szeman, Imre. "System Failure: Oil, Futurity and the Anticipation of Disaster." *South Atlantic Quarterly* 106, no. 4 (2007): 805–23.

Tanke, Joseph. "The Care of Self and Environmental Politics: Towards a Foucaultian Account of Dietary Practice." *Ethics & the Environment* 12, no. 1 (spring 2007): 79–96.

Thomas, Lyn. "Alternative Realities: Downshifting Narratives in Contemporary Lifestyle Television." *Cultural Studies* 22, no. 5 (September 2008): 680–99.

Thoreau, Henry David. *Walden and Other Writings of Henry David Thoreau*. Edited by Brooks Atkinson. Modern Library ed. New York: Modern Library, 1992. First published 1854 by Ticknor and Fields.

Tol, R.S.J, and G.W. Yohe. "A Review of the Stern Review." *World Economics* 7, no. 4 (2006): 233–50.

Trubek, Amy B. *The Taste of Place: A Cultural Journey Into Terroir*. California Studies in Food and Culture, edited by Darra Goldstein. Berkeley: University of California Press, 2009.

Vallianatos, M., R. Gottlieb, and M.A. Haase. "Farm-to-School." *Journal of Planning Education and Research* 23, no. 4 (2004): 414–23.

Vidal, John. "Time Is Running Out: The Doha Climate Talks Must Put an End to Excuses." *The Guardian*, 26 November 2012. http://www.guardian.co.uk/commentisfree/2012/nov/25/doha-climate-talks-end-to-excuses

Ward, Barbara. *Progress for a Small Planet*. 2nd ed. London, UK: Earthscan, 1988.

Watson, James L., and Melissa L. Caldwell, eds. *The Cultural Politics of Food and Eating: A Reader*. Blackwell Readers in Anthropology. Oxford: Blackwell, 2005.

Weisman, A. *The World Without Us*. New York: Picador, 2008.

Wheeler, David, and Jane Thomson. "Brand Barons and the Business of Food." In *Feeding the Future: From Fat to Famine: How to Solve the World's Food Crises*, edited by Andrew Heintzman and Evan Solomon, 192–235. Toronto: House of Anansi Press, 2004.

White, Richard. "'Are You an Environmentalist or Do You Work for a Living?': Work and Nature." In *Uncommon Ground: Toward Reinventing Nature*, edited by William Cronon, 171–85. New York: W.W. Norton & Co, 1996.

Williams, Raymond. *The Country and the City*. London: Chatto & Windus, 1973.

– *Culture and Society, 1780–1950*. New York: Columbia University Press, 1983.

Wilson, Alexander. *The Culture of Nature: North American Landscape from Disney to the Exxon Valdez*. Toronto: Between the Lines, 1991.

Wilson, Edward O. *Biophilia*. Cambridge: Harvard University Press, 1984.

Woodhouse, Keith. "The Politics of Ecology: Environmentalism and Liberalism in the 1960s." *Journal for the Study of Radicalism* 2, no.2 (2008): 53–84.

Woolf, Aaron. *King Corn*. New York: Docurama Films, 2006. DVD.

World Commission on Environment and Development. *The Danish Government's Action Plan: Environment and Development: Follow Up to the Recommendations in the Report of the World Commission on Environment and Development and the UN Environmental Perspective to the Year 2000*. Copenhagen: Ministry of the Environment: State Information Service, 1988.

Worster, Donald. *Nature's Economy: A History of Ecological Ideas*. 2nd ed. Studies in Environment and History, edited by Alfred Crosby and Donald Worster. Cambridge: Cambridge University Press, 1994.

Zapf, Hubert. "Literary Ecology and the Ethics of Texts." *New Literary History* 39, no. 4 (autumn 2008): 847–68.

Ziser, Michael, and Julie Sze. "Climate Change, Environmental Aesthetics, and Global Environmental Justice Cultural Studies." *Discourse* 29, no. 2/3 (spring & fall 2007): 384–410.

Zizek, Slavoj. "Nature and Its Discontents." *SubStance* 37, no. 3 (2008): 37–72.

Index